The Earliest Version of John's Gospel

The Earliest Version
of John's Gospel

Recovering the Gospel of Signs

by

Urban C. von Wahlde

Michael Glazier
Wilmington, Delaware

About the Author

Urban C. von Wahlde is a chairperson of the theology department at Loyola University of Chicago. He is an associate editor of Catholic Biblical Quarterly, and has contributed numerous articles on the gospel of John to scholarly journals in the U.S. and Europe.

BS
2615.2
.V66
1989

First published in 1989 by Michael Glazier, Inc., 1935 West Fourth Street, Wilmington, Delaware 19805.

Copyright © 1989 by Michael Glazier, Inc. All rights reserved.

Library of Congress Cataloging-in-Publication Data

Von Wahlde, Urban C.
   The earliest version of John's Gospel: recovering the Gospel of signs/ Urban C. von Wahlde.
     p.   cm.—
Bibliography: p.
Includes index.
ISBN: 0-89453-694-X
1. Bible. N.T.   John—Criticism, Textual.   I. Title   II. Series.
BS2615.2.V66   1989
226'.5066—dc19   88-82468
                                                                          CIP

The Bible text in this publication is from the Revised Standard Version of the Bible, copyrighted 1946, 1952, © 1971, 1973 by the Division of Christian Education of the National Council of the Churches of Christ in the U.S.A., and used by permission.

Typography by Phyllis Boyd LeVane
Printed in the United States of America

For
Urban Bernard von Wahlde
(1896-1987)
and
Louise Catherine Reeves von Wahlde
(1902-1986)

Table of Contents

ACKNOWLEDGEMENTS

The present work had its beginnings in a dissertation at Marquette University under the direction of Dr. Noel Lazure. To him is due the deep gratitude for ingraining in me the methodological questions that have led to this study. Also among those who greatly encouraged me in continuing this research is Dr. William J. Parente, formerly Dean of the College of Arts and Sciences at the University of Scranton.

I wish to thank my colleagues at Loyola University of Chicago who by their interest and example have helped this work along. Particularly I would like to thank Dr. Pauline Viviano and Dr. John White, both of Loyola, who have read versions of the manuscript and made suggestions. I would also like to thank my graduate assistant Mr. David Livingstone who has done much of the proofreading and who has prepared the indices.

I am deeply grateful to Dr. Mary Ann Getty who invited me to write this volume and to Mr. Michael Glazier, the publisher, whom I have found to be constantly accessible, supportive and helpful; he is a true patron of theological publishing in the United States.

A father could not be more proud of his children than I am of mine. Michael and Lisa also have been very patient with Dad and by their enthusiasm and interest in "Dad's book" have helped in more ways than they know. But most of all I owe a debt of gratitude to my wife Carol who in innumerable ways all through the years of our marriage has provided the loving and supportive atmosphere which in turn made it possible for me to begin and to complete this project.

Abbreviations of Books of the Bible

Num Numbers
Deut Deuteronomy
Sam Second Samuel
1 Chr First Chronicles
Ps Psalms
Wis Wisdom

Is Isaiah
Jer Jeremiah
Hos Hosea
Mt Matthew
Mk Mark
Lk Luke
Jn John

Principle Abbreviations Periodicals and Series

AB Anchor Bible
ATR Anglican Theological Review
BJRL Bulletin of the John Rylands University Library of Manchester
BU Biblische Untersuchungen
BZ Biblische Zeitschrift
CBQ Catholic Biblical Quarterly
CD Cairo (Genizah text of the) Damascus (Document)
DSSE Dead Sea Scrolls in English
EKK Evangelisch-katholischer Kommentar zum Neuen Testament
ETL Ephemerides theologicae lovanienses
FRLANT Forschungen zur Religion und Literatur des Alten und Neuen Testament
JAAR Journal of the American Academy of Religion
JBL Journal of Biblical Literature
JTS Journal of Theological Studies

LXX Septuagint
NovT Novum Testamentum
NovTSupp Novum Testamentum, Supplements
NT New Testament
NTS New Testament Studies
RB Revue biblique
RevQ Revue de Qumran
RSV Revised Standard Version
SANT Studien zum Alten und Neuen Testament
SBLSBS SBL Sources for Biblical Study
SNTSMS Society for New Testament Studies Monograph Series
ST2 Studia Theologica, 2nd Series
TDNT G. Kittle and G. Friedrich (eds.) Theological Dictionary of the New Testament
TZ Theologische Zeitschrift
VD Verbum Domini
ZNW Zeitschrift fur de neutestamentlich Wissenschaft

INTRODUCTION

In the theological vocabulary of John's gospel, there is no more distinctive term than John's use of the word "sign" to refer to the miracles of Jesus. Although it is not the only word for miracle in the gospel (the miracles are referred to also as "works"), sign certainly is the term that is most closely associated with the gospel's portrayal of Jesus' miracles.

The traditional interpretation of the signs is that they are symbols which point beyond themselves to some spiritual reality. The focus thus is not on the miracles themselves but on something beyond them. If Jesus multiplies bread for the hungry in the desert, it is really a symbol of his desire to give the living bread—himself—to all persons. If Jesus heals a blind man, this is symbolic of his desire to heal the deeper, spiritual blindness.

This book argues against that interpretation. While it is true that some of the miracles in the gospel are developed symbolically within the gospel in its present form, this is certainly not true of them all. There is no symbolic elaboration of the healing of the official's son, for example. Nor was such symbolism the intention of the original author.

To fully understand the signs in the gospel of John, we must begin to take seriously the distinctions contained in the previous paragraph. There it was said that the signs may be symbolically developed in the gospel "in its present form" but that such symbolism, where it is present, was not the intention of the original author.

Implicit in this is the conviction that the gospel in its present form is not the product of a single individual but rather the end-product of a series of editings. To understand a document such as the gospel of John with precision and without a harmonization which forces ideas and passages into a meaning they were not originally intended to have, we must take seriously these disjunctures (the so-called "Johannine problem"). When viewed properly, these disjunctures are not only the clue that the gospel has been edited but also a clue to how this editing was done.

Although these literary features are evident enough within the gospel, there has been as yet no commonly accepted solution to the problem they pose. While most scholars would recognize that the gospel has been edited, there is relatively little agreement about the precise nature and extent of that editing. Some scholars have despaired of ever being able to reach a satisfactory solution to the problem.

But the identification of the various editions of the gospel of John is not a project beyond reach. Just as the study of the Pentateuch has revealed the characteristics of the various traditions woven into the Pentateuch, so it is possible to discover the characteristics both of language and thought which mark and distinguish the various editions of the gospel of John. This book presents a new set of evidence for distinguishing and separating from each other the material of these various editions. While in some ways this proposal is radically new (it shows with greater clarity the nature and extent of these various sets of material), in many ways the view provided here is not new. The reader will find in the footnotes references to the many other scholars whose observations have aided in the present project. So in chapter two we will set out the linguistic and theological tools we have for "Recovering The Gospel of Signs."

Chapter three will be the heart of the book. There, applying the criteria of chapter two, we will actually separate out the material which formed the first edition of the gospel, "The Earliest Version of John's Gospel." This chapter is a detailed study of the theological and linguistic characteristics of the earliest version of the gospel. It is argued throughout the book that the characteristics of the signs material occur consistently and exclusively within the material of the first edition. The full impact of this cannot be appreciated without a comparison between characteristics of the signs material and those of the surrounding material in the gospel. While this has been done to a great extent in chapter two, the comparison there will not substitute for the reader's own comparison of the signs material with the full text of the gospel. Once the reader has become familiar with the characteristics of the signs material as described here, it will be fruitful to return to a reading of the entire gospel, seeing from a new perspective how consistent the viewpoint of the earliest edition is and also how different it is from the remainder of the material of the gospel.

Chapter four provides a synthetic view of the theology of the signs gospel as it is still in evidence in the gospel. Here we will see that enough of the first edition remains in the present state of the gospel to enable us to see with a great deal of clarity the structure and the theology of the first edition. We will examine its structure, its christology, the details of its date, the locale of its origin, and the character of the community that gave birth to it.

Finally, in chapter five, we will look beyond the signs material briefly to the second edition of the gospel. For while the identification of the signs material in John is crucial for understanding the growth of the gospel, the signs material is only the first of these stages of growth. A glimpse at some of the ways the second edition made use of the signs material will orient the reader to a fuller reading of the gospel in its present state.

In what follows we will of course concentrate on the signs in John. Consequently we are not in a position to explore the full development of the Johannine gospel and the Johannine theology. However a word may be in order here about the general view of the composition of all three stages of the gospel presumed in this book.

The first edition of the gospel was a document which treated the ministry of Jesus from the baptism of Jesus to the resurrection. It focused on the miracles of Jesus and the reaction of both the people and the religious authorities to these miracles. The details of public ministry and the role of the signs in the ministry within this edition of the gospel are the subject of this book. This edition shows considerable familiarity with Palestine and with Judea in particular; it was written sometime prior to 90AD, perhaps in the seventies or eighties.

The second edition of the gospel took place about the year 90 AD when the Johannine community (a Jewish-Christian community) was undergoing expulsion from the synagogue. This version of the gospel once again addressed the question of the grounds for belief in Jesus and for the failure of belief on the part of the Jewish religious authorities. It presents a more complex view of the reasons for belief and unbelief than that found in the earlier edition. This edition focused on the importance of the Spirit for belief and at the same time extended the basis for belief (what the second edition of the gospel calls the "witnesses" to Jesus) to more than just miracles. This edition of the gospel has for one of its aims the demonstration of how these witnesses were accepted by some (notably the disciples) and how they were rejected by others (notably the "Jews"). In the final chapter of the book, something more will be said of the way this perspective developed the material of the first edition.

The third edition of the gospel came about as a result of a misinterpretation of the gospel as it existed at the end of the "second" edition. As Raymond Brown has cogently argued,[1] what had been written in a polemical way to deal with the expulsion of the community from the synagogue was easily misunderstood when read in other circumstances. This misunderstanding became the basis of the conflict evident in the pages of 1 Jn. At about the same time as the writing of 1 Jn, the gospel was edited for a third time by someone, other than the author of 1 Jn, who clearly shared his theological viewpoint. Thus the third edition clarified the tradition as it was understood "from the beginning," removing ambiguities and producing the gospel in the form it stands today. The study of the second and third editions of the gospel are the topic of another time.[2]

Although the first "stratum" is not intact within the present gospel, nevertheless enough of it remains for us to be able to identify and describe its theological structure as well as its religious background and christology.

There is in the literature on the signs in John no little discussion of minor features within the signs material which may or may not be editorial additions. In most cases, I have not paused to debate whether these minor features belong to this or that edition. These features almost inevitably are of relatively little consequence and they are by their very nature more difficult to identify with any certainty. It has been one of the lessons of OT research into such problems that although the major bodies of material can be identified with great certainty, the possibility of minor modifications provide grist for many mills for many years. If we are able to identify the nature and extent of

[1]R. Brown, *The Johannine Epistles* (AB 30; New York: Doubleday, 1982) 69; *The Community of the Beloved Disciple* (New York: Paulist, 1979) 108.

[2]The author is currently at work on a commentary on the gospel of John for Michael Glazier, Inc. which will involve such a complete analysis.

the major body of signs material with some certitude, our gain will be considerable.

One of the accidental benefits of the view presented in this book is that it deals with features of the gospel which, by and large, are evident even within an accurate English translation, although at times some slight modifications of the text may be necessary in order to more literally reflect the original. Thus the process of editing can be demonstrated to a larger audience than if the characteristics were evident only in the critical Greek text. Nevertheless the reader should be assured that the work has in fact been done on the critical Greek text of the UBS version of the New Testament.[3] Many facets of the work have previously been presented in scholarly papers and articles by the author although much appears here for the first time.

The author of this book has found the journey back through the various editions of John an exciting venture. The recovery of the first edition of John brings the reader into a "new land," into intimate contact with what must be the very roots of the Johannine tradition, and into contact with some of the earliest Jewish-Christian views of the meaning and identity of the person of Jesus. It is hoped that the trip will be as exciting for the reader!

[3]B. Metzger, et al. *The Greek New Testament* (London: The United Bible Societies, 3rd ed., 1975).

1

The Johannine Problem

It has long been recognized that the gospel of John contains many peculiar features which make for uneven reading and which indicate that the history of the gospel's formation is not a simple one. Indeed, these features form the single greatest obstacle to a complete and precise understanding of the Johannine theology. Until these inconsistencies can be accounted for and the stages by which the gospel was composed can be identified with certainty, the profundity of Johannine theology will never be fully grasped. Without a full accounting for these puzzling literary features, explanations of Johannine theology will always run the risk of failing to understand the mind of the author and of putting theological emphasis where it was not intended. It is obvious then why, for a proper understanding of Johannine theology, one must come to grips with the essential "Johannine problem": the literary inconsistencies.

These literary inconsistencies, frequently called "aporias" (a Greek word meaning "block" or "obstruction") are of various sorts.[1] There are, for example, "sequence" problems. That is, the sequence of the narrative is interrupted, giving the impression that some disruption has occurred. Sometimes it seems that material is simply out of order.

[1]The article of E. Schwartz ["Aporien im vierten Evangelium," *Nachrichten von der königlichen Gesellschaft der Wissenschaften zu Göttingen* (1907) 342-372; (1908) 115-148; 149-188; 497-560] is generally considered to mark the beginning of the identification and listing of such problems within the modern critical period.

17

Other times it seems that the original sequence has been disrupted by material added by a later author.

The most well known of these aporias concerns the sequence of the material in chapters 5 and 6. At the end of chapter 4, Jesus is in Cana in Galilee. At the beginning of chapter 5, there is an abrupt notice that Jesus makes a journey to Jerusalem for a feast. Jesus remains at the feast throughout chapter 5. Then at the beginning of chapter 6, without explanation, Jesus is described as crossing "to the other side of the sea of Galilee." That is, Jesus is now suddenly back in Galilee without mention of a return journey. In addition the text seems to presuppose that he had been there previously and was simply crossing from one side of the lake to the other! The common explanation of this peculiar state of affairs is that the two chapters have been switched around either deliberately or accidentally.[2]

If chapter 5 occurred *after* chapter 6, two problems would be solved. First, the crossing to the other side of the Sea of Galilee would fit well with the sequence at the end of chapter 4 since Jesus was in Galilee at that time. Second, the unnamed feast in chapter 5 would be identified with the coming feast of Passover mentioned in 6:4. There are many other instances of this sort of problem in the gospel. We will have occasion to notice them in time.

Another type of problem which occurs is one of contradiction or lack of consistency. Perhaps the most famous of the contradictions within the gospel occurs soon after the beginning of the Last Discourses. When Jesus speaks of his departure, Peter asks Jesus where he is going (13:36); yet later in the Last Discourse (16:5), this is contradicted by Jesus' remark that no one asks him where he is going. In 7:21, Jesus speaking to a group at Tabernacles says that he has performed only one work, a remark that is clearly inconsistent with the report of the miracle at Cana and the healing of the official's son.[3] In addition, it is peculiar that Jesus would refer so casually to a miracle, presuming that his audience would know what he was referring

---

[2]An additional curiosity connected with the material in chapter five is that of all the feasts mentioned in the gospel (three Passovers, Tabernacles, and Dedication—plus two mentions of the Sabbath) it is the only feast not identified specifically. This fact has increased suspicion that some disruption of the sequence has occurred.

[3]If the statement is construed to refer to one miracle *in Jerusalem*, it is inconsistent with the report of Jesus' many miracles at Passover in Jerusalem in 2:23.

to, although the miracle had occurred at a feast before Passover and it was now Tabernacles.[4]

12:44-50 is almost certainly not in its original location. In 12:36, after talking to the crowd, it is said that Jesus "departed and hid himself." But then without preparation or explanation, Jesus is presented as beginning to speak again in 12:44.

There are two concluding statements for the gospel. The first ending occurs in 20:30-31, where after the reports of post-resurrection appearances of Jesus over a period of eight days, it is said:

> "Now Jesus did many other signs in the presence of the disciples, which are not written in this book; but these are written that you may believe that Jesus is the Christ, and that believing you may have life in his name."

Yet the text then continues with chapter 21 which also ends with the statement:

> "But there are also many other things which Jesus did; were every one of them to be written, I suppose that the world itself could not contain the books that would be written."

There are also unexplained shifts in terminology within the gospel. In some texts the miracles of Jesus are called "signs" (*sēmeia*) and in other passages "works" (*erga*). In some passages the religious authorities are referred to as "Pharisees," (*Pharisaioi*) "chief priests," (*archiereis*) and "rulers" (*archontes*) while in others they are referred to as "Jews," (Ioudaioi) a term that is peculiar in that it is usually intended as a designation of the entire nation. These various alternations seem random and cannot to be explained as the result of nuances in meaning.

Another type of literary feature which needs to be explained is the existence of passages which seem to occur in duplicate or near duplicate

---

[4]As we shall see in chapter 3, it is a common occurrence for someone to ask Jesus a question or to make a comment; yet when Jesus responds, the response seems not to deal at all directly with the topic that had been introduced by the other. Examples of this occur in Jesus' words of 3:3; 7:28, 33; 12:21, etc., and in the words of the Baptist in 3:27. It is as if the question or comment belonged to the original edition of the gospel and the response in the current text has been supplied by a later editor.

versions. The most striking example of this is in the Last Discourses where there are extensive similarities between 13:31-14:31 and 16:4-33.[5] A shorter example of duplicate versions is 5:19-25 which is repeated in 5:26-29.

There are also theological problems. For example, it is not certain from a close reading of the gospel whether many people believe in Jesus (as in 2:23; 4:42; 7:32; 11:45) or whether almost no one believes in him (2:24-25; 12:37). How are we to account for these differences?

In some passages the authorities debate whether Jesus is "from God" (cf 3:2). This concern is evident as late as chap. 9 (vv 16, 24-25, 29). In chap. 7, they debate whether "the prophet" could come from Galilee (v52). Yet in other earlier passages the context of the debate among the religious authorities is on a much more advanced level and involves charges of an entirely different order. As early as 5:18, the religious authorities confront Jesus with a much more serious charge of "making himself equal with God."

As the reader can see, these various literary features are not a minor problem for understanding the gospel! They occur in such quantity and diversity that they constitute a major obstacle to a precise understanding of the gospel of John. We can hardly say that we understand the gospel of John if we are not able to explain these puzzling inconsistencies.

Accounting for These Problems

Scholars have attempted to deal with these features of the gospel in various ways.[6] Some have tried to explain the problems as only apparent and so harmonize the differences. Others have tried to historicize the accounts by saying for example that 14:31 (the command to "arise and leave" the Last Supper) marked the end of the supper and that the

---

[5]For a detailed description of these similarities, see R. Brown, *The Gospel According to John* (AB 29, 29a; New York: Doubleday, 1966, 70) 586-597.

[6]R. Kysar [*The Fourth Evangelist and His Gospel. An Examination of Contemporary Scholarship* (Minneapolis: Augsburg, 1975) 9-81] gives a balanced review of recent critical attempts to deal with the question of the sources and editing involved in the gospel. H. Teeple [*The Literary Origins of the Gospel of John* (Evanston: Religion and Ethics Institute, 1974) 1-116] provides a survey before presenting his own analysis.

remainder of the last discourses took place along the road to Gethsemane!

As we have already seen, some have claimed that there are accidental dislocations within the gospel and that the commentator should rearrange the text before interpreting it.[7]

But most commentators today see these various features as evidence that the gospel as we have it is not the work of a single author![8] Most see the gospel as the result of two or more major stages of composition, each of which has left various of the awkward features. Two types of these theories have been proposed. One theory proposes that the evangelist used written sources (e.g., a collection of miracles) and composed his gospel around the material of those sources. This edition was then finally edited by another hand. The second type of theory is that the earliest version of John was not just a "source" but a complete gospel. This gospel then was re-edited, with the editor(s) both deleting some material from the original and adding new material.[9] These

---

[7]The most famous and extensive of these is the theory of R. Bultmann [*The Gospel According to John. A Commentary.* (ET; Philadelphia: Westminster, 1970)]. However, others as early as J.H. Bernard, *A Critical and Exegetical Commentary on the Gospel of St. John* (ICC; 2 Vols; Edinburgh: Clark, 1929) and as recently as R. Schnackenburg [*The Gospel According to St. John.* (Vol. 1; New York: Herder and Herder, 1966; Vol. 2-3; New York: Crossroad, 1980-82)] have advanced theories of moderate rearrangement.

[8]There are those who, although they consider the gospel to have been edited, do not think it is possible to recover the original. C.K. Barrett is a striking example of this position [*The Gospel According to St. John* (2nd ed.; Philadelphia: Westminster, 1978) 18-21].

[9]The first critic in this century to take this view was H.H. Wendt, *The Gospel According to John* (ET; Edinburgh: Clark, 1902); *Die Schichten im vierten Evangelium* (Göttingen: Vandenhoeck & Ruprecht, 1911). It was also taken by J. Wellhausen, *Das Evangelium Johannis* (Berlin: Georg Reimer, 1908). More recently it has been espoused by W. Wilkens, *Die Entstehungsgeschichte des vierten Evangeliums* (Zollikon: Evangelischer Verlag, 1958); and *Zeichen und Werke* (Zurich: Zwingli, 1969) and especially by R. Fortna, *The Gospel of Signs. A Reconstruction of the Narrative Source Underlying the Fourth Gospel* (SNTSMS 11; Cambridge: Cambridge University, 1970). This approach has been extended to four levels of editing by M.E. Boismard and A. Lamouille, *L'Évangile de Jean* (Synopse de quatre Évangiles, Vol III; Paris: Cerf, 1977). It is reduced to two levels by E. Hirsch, *Das vierte Evangelium in seiner ursprünglichen Gestalt, verdeutscht und erklärt (Tübingen: Mohr, 1936); Studien zum vierten Evangelium* (Tübingen: Mohr, 1936).

Wilkens should be distinguished from the other scholars mentioned here since he proposes that the successive editing has been done by the same individual rather than

theories are sometimes combined with a theory of rearrangement, and unfortunately not all treat the problem with the same degree of thoroughness.

The most detailed, and at the same time the most famous, attempt to explain the origin of the gospel is that of Rudolf Bultmann.[10] Bultmann claimed that the gospel was a result of the work of the evangelist who combined material from a signs source (which contained miracles), a discourse source (which contained much of the discourse material of the gospel)[11] and finally a Passion source. In addition, Bultmann claimed that after the evangelist had finished his work, the gospel was redacted by a so-called "ecclesiastical redactor," that is, by an editor who saw the need to correct certain tendencies in the gospel and so to bring its thought into line with that of the rest of the early church.

Finally, Bultmann believed that the gospel had been accidently put into disarray sometime during its history. Consequently, before proceeding to his commentary he put forward a proposed rearrangement of the text of the gospel which then was the basis of his commentary. Thus Bultmann attempted to solve the literary problem not only by theories of sources and re-editing, but also by the theory of accidental displacement.

However, apart from his isolation of a signs source, Bultmann's theory is no longer widely accepted because, in spite of its ingenuity, there simply is not enough evidence for the sources or the disarrangement as Bultmann proposed them.

Rudolf Schnackenburg also produced a massive commentary on the Fourth Gospel. Although he was quite conservative on literary matters at the beginning of his work, as he progressed he became convinced that editing played a larger part in the formation of the gospel than he had originally thought.

by separate authors and that the dislocations are a result of the evangelist's intentional rearrangement. Wilken's theory has not met with wide acceptance.

[10]Bultmann, unfortunately, did not deal with the issues of literary history in a unified way but simply made comments on the issue in his footnotes. A very helpful book which provides a synthetic treatment of Bultmann's literary theory is D.M. Smith's *The Composition and Order of the Fourth Gospel. Bultmann's Literary Theory* (New Haven: Yale University Press, 1965).

[11]Bultmann claimed in addition that this discourse material had been composed by a gnostic group and then converted to use by Christians and applied to Jesus.

Schnackenburg included a brief consideration of a signs source used by the evangelist.[12] He also chose to invert the order of chapters 5 and 6, to provide a better sequence, and to move 7:15-24 to the end of chapter 5. In addition to various minor alterations, he came to see 12:44-50 and chapters 15-17 as additions by editors, chapters 15-17 he ascribed to other members of the Johannine circle.[13]

Raymond Brown posited five stages for the development of the gospel, three of which are *written* stages.[14] The evangelist has taken a body of traditional material which was independent of the synoptics (Stage 1) but which had been shaped into Johannine patterns through oral preaching and teaching (Stage 2) and has organized it into a consecutive gospel (Stage 3). The edition was then re-edited by the same evangelist (Stage 4) and then later given a final editing by someone other than the original author (Stage 5).

The editor was responsible for adding material originally composed by the evangelist but which duplicated material incorporated into the gospel at Stage 4. The editor also added chapters 11 and 12, and much of the material in the Last Discourse section.[15]

Brown's notice of the duplicate discourses is one of the most lasting contributions of his literary analysis, but his theory that the gospel originally ended at 10:42 and that chapters 11-12 have been added has not found much acceptance. In spite of his conviction about the literary origin of the material, Brown did not propose a theory of a "signs source" as others had done. In addition, he chose to comment on the gospel in the form in which it now stands rather than to explain its theology "genetically."[16]

---

[12]Schnackenburg's recognition of the importance of a "literary" solution to many of the problems within the gospel grew as his commentary progressed, as he himself admits. See his prefatory remarks (*Gospel* 1, 64-74) and his concluding review (3, 387-388) but also at various places throughout.

[13]Schnackenburg, *Gospel* 3, 387-388.

[14]Brown, *Gospel* xxxiv-xxxix.

[15]The material added by the redactor (culled from Brown's discussion on pp. xxxvii-xxxix and from throughout the commentary) includes: 1:1-18; 3:31-36; 5:26-30; 6:51-58; 11:1-12:50; 15:1-17:26; 21:1-25.

[16]Brown is certainly not the only commentator to choose to comment on the present form of the gospel in the conviction that the present text must have made sense to the final redactor. This is an important principle. Nevertheless, unless one is able to see clearly the stages by which the gospel was composed, one is not able to see clearly

Today the most respected proponent of the theory of a gospel built around a "signs source" is R. Fortna.[17] Fortna reconstructed a narrative source which was used by the evangelist as a basis for the remainder of his work. In Fortna's view this narrative gospel (rather than a simple collection of miracles) is the basis of the evangelist's later work. Although Fortna's theory has gained considerable acceptance among scholars, several individual elements of the theory have not gained acceptance (e.g., that the miraculous catch of fish during the resurrection appearance of Jesus to the disciples in chapter 21 was, in the source, a Galilean miracle of the public ministry).[18]

Two years after the appearance of Fortna's book, W. Nicol also attempted to describe the signs in the gospel. His short book did not analyze the signs in the same detail as the previous scholars. In addition, he attributed only nine passages to his signs source.[19] Never-

what the perspective of the final redactor was and consequently runs the risk of confusing earlier viewpoints with that of the final editor.

[17]R. Fortna, *Signs*. This scholarly monograph was the first detailed attempt to deal with the signs' source after Bultmann.

Fortna's sequel to his earlier work, *The Fourth Gospel and Its Predecessor: From Narrative Source To Present Gospel* (Philadelphia: Fortress, 1988) appeared after the present book was in press. Consequently detailed discussion of it is not possible outside of this note.

Two important points however should be made about Fortna's second volume. Regarding the analysis of the signs themselves, Fortna indicates (*Gospel* xi) that the previous findings have been altered only slightly in the sequel. This means that we are able to use the previous book with confidence regarding the discussion of the signs themselves.

Secondly, Fortna's second book does not, although the title would seem to indicate otherwise, attempt to describe the signs material in relation to the full text of the Fourth Gospel. The second book seeks only to discuss the redactional additions within the signs material itself. This is an important fact. As Fortna himself says (*Gospel* 3): "In this book we are concerned only with the narratives in 4G, for obviously the narratives and discourses stem from radically different origins (and so far a precise way to explain the discourses' provenance and development has not been found), and they reflect distinct periods in the development of 4G." While I would agree that there can be a rough division between narrative and discourse in the gospel of John, the distinction is not an absolute one. More importantly, the criteria that I propose in this book do claim to be applicable to both narrative and discourse material. In that sense, the present book is considerably different from and considerably more comprehensive than Fortna's treatment.

[18]See for example the reviews by D. Moody Smith [*JBL* 89 (1970), 498-501], Jerome Murphy-O'Connor [*RevBib* 77 (1970), 603-606], C.K. Barrett [*JTS* 22 (1971), 571-574], J.M. Robinson [*JAAR* 39 (1971), 339-348].

[19]W. Nicol *The Semeia in the Fourth Gospel* (NTSupp 32; Leiden: Brill, 1972).

theless, there are valuable insights in his longer study of the background of the signs.

From our brief review of past approaches to the literary question of the gospel, two things should be apparent. First, it should be clear that any thorough understanding of Johannine theology must come to grips with the literary problems of the gospel. Second, it should be clear that there is a reasonable consensus that the gospel has probably undergone three literary stages in its development. In addition, most scholars would agree that the miracles in the gospel belong to the earliest "stratum," and that at least some of the material of the discourses reflect a second stage. Finally, there is considerable agreement that there is an additional level of theology in the gospel. However, there still is no agreed upon means of identifying and isolating these bodies of material with any precision. Without that precision, precision in the discussion of the theology is impossible. This book is a modest attempt to correct that situation.

Because attempts to discover the nature and extent of the various editions of the gospel of necessity involve a detailed study of the numerous details of the Greek text, it is impossible to discuss in detail the positions of all the critics who have studied these verses before me. I have attempted to remedy this problem in a variety of ways. In this chapter I have provided the reader with a summary of the major types of theories that have been advanced. In chapter two I have attempted, in the notes, to indicate and to give credit to those scholars whose observations are in some respects similar to mine and whose observations were in fact helpful in the formulation of my own view of the text. In addition, there will be considerable reference to the positions of other scholars in the notes of chapter three.

2

Recovering the Signs
and Their Context

In the previous chapter we saw the variety of literary features that characterize the gospel of John and how these features indicate that the present form of the gospel is the result of two or more editings. This is of importance for our understanding of the Johannine signs because, in order to accurately describe the theology of signs, we must be able to identify this material and then separate it from that of the other layers in the gospel. Identifying the original context of the signs also enables us to understand more precisely the other material of the gospel and how the signs were incorporated into the later edition(s). Thus the process we are embarking on will in the end give a new clarity and a new richness to our understanding of this beautiful gospel.

We will see in this chapter that in spite of past difficulties in identifying the signs material of the gospel, there are numerous features which enable us to recover the signs and their original theological and literary context. In this chapter we will examine those features; in the next chapter we will use these criteria to recover the signs material of the gospel of John.

The Literary Seams

Scholars are in general agreement that the surest means for telling where one stratum of the gospel stops and another commences (the so-called "literary seams") is the presence of aporias. These literary seams are usually marked by contextual aporias, that is, sudden changes in thought, chronology, theology, or other forms of narrative sequence. Consequently, these breaks in thought not only indicate that there is a problem of multiple authorship in the gospel but, if viewed correctly, can be used as indicators of where the authorship changes. In what follows, such aporias will be the chief indicator of such changes in authorship.

A more specific form of aporia which should be mentioned is the occurrence of the "repetitive resumptive" (or "framing repetition"). This technique was an attempt to re-establish and resume the original literary sequence after an editorial insertion. In it, the editor repeats a brief fragment of original material from immediately before his insertion at the end of the insertion as a way of marking off and "framing" the intervening material. This technique occurs frequently throughout the books of the Hebrew and Greek testaments but occurs with some regularity in the gospel of John.[1] Within the gospel of John, it occurs in both narrative and discourse although the precise means of framing is somewhat different in each case.[2]

In narrative, it is common to repeat part of the prior narrative sequence in order to resume the original (compare, for example, 4:40 with 4:30, which it repeats in order to resume).[3]

In discourse or dialogue material, the addition is sometimes marked only at the end by such awkward phrases as "Having said this..." (*Tauta eipōn*) (cf e.g., 9:6).[4] Of course each case must be judged

---

[1] Its use in the Hebrew Scriptures has been studied by H. van Dyke Parunak, "Oral Typesetting: Some Uses of Biblical Structure," *Biblica* 62 (1981) 153-168.

[2] The technique is known by a variety of names: "repetitive resumptive," "resumptive repetition," "framing repetition." In German it is called *Wiederaufnahme;* in Greek, *epanalepsis.* The study of this technique in relation to the gospel of John has been thoroughly surveyed by F. Neiranck, "L'Epanalepsis et la critique littéraire à propos de lévangile de Jean," *ETL* 56 (1980), 303-338.

[3] I have studied the technique in relation to narrative in "A Redactional Technique in the Fourth Gospel," *CBQ* 38 (1976) 520-33. M.-E. Boismard has studied it in his "Un procédé rédactionnel dans le quatrième évangile: la Wiederaufnahme," in *L'Évangile de Jean: Sources, rédaction, théologie* (Bibliotheca Ephemeridum Theologicarum Lovaniensium 44; Leuven: University Press, 1977) 235-241. He has made it a major tool of his literary analysis in M.-E. Boismard, A. Lamouille, L'Évangile de Jean (Synopse de quatre Évangiles, Vol. 3; Paris: Cerf, 1977)).

[4] I have studied the technique in relation to discourse material in "*Wiederaufnahme* as a Marker of Redaction in Jn 6, 51-58," *Biblica* 64 (1983) 542-49.

individually since repetition can also be used as a stylistic device. But it should be clear that such repetition, in conjunction with other literary features, can be quite helpful in identifying literary seams. More will be said of the technique at the time of its first occurrence (4:40-42).

Unfortunately, identifying where a change in authorship occurs is not the same as being able to identify to which edition of the gospel a given passage belongs. For this we must depend upon other features.

Identifying the Signs Material

We have seen that the contextual aporias indicate where the literary seams occur. In order to identify the various bodies of material within the gospel, we must depend upon other criteria. These will be of the same type as those used in the identification of the various strands of tradition in classical Pentateuchal analysis.[5] The success of Pentateuchal analysis indicates that such criteria will provide a solid basis for analysis of the signs also. The first type of criterion is the variation in vocabulary employed for the same realities in cases where this alternation is not due to changes in connotation or to stylistic variety. These differences in vocabulary are called "linguistic" differences. The variation in the divine names in Genesis is the most famous example of this type of linguistic criterion.[6]

The second of the criteria is "ideological differences"[7] or differences in "thought." Ideological features refer to those elements of thought

---

[5]The criteria used in Pentateuchal analysis are aptly summarized in O. Eissfeldt, *The Old Testament: An Introduction* (New York: Harper and Row, 1965) 182-188.

[6]Fortna (Signs 15) includes linguistic criteria within his listing of "style" characteristics. This is a significant methodological error. As the study of the Hebrew Scriptures indicates, there are no more objective criteria than duplicate sets of terms for the same entities. But the use of "style" in the restricted sense is much more open to criticism precisely because it is so lacking in objectivity.

Without the presence of alternating terms for the same entities, it is doubtful whether the analysis of the literary history of the Hebrew Scriptures would have been able to make significant progress. Yet the use of style in the strict sense has not been of comparable value. For a further discussion of style see note 8 below.

[7]This term is borrowed from Fortna, *Signs* 15-17. However, Fortna understands "ideological" to include both theological and other more general characteristics of thought. I would distinguish ideological differences from theological differences in that ideological characteristics do not involve the manifest theological interests of the

within the gospel which are not directly theological but which indicate the author's perspective on a particular topic. Where these features occur in ways which are contradictory or inconsistent with one another, especially if such differences are frequent and consistent, we can be certain that we are in touch with different authors. For the most part these differences in thought or in presentation give evidence of not being in the focus of the author's intention. This fact suggests that it is unlikely that such features would be imitated by another editor. This makes them quite reliable. For example, we will point out below that in some material in the gospel, the hostility to Jesus is presented as growing throughout the ministry, yet in other material, there is a clear portrayal of this hostility as of great intensity from the beginning and throughout the gospel.

The third of the criteria is differences in theology. It is generally said that theological differences are the most unreliable guides to identifying the various literary strata within the gospel because they are the most subjective and because they are the most susceptible of imitation. Yet as will be seen in what follows, the differences in theology between the first and the second editions of John are so considerable that there can be no question of imitation.[8]

document. A review of the ideological criteria listed below in this chapter will reveal how different such characteristics are from those listed under the category of "theology."

[8]A fourth criterion is that of style. This has been employed by a number of scholars: E. Schweizer, *Ego eimi* (FRLANT 38; Goettingen: Vandenhoeck und Ruprecht, 1939); E. Ruckstuhl, *Die literarische Einheit des Johannesevangeliums* (Studia Friburgensia, n.f. 3; Freiburg; S. Paul, 1951); W. Nicol, *Semeia*; H.M. Teeple, *Origin*; M.-E. Boismard, A. Lamouille, *L'Évangile de Jean.*

However, this book has not incorporated a study of style as a means of identifying the material in John because of the myriad problems connected with its use as a criterion. First, there has been little agreement regarding what constitutes the Johannine style. Lists have ranged from thirty-three (Schweizer) to over four hundred (Boismard-Lamouille). Many of the concerns for style are, it would seem, ill-conceived. Since "Johannine style" is frequently determined by comparison with the synoptics, much of what is described as style could be attributed also to dialectical idiosyncracies or theological differences or simply described as peculiar vocabulary demanded by the topic rather than evidence of personal style. Secondly, some elements of style are so superficial that they could well be "laid over" material of earlier editions without disturbing the major orientation of the original material.

Many see what are considered to be characteristic features of "Johannine style" as evenly distributed throughout the gospel. As a result these scholars feel compelled to either of two alternatives in their analysis. Some have proposed theories which are

Thus just as contextual aporias helped us identify where the changes in authorship occur, so these various shifts in vocabulary, "ideology," and in theology, if they occur with sufficient frequency in the gospel, enable us to identify material as belonging to a given edition.

As was mentioned above, these kinds of criteria are identical to those used in the study of the Pentateuch, those which enabled us to see for the first time with clarity how the various Israelite traditions had been edited together to form our current version of the Pentateuch. Just as the presence of two sets of divine names in Genesis signalled the presence of distinct traditions and just as these occur in groups with other terms particular to the various traditions (such as the two names for the sacred mountain: Sinai and Horeb), so the presence of such differing sets of terms in the gospel of John will provide a starting point for identifying the signs and their original context within the gospel of John.

The Linguistic Differences

In the gospel of John, there are three primary and one secondary linguistic characteristics which mark the first edition and distinguish it from the second.[9] These linguistic characteristics are the most objective criteria available and therefore the most reliable.

complex, in many cases dissecting sentences and attributing a few words to one author and a few to another (Teeple, Boismard). The resulting reconstructions propose a process so complex that it is sometimes difficult to imagine how the process would have taken place. Others have argued that the alleged homogeneous style of John is the result of the evangelist's "imitation" of the style of the source. This objection has been advanced by, among others, B.W.Bacon, *The Fourth Gospel in Research and Debate* (New Haven: Moffat, Yard, 1910) and E. Hirsch, "Stilkritik und Literaranalyse im vierten Evangelium," *ZNW* 43 (1950-51) 129-43. Such theories of imitation make any attempt at source analysis almost impossible because of the a priori difficulty in determining whether a given characteristic is typical of the original author or simply a result of imitation by a redactor.

Of course the greatest argument against the use of style would be the development of a set of clear and consistent criteria apart from "style." This book hopes to present such criteria.

[9]Although there is significant evidence that the gospel of John in its present form is a result of three stages of editing (an original edition plus two re-writings), only those characteristics which are useful in identifying and isolating the signs material and distinguishing it from the remainder of the gospel will be studied here. In all cases these comparisons are with material from the second edition. We will not discuss at any length the criteria for identifying the third edition.

1. THE TERMS FOR RELIGIOUS AUTHORITIES[10]

In the gospel, there are two sets of terms for religious authorities. Within the first set, three terms occur: "Pharisees," (*Pharisaioi*) "chief priests," (*archiereis*) and "rulers" (*archontes*). These terms occur frequently throughout the gospel and are commonly intermixed with one another. "Pharisees" occurs nineteen times (excluding its occurrence in the pericope of the woman taken in adultery).[11] "Chief priests" (in the plural, referring to a group rather than to the individual high priest) occurs ten times.[12] "Rulers" occurs four times in the sense of "religious authority."[13]

[10]The first to suggest that the terms for religious authorities derived from different authors was J. Wellhausen, *Das Evangelium Johannis*. He was followed by F. Spitta, *Das Johannesevangelium als Quelle der Geschichte Jesu* (Göttingen: Vandenhoeck & Ruprecht, 1910), 202-03. It was also noticed by M.C. White in his unpublished dissertation *The Identity and Function of Jews and Related Terms in the Fourth Gospel* (Ann Arbor: University Microfilms, 1972). However, in both cases the authors did not pursue the observation in a consistent way. Fortna also proposed ["Theological Use of Locale in the Fourth Gospel," *ATR Supp. Series 3* (1974) 91] that the term "Jews" was the evangelist's insertion into his source, but also suggested that "Pharisees" was John's insertion. The treatment here follows that which I proposed in "The Terms for Religious Authorities in the Fourth Gospel: A Key to Literary Strata?" *JBL* 98 (1979) 231-53. John Aston ["The Identity and Function of the *Ioudaioi* in the Fourth Gospel," *NovT* 27 (1985) 40-75] also attributes the terms to separate authors much as I would. However, his treatment is less thorough and does not attempt to deal with all the instances of the term within the gospel.

The majority of modern scholars do not sufficiently distinguish between the two sets of terms. For example, Bultmann attributes both material containing Pharisees (7:25-32, cf *Gospel* 306; 11:45-47, cf ibid. 409, n.8) and material containing Jews (9:19-23, cf ibid. 335, n.1) to the Evangelist. Yet he gives no explanation for the shift in terminology. Brown labels some of the references to Pharisees as "editorial" (e.g., 12:9-11, 17-19), yet does not think the shift in 9:18-23 is sufficient to indicate that the material comes from a different hand (cf *Gospel* 373, 459, 463-64).

Dodd [*Tradition* 242, n.1] speaks of the author using the term "imprecisely." Dodd then continues by pointing out the three meanings for the term. Nowhere does he suggest that the meanings are the result of editing. E. Graesser ["Die antijuedische Polemik im Johannesevangelium," *NTS* 10 (1964-65) 76], although careful in distinguishing various uses of the term "Jews," states that "the term can be used for religious authorities, but, in this sense, the Evangelist occasionally uses the traditional designations of chief priests, Pharisees, and rulers" (translation mine).

[11]1:24; 3:1; 4:1; 7:32 (twice), 45, 47, 48; 8:13; 9:13, 15, 16, 40; 11:46, 47, 57; 12:19, 42; 18:3.

[12]7:32, 45; 11:47, 57; 12:10; 18:3, 35; 19:6, 15, 21.

[13]3:1; 7:26, 48; 12:42. The use of "ruler" in the phrase "ruler of this world" is clearly a different sense and is not included here.

The second set of terms is the designation of the authorities as "Jews." The word "Jews" (*Ioudaioi*) occurs seventy-one times in the gospel, more frequently than in any other work of the New Testament. However, not all uses of the word are the same. Consequently, before this term can be of use in identifying material of the gospel, the various meanings of the word must be separated from one another.

The term is used first of all to refer to Jews in the national or religious sense.[14] This use seems to occur throughout the gospel and is not characteristic of one or the other edition of the gospel. Nor is this use unique to the gospel of John.

The second meaning of *Ioudiaos* in the gospel is "Judean." In Greek the same word can mean both Jew as in the sense above and also "Judean" referring both to the inhabitants of Judea and to the land of Judea itself. The word with this meaning occurs twelve times in the gospel.[15] This usage also is not unique to John and so must be distinguished from the characteristic Johannine use.

The third use of *Ioudiaos* in the gospel is the characteristic Johannine use and is without parallel in the ancient world. This use is entirely different from those described above. In these passages, the term is used to refer to religious authorities in a way that is unique to the gospel of John. This Johannine (or "hostile"[16]) sense of Jews occurs

---

[14]This would include references to Jewish religious/national customs (2:6; 19:40, 42), feasts (2:13; 5:1; 6:4; 7:2; 11:55) or to their authorities (e.g., "ruler of the Jews") (3:1; 18:20; 19:21a); references to individuals as "Jews" in a context which distinguishes them from non-Jews such as Samaritans or Romans (4:9a, 9b, 22; 18:35); references to Jesus as "King of the Jews" (18:33, 39; 19:3, 19, 21b, 21c).

[15]3:22 speaks of Jesus going into the Judean countryside (*eis tēn Ioudaian gēn*). References to "Judeans" occur in 1:19; 3:25; 11:19, 31, 33, 36, 45, 54; 12:9, 11; 19:20. Raymond Brown who noticed this usage in chapters 11 and 12 attributed those chapters to a special source but failed to notice that the same usage also occurred earlier in the gospel (*Gospel* xxxvii).

[16]This use is described as a "hostile" sense because in all of these instances where "Jews" refers to the religious authorities, the authorities are consistently portrayed as being hostile to Jesus. Detailed discussion of this is available in U.C. von Wahlde, "The Johannine 'Jews': A Critical Survey," *NTS* 28, 1 (1982), 33-60, esp. 47-48. This analysis has been accepted by Ashton ("Jews" 56-57). Ashton distinguishes between the sense and the reference of the term. I am not sure that either of these categories would aptly describe what I set out to describe. Although I am inclined to believe that these hostile Johannine "Jews" are symbolic of an attitude which is hostile to Jesus (as Ashton and Bultmann before him would hold—and what Ashton would call sense). In the above mentioned article I chose to omit that question from consideration. Nor did

thirty-seven times in the gospel.[17] It is this use of the term which contrasts with the designation of the religious authorities as Pharisees, chief priests, and rulers.

That this "hostile" sense of Jews is intended to refer to religious authorities is apparent from several features of its usage. First, the term occurs in contexts where it alternates with the other terms for religious authorities (e.g., 7:32-36; 9:13-41; 18:3-14).

Second, passages where the term Pharisees has been used to designate the authorities are referred to elsewhere but with the term Jews used for religious authorities. In 11:45-52, the authorities are designated as Pharisees; in 18:12-14 that passage is recalled but the authorities are there identified as Jews. The same is true of 18:3 where the attendants who arrest Jesus are identified as being "of the Pharisees"; in 18:12-14, they are described as attendants "of the Jews."[18]

A third indication is that persons who are ethnically Jews are said to "fear the Jews" (e.g., 7:13; 9:22; 20:19). These "Jews" are clearly not the common people but some authoritative group. The common people are also said to report to "the Jews" as to people in authority in 5:15. Finally, the crowd of 7:20 is contrasted with the "Jews" in that the crowd is not aware of the intention of the Jews to kill Jesus. A distinction is obviously intended between the two groups!

A fourth indication of the identity of the Jews as authorities is found

I choose to enter into the discussion of the historical "reference" of the characteristic Johannine usage ("Jews" in the national sense or "Judeans"). Rather I confined myself to the more limited issue of whether all instances of the word Jews *functioned* the same within the gospel. Ashton would agree with my conclusion that they do not. He also agrees that the hostile sense would refer only to authorities. These are two important advances in the understanding of the term. When these facets of the usage are coupled with the realization that the "neutral" and the "hostile" terms come from separate literary strata and that those which refer to authorities are to be distinguished from passages where the authorities are referred to as "Pharisees, chief priests, and rulers," then one has achieved sufficient precision to enable one to use them as criteria for separating the material of these two strata!

Finally, it is only when the editorial process is clear and both the theology and the historical circumstances of the community at the time of the second edition are clear that one is able to give a definitive answer to the question why the author chose this term to represent such an attitude and to the question of what meaning the term itself would have had to its contemporary readers ("Jew" or "Judean").

[17]2:18, 20; 5:10, 15, 16, 18; 6:41, 52; 7:1, 11, 13, 15, 35; 8:22, 31, 48, 52, 57; 9:18, 22; 10:19, 24, 31, 33; 11:8; 13:33; 18:12, 14, 31, 36, 38; 19:7, 12, 14, 31, 38; 20:19.

[18]See the more detailed discussion of this below.

in the function they are said to perform. In 9:22, it is said that these Jews have already passed an edict of excommunication against those who would confess Jesus as the Christ. Thus there can be no doubt that these "Johannine Jews" are intended to identify religious authorities.

These two sets of terms for religious authorities constitute separate frames of reference within the gospel. That is to say, the terms from the two groups are never intermixed. Although Pharisees, chief priests, and rulers are used with one another in various combinations throughout the gospel, they are never mixed with the term Jews as religious authorities. Second, where terms from the two sets are juxtaposed, contextual aporias occur indicating the presence of literary seams between the material. Finally, one of the most striking features of these two sets of terms is that there are some passages which were first narrated in the first stratum (which used Pharisees, chief priests and rulers) which are referred to in the second stratum. But when referring back to this earlier material, the author consistently substitutes the term Jews, the term appropriate to the second stratum.

The clearest example of this is 18:12-14 a passage which refers back to both 18:3 and to 11:49-50. In 11:45-50 the chief priests and Pharisees are said to convene the council and in v49 Caiaphas advises them that Jesus should die:

> "...some of them [the people from Judea] went to **the Pharisees** and told them what Jesus had done. So **the chief priests and the Pharisees** gathered the council, and said, 'What are we to do? For this man performs many signs. If we let him go on thus, everyone will believe in him, and the Romans will come and destroy both our holy place and our nation.' But one of them, Caiaphas, who was chief priest[19] that year, said to them, 'You know nothing at all; you do not understand that it is expedient for you that one man should die for the people, and that the whole nation should not perish'" (RSV modified as noted).

In 18:3 we see the following:

> "So Judas, procuring a band of soldiers and some officers from

[19]This is a literal rendering of the Greek. The RSV translates as "high" priest.

the chief priests and the Pharisees, went there [to the garden] with lanterns and torches and weapons." (RSV)

However, in 18:12-14, reference is made back to these two passages. Notice the substitution of different terms for the authorities:

> "So the band of soldiers and their captain and the officers of **the Jews** seized Jesus and bound him. First they led him to Annas; for he was the father-in-law of Caiaphas, who was high priest that year. It was Caiaphas who had given counsel to **the Jews** that it was expedient that one man should die for the people." (RSV)

Because of all these factors there can be no doubt that these two sets of terms for religious authorities stem from separate authors.[20] In addition, because the terms are so numerous in the gospel, they provide a means which is both objective and at the same time widespread within the gospel for determining a core of the first two editions of the gospel. It is because of the importance of these terms that we have spent so much time on the analysis of their use. In all that follows, we will see that the other characteristics of the two earliest editions of the gospel are associated consistently and exclusively with one or other of these two sets of terms.

Failure to distinguish various meanings of the same words has more than any other single factor crippled past attempts to use changes in language as a criterion for determining authorship. For example, both Fortna and Nicol list all instances of the "Jews" as typical of the evangelist.[21]

---

[20]For a detailed survey of past attempts to solve the puzzle of the Johannine Jews as well as the author's own analysis, see von Wahlde, "Jews" 34-41.

[21]Fortna, *Signs* 80, 82, 84; "Locale" 89-95. Fortna speaks of a complex use of *Ioudaioi* but sees this as a theological complexity rather than as a lexical complexity. He associates all uses of *Ioudaioi* with Judea and so makes these Jews/Judeans representative of unbelief ("Locale" 76-81). Consequently he does not distinguish the "neutral" use of the term from the "hostile." In chapter eleven, where the majority of the "neutral" uses occur, Fortna would see the term as a Johannine insertion just as he does for the remainder of the "hostile" uses ("Locale" 89). W. Nicol also attributes all occurrences of Jews to the evangelist (*Semeia* 17). The only contemporary proposal to consistently distinguish differences in usage is that of R. Brown. He, however, allows for the term in the sense of "Judean" only in chapters 11 and 12 (*Gospel* xxxvii).

In what follows we will see that distinctions must be made not only in the meanings of "Jew" (*Ioudaios*) but also in the various uses of "sign" (*sēmeion*) and "work" (*ergon*). When such distinctions in meaning are established and maintained, the consistency of usage for each of the terms becomes quite clear. But it is only when such distinctions are made that these various terms can be useful as criteria in determining literary strata.

2. THE TERMS FOR MIRACLE[22]

The second linguistic criterion is the shift in terminology for miracles in the first and second editions of the gospel. In passages where the terms Pharisees, chief priests, and rulers occur, the miracles are referred to as signs (*sēmeia*). In passages where the authorities are referred to as Jews, the miracles are referred to as works. (*erga*).[23] However, as was

---

[22]The first attempt to make the difference in terms for miracle a means of distinguishing authorship was by H.H. Wendt, *The Gospel According To John* (ET; Edinburgh: Clark, 1902) and *Die Schichten im vierten Evangelium* (Göttingen: Vandenhoeck & Ruprecht, 1911). Wendt rightly observed that "the 'signs' of Jesus, on which such special stress is laid in the narrative parts of the Fourth Gospel, do not play the same important part in the discourses: indeed they play no part at all" (*Gospel* 58). The purpose of Wendt's analysis was to determine the historical accuracy of the fourth gospel, using the synoptic outline as a norm (see *Gospel* 7-9, 31-32). On this basis Wendt concluded that the viewpoint of the signs was secondary (non-historical and that of the evangelist) and that the theology of the "works" represented the view of an older source the evangelist used for the discourses (*Gospel* 58-66; *Schichten* 49-53). Of course it is now recognized that the signs are in fact the older material.

Wilkens (*Entstehungsgeschichte, Zeichen*) attributed the two terms to separate editions but claimed that they were simply intended to reflect different theological views. Like Wendt, Wilkens recognized the association of the term signs with the narrative and works with the discourse material.

[23]Schnackenburg (*Gospel,* 515-528) struggles with the problem of the two terms: "...the question is why does the evangelist, whose style is mature and whose choice of words is deliberate, now use one term and now another. The difference cannot be explained by the use of various sources or on other grounds of literary criticism, since the terms are interchanged for no apparent reason within a given chapter." (p. 518). Brown (*Gospel,* 526) proposes that these two terms are distinguished by the fact that work appears only on the lips of Jesus (except at 7:3) and that others refer to them as signs. This is factually incorrect. In addition to 7:3, others speak of works in 10:33; Jesus himself uses the term sign in 4:48 and 6:26 and although the use in 4:48 can be said to be disparaging, the same is not true of 6:26. The gospel itself does not take a disparaging view of them as can be seen in the author's use of the terms in 12:37 and 20:30-31. Clearly then Brown's explanation is not sufficient.

the case with the term Jews, we cannot simply look to *all* uses of the words; a critical differentiation of the various uses of these terms is necessary.

The usage of signs in the gospel is relatively uncomplicated. All uses of the word occur in the sense of miracle except for the instances of 2:18 and 6:30.[24] As we shall see in greater detail in chapter 4, this use of sign to refer to miracles is cast against the Old Testament background of the signs at Exodus. The usage of sign in 2:18 and 6:30 however is a different usage.[25] Two things are noteworthy about these texts. First, in both, the religious authorities (identified as Jews) *demand* a sign. Throughout the gospel tradition such a demand for a sign is refused.[26] Thus even though the sign would presumably be a proof that Jesus was from God and thus would be not unlike the many other signs he performed, the fact that it was demanded and stemmed from unbelief puts this kind of sign in a separate category. As Schnackenburg says, "There is no continuity between this very negative concept of sign and the positive understanding of it in the fourth Gospel."[27] The use of sign in this sense of apologetic sign occurs in both instances with the term Jews (cf 2:18, 6:41) whereas sign in the sense of miracle always is associated with the terms Pharisees, chief priests and rulers.

The word "work" also occurs with two meanings. These must be differentiated if their use for the separation of editions is to be valid. First, work is used to refer to the miracles of Jesus. Jesus performs the works (7:21; 9:4(?); 10:25; 14:11, 12; 15:24) that the Father has given him (5:36; 10:32, 37; 14:10). These works are his miracles. Thus Jesus can be said to work (5:17) just as the Father works. But the individual

---

[24]The texts where the term refers to miracles are: 2:11, 23; 3:2: 4:48, 54; 6:2, 14, 26; 7:31; 9:16; 10:41; 11:47; 12:18, 37; 20:30.

[25]This is commonly pointed out by commentators. For example, Schnackenburg, *Gospel* I, 517; Brown, *Gospel* 527-28; Barrett, *Gospel* 199; Wilkens, *Zeichen,* 62-65. Wendt (*Gospel* 58-59) does not see a different meaning in these cases but attributes them to the same edition as the remaining instances of signs. This is unlikely as we shall see below.

[26]In Mt 12:38-39, the scribes and Pharisees demand a sign and Jesus refuses saying that "an evil and adulterous generation seeks for a sign but no sign shall be given it except the sign of the prophet Jonah." Similarly, in 16:1-4 and in Lk 11:16 and 29-32. In Mk when the Pharisees demand a sign (8:11-13), Jesus refuses: "No sign shall be given to this generation."

[27]Schnackenburg, *Gospel* 1 517.

works are also said to be part of a larger work given him by the Father. Work in this sense (always in the singular) is a theological conceptualization for the ministry of Jesus as a whole. So, for example, in 4:34 Jesus says that his food is to do the will of him who sent him and "to accomplish his work." The description of the ministry as a work also occurs in 17:4. In both of these instances, the verb translated "accomplish" can also mean "to bring to completion or perfection."[28] Not only are the individual works of Jesus related to the overall work given him by the Father, but in doing this he cooperates with the Father and so brings the work of the Father to completion and perfection.[29]

However, alongside of this complex of ideas, which echoes the Old Testament description of the action of Yahweh,[30] there is another complex which does not have a parallel in the Old Testament but which rather derives from apocalyptic.[31] This is the usage of the word work in the phrase "to work the works of someone" or "to do the works of someone." It is clear from the context where such usage occurs that this usage does not intend to refer to miracles but simply to human acts or deeds which are done to fulfill the request of another.[32] In this sense it is synonymous with "doing the will" of someone and reflects the conviction of apocalyptic that all human acts are done

[28]The same verb is used of the works (plural = miracles) of Jesus in 5:36; but more often it is the simple verb "perform" (*poiein*) (7:3, 21; 10:25, 32, 33, 37, 38; 14:10, 12; 15:24).

[29]The complete listing of the occurrences of "work" referring to miracles is: 5:20, 36; 7:3, 21; 9:3, (4?); 10:25, 32, 33, 37, 38; 14:10, 11, 12; 15:24. To be grouped with these is the use of "work" (both noun and verb) to refer to the ministry as a whole: 4:34; 5:17; 9:4; 17:4.

[30]The background of work as a designation of miracle is discussed in more detail in G. Bertram, "ergon" *TDNT* 635-52, esp 642-43.

[31]I have discussed this at greater length in "Faith and Works in Jn vi 28-29" *NovT* 22, 4 (1980) 304-315. Such a use which stems from the world of dualistic thought was suggested previously by R. Bergmeier, "Glaube als Werk? Die 'Werke Gottes' in Damaskusschrift II, 14-15 und Johannes 6, 28-29," *RevQ* 6 (1967) 253-60. However, this important distinction in the use of the term has not been recognized by commentators in the past. This dualist usage occurs exclusively in the third stratum of material in the gospel which is the only stratum typically marked by elements of apocalyptic.

[32]This usage occurs in 3:19, 20, 21; 6:28, 29; 7:7; 8:39, 41. 9:4 may also be an example of this use. However it is at least possible that the use in 9:4 belongs to the "Johannine" use to refer to miracles.

under the influence of either good or evil spirits. A clear example of this use is 8:39. In reply to the Jews' claim that Abraham is their father, Jesus says, "If you were children of Abraham you would do the works of Abraham (*ta erga tou Abraam epoieite*). Now you seek to kill me ... this Abraham would not have done. You do the works of your father. (*hymeis poieite ta erga tou patrous hymōn*)." The Jews then respond, "We are not born of fornication, we have one father, God." Jesus responds, "If God were your father, you would love me. . . . You are of the devil your father and you do his wishes (*tas epithymias tou patros hymōn thelete poiein*)." (my translation) In all of this we see clearly that the works here are really paralleled with "what Abraham would have done" and "doing his wishes."

This same expression is found throughout apocalyptic literature with clear parallels attested at Qumran and in the pseudepigrapha.[33] For example:

> And now, children, harken unto me, and I shall uncover your eyes to see and consider the works of God; to choose that in which he delights and to reject that which he hates, to walk uprightly in all his ways and not to wander according to the designs of a guilty inclination and the allurement of lust (CD2:14-16 DSSE 98).

Here the phrase "works of God" does not refer to anything miraculous; rather it refers to his wishes, to those works which when performed would be pleasing to God. These instances do not represent the same usage as that of the first group and are not to be grouped with those.

This brief review of the use of sign and work in John provides several valuable insights. Like the terms for religious authorities, the two sets of terms for miracles are never used together, but on the other hand, they do occur consistently and exclusively with the same sets of terms for religious authorities. So signs (in the sense of miracle, excluding 2:18; 6:30) occurs consistently with Pharisees, chief priests, and rulers, while works (in the sense of miracle and in the related sense describing the ministry of Jesus) occurs consistently in passages where the religious authorities are called Jews. Let us look at some examples.

---

[33]For other examples see my article referred to above.

In material of the first edition[34] (3:1-2):

> "Now there was a man of **the Pharisees**, named Nicodemus, **a ruler of the Jews**. This man came to Jesus by night and said to him, "Rabbi, we know that you are a teacher come from God; for no one can do **these signs** that you do, unless God is with him." (RSV)

Again in 7:31-31:

> "Yet many of the people believed in him; they said, 'When the Christ appears, will he do more **signs** than this man has done?' The **Pharisees** heard the crowd thus muttering about him, and **the chief priests** and **Pharisees** sent officers to arrest him" (RSV)

In the discussion regarding the man born blind (9:16), we read:

> "Some of the **Pharisees** said, 'This man is not from God, for he does not keep the sabbath.' But others said, 'How can a man who is a sinner do such **signs**?' There was division among them." (RSV)

But when we turn to the material of the second edition we see both a change in terms for authorities and in the terms for miracles. Following the healing of the paralytic, we read (5:15):

> "The man went away and told **the Jews** that it was Jesus who had healed him. And this was why **the Jews** persecuted Jesus, because he did this on the Sabbath. But Jesus answered them, 'My Father is **working** still, and I am **working**.' This is why **the Jews** sought all the more to kill him, because he not only broke the sabbath, but also called God his own Father..." (RSV)

And in 10:24-38:

> "So **the Jews** gathered round him and said to him, 'How long will you keep us in suspense? If you are the Christ, tell us plainly.' Jesus

---

[34]It will become clear as we proceed that the material marked by "Pharisees, chief priests and rulers" and by the term "sign" for miracle belong to the first edition of the gospel. The material identified by the term "Jews" has been added to this other material and constitutes the core of the second edition.

answered them, 'I told you, and you do not believe. **The works** which I do in my Father's name, they bear witness to me; but you do not believe....' ... **The Jews** took up stones to stone him. Jesus answered them, 'I have shown you many good **works** from the Father; for which of these do you stone me?' **The Jews** answered him, 'It is not for a good **work** that we stone you....' ... 'If I am not doing **the works** of the Father, then do not believe me; but if I do them, even though you do not believe me, believe **the works**, that you may know and understand that the Father is in me and I am in the Father.'"

The correlation of these terms with one another is both consistent and exclusive throughout the gospel, provided the proper distinctions are maintained regarding the meaning of the terms. Consequently they clearly identify the material of the first two strata of the gospel and provide a basis for further exploration of the gospel.

The determination that the two terms come from separate authors also enables us to provide a more satisfactory solution for a continuing theological tension in Johannine theology. As early as 1900, Wendt[35] pointed out such a distinction and demonstrated that "signs" occurred in the narrative, and "works" occurred in the discourses. However, the parallel observation, that signs never (6:26 is an exception) occurs on the lips of Jesus while works does, led many scholars to suspect that the solution lay in the area of theological distinctions rather than in the area of separate authorship. Thus the view of the miracles as works would be the view of Jesus which corrected the insufficient view of the miracles as signs. Yet in other ways signs was always considered to represent a characteristic of Johannine theology in that the miracles were meant to be signs in the sense of being symbolic of a deeper reality. As long as both were seen to be the work of the same individual there resulted a continuing tension about which term (or whether both terms) represented the theology of the evangelist. The recognition that the terms stem from different authors with different theological viewpoints will finally enable us to relate the two terms theologically in a more critical way.

[35]Wendt, *Gospel* 58.

3. THE USE OF 'JEWS' TO REFER TO JUDEANS

We have already seen that the word Jews in the gospel can have the meaning of "Judean" as well as "Jew." This use of the term does not occur in passages where the term also means "religious authorities." However, it does occur in passages where the terms Pharisees, chief priests, and rulers occur.[36] That the term is intended to refer to Judeans is apparent first by the absence of the hostility present in the characteristic Johannine instances but more important by its close association with the mention either of Judea itself (3:22) or with Jerusalem (11:18; 12:12). This use is apparent particularly throughout the story of the raising of Lazarus and its aftermath. In addition, its combination with the other terms characteristic of the first edition is clear. For example:

> "Many of **the Judeans**[37] therefore, who had come with Mary and had seen what he did, believed in him; but **some of them** [the people from Judea] went to **the Pharisees** and told them what Jesus had done. So **the chief priests** and the **Pharisees** gathered the council, and said, 'What are we to do? For this man performs many **signs**. If we let him go on thus, everyone will believe in him, and the Romans will come and destroy both our holy place and our nation.' But one of them, Caiaphas, who was chief priest[38] that year, said to them, 'You know nothing at all; you do not understand that it is expedient for you that one man should die for the people, and that the whole nation should not perish.'" (RSV, modified as noted).

Notice also 12:9-11:

> "When the great crowd of **the Judeans**[39] learned that he was there, they came, not only on account of Jesus but also to see Lazarus, whom he had raised from the dead. So **the chief priests** planned to put Lazarus also to death because on account of him many of **the**

---

[36]In 3:22 it refers to the territory of Judea. In 3:25; 11:19, 31, 33, 36, 45, 54; 12:9, 11; 19:20, the term refers to Judeans.

[37]This is a literal rendering. The RSV has "Jews."

[38]RSV: high priest.

[39]RSV: Jews.

Judeans[40] were going away and believing in Jesus" (RSV, modified as noted).

CONCLUSIONS FROM THE STUDY OF THE PRIMARY LINGUISTIC CRITERIA

This detailed study of the language of the gospel of John, while it may at first sight seem to be technical and uninteresting, should by now have awakened the interest of the reader. For it should be clear how consistent this use of language is within the gospel (when the usage is critically defined) and how clearly it identifies distinct bodies of material within the gospel!

Looking back at the gospel from the point of view of the differences in terminology described above, it may seem curious that such distinct differences in terminology have not regularly been the basis upon which literary analysis of the gospel is founded. However, it should be noticed that using these terms as criteria is not possible if all instances of a given term are taken together indiscriminately. Past attempts to use the two sets of terms for religious authorities and for miracles did not include such distinctions in a sufficiently thorough way. It is only recently that we have achieved a sufficiently nuanced sense of the difference in meanings given to the same terms by different authors. When these differences in meaning are attended to, then we have a sufficiently critical basis for separating the literary strata of the gospel.

What is particularly helpful is that the three sets of primary linguistic criteria are sufficiently frequent within the gospel to mark off large bodies of material within the gospel. Although one other linguistic characteristic of the gospel is evident and will be discussed immediately below, this is not a primary criterion since it does not occur in passages marked by the other distinctive vocabulary.

In Appendix A the reader is given a listing of the texts identified by the primary linguistic criteria. It is these passages which will be used in the establishment of the ideological and theological criteria below.

[40]RSV: Jews.

A Secondary Linguistic Criterion

4. THE TRANSLATION OF PLACE NAMES AND RELIGIOUS TERMS

Ten times in the gospel of John terms are translated for the reader. These terms are of two types and, curiously, each is handled differently but consistently. Words which refer to Jewish religious concepts are first given in Hebrew and then translated into Greek (1:38, 41, 42; 2:33;[41] 20:16); place names are first given in Greek and then translated into Hebrew (Aramaic) (5:2; 6:1;[42] 9:7; 19:13, 17[43]). Of these latter the Aramaic version is given first only in 6:1 and 9:7.

First, let us look at the translations of religious terms. The most frequent occurrence of these translations occurs in the gathering of the first disciples. The text of 1:38 states: "And they said to him, 'Rabbi' (which means Teacher)." When Andrew tells Simon of Jesus, he says (1:41): "'We have found the Messiah' (which means Christ.)" When Jesus changes Simon's name (1:42), we see: "You shall be called Cephas (which means Peter)." In 2:23, a literal translation of the Greek states: "When he was in Jerusalem, in the Pasch, in the feast, many believed in his name, seeing the signs which he was performing." In 20:16, when the risen Jesus addresses Mary we read: ". . . [s]he turned and said to him in Hebrew, 'Rabboni!' (which means Teacher)."

Place names are generally handled in the reverse order. The first of

---

[41]The RSV has eliminated the awkardness of the Greek. The original reads "While he was in Jerusalem at the Pasch, at the feast. . . ." This is the same technique as is operative in the other more extensive translations.

[42]This is not precisely a translation but rather a juxtaposition of the Jewish and secular names for the same location. It seems to be simply a variant of the technique operative in the other translations.

[43]The editing here has juxtaposed material with the term "Jews" to material from the early stratum. 18:39-19:6a seem to be derived from the early edition. But 19:6b-12 come from the middle edition as clearly identified by the terms for authorities as well as by the religious concerns and the interest in high christology. The original version of the scene probably continued in 19:13-14 (which follows well on 19:6a). Then the author of the second edition added 19:14b-15a to re-establish the context of the cry for crucifixion (which had to be re-introduced after the long interruption of 19:6b-12) and the answer to the cry for crucifixion is then resumed from the early edition where the concern was political ("We have only one king—Caesar"). The basic narrative of the passion then continues in the material of the first edition through 19:22. (See below chap. 3 for detailed analysis.)

these occurs in 5:2: "Now there is in Jerusalem by the Sheep Gate a pool, in Hebrew called Bethzatha.... In 6:1, the order is reversed and the Jewish name is given first: "After this Jesus went to the other side of the Sea of Galilee, (which is the Sea) of Tiberias."[44] In 9:7, although the text of the gospel is verbally identical to the other instances, the purpose is not to give the secular name but to explain the meaning of the term. Jesus addresses the blind man and tells him, "'Go, wash in the pool of Siloam' (which means Sent)."[45] 19:13 describes the place where Pilate renders judgment: "...and [he] sat down on the judgment seat at a place called The Pavement, in Hebrew Gabbatha." 19:17 describes the place of the crucifixion: "...and [Jesus] went out ... to the place called the place of a skull, which is called in Hebrew Golgotha."

The purpose of these frequent translations seems simple: to provide religious and geographical terminology in the language familiar to Jewish readers and also to provide the secular Greek equivalents.[46]

Relatively few of these occur in passages identified by primary criteria (i.e., the linguistic features just discussed) as material from the early edition.[47] Nevertheless, all occur in material which is identified either by primary criteria or by secondary criteria (i.e., the ideological and theological criteria to be discussed in the following sections of this chapter).[48] These various translations are listed here since they are

[44]The parentheses here are mine to indicate that in the Greek only the double names of the sea itself appear: *peran tēs thalassēs tēs Galilaias tēs Tiberiados.*

I am inclined to think that the references to the various feasts and customs as "of the Jews" are also to be related to this practice of translating terms. However, I do not intend to imply that they are exactly the same technique. They are more properly related to instances such as 3:1 (where Nicodemus is referred to in the signs material as a "ruler of the Jews") and 19:21 ("chief priests of the Jews").

[45]The Greek *ho hermēneuetai Apestalmenos* is exactly the same as that in 1:42 and a variant of *methermēneuein* used in 1:38, 41.

[46]Only in 9:7 is there any indication that the translation is intended to bring out a symbolic meaning. That such symbolism is not developed within the miracle may indicate that the later exegetical attempts to find such symbolism here are misguided and that the original intention may simply be translation!

It is not possible to tell whether these translations are the work of an editor providing a translation for a term that was not translated in the original. All it is possible to say with certainty is that the phenomena are distributed consistently within the gospel. It is this consistency that allows their use as a criterion.

[47]Only 2:23; 5:2; and 6:1 occur in passages containing primary criteria.

[48]Of course this list does not account for all of the religious terminology or place

specific linguistic characteristics. They will be discussed in detail in chapter 3 in relation to the passages in which they occur.

The Ideological Differences

As was indicated above, ideological differences are those differences in the thought of the author which are not directly theological but which reflect in a less deliberate way the perspective of an author. There are a considerable number of these ideological differences between the signs material and the remainder of the gospel. In each case, the material is also identified by the specific linguistic characteristics which have just been discussed.

5. STEREOTYPED FORMULAS OF BELIEF

One of the most striking ideological features of the material of the early edition is that it contains repeated statements of belief in Jesus which occur in stereotyped form. This belief always occurs after the miracle rather than before it, is always as a result of "signs", and occurs in either of two set forms: ". . . many of the (name of group) believed in him" or ". . . and 'they' (with or without the name of group) believed in him." In almost all cases there is explicit mention of the miracles as "signs"—or other characteristics of the signs material. For example:

> 2:11. This, the first of **his signs,** Jesus did at Cana in Galilee, and manifested his glory; **and his disciples believed in him. (RSV)**

> 2:23 Now when he was in Jerusalem at the Passover feast, **many believed in his name,** when they saw **the signs which he did.** (RSV)

> 4:39 **Many Samaritans from that city believed in him** because of the woman's testimony, "He told me all that I ever did."[49]

names in the gospel or even in the signs material. Only *some* terms were treated this way and it is not possible to discover the reason why some were translated and others were not. My purpose here is to show that those which were translated occur consistently in the signs material.

[49]Although this incident is not identified as a sign within the passage itself, it is identified as such in 4:54. See the full discussion of the passage in chapter 3.

4:53 . . . and **he himself (the official) believed and all his household.**[50] (RSV)

7:31. Yet **many of the people believed in him;** they said, "When the Christ appears, will he do **more signs** than this man has done?" **The Pharisees** heard the crowd thus muttering about him, and **the chief priests and Pharisees** sent officers to arrest him. (RSV)

10:41-42 And many came to him; and they said, "John did **no sign,** but everything that John said about this one man [Jesus] was true." **And many believed in him there.** (RSV)

11:45 **Many of the Judeans** [RSV: Jews], who had come with Mary **and had seen those [things] which he had done** [RSV: what he did[51]], **believed in him;** but some of them went to the **Pharisees** and told **them those [signs] which Jesus had done.**[52] So **the chief priests and Pharisees** gathered the council, and said, "What are we to do? For this man **performs many signs.**"(RSV)

12:11 So **the chief priests** planned to put Lazarus also to death, because on account of him **many of the Judeans** [RSV: Jews] **were going away and believing in Jesus.** (RSV).

12:42 Nevertheless **many even of the rulers believed in him,** but **for fear of the Pharisees** they did not confess it, lest they should be put out of the synagogue.[53] (RSV, modified)

The fact that these stereotyped expressions of belief can be identified so clearly with the first edition is important because of the role of these expressions in the gospel. First, they are of importance theologically because they demonstrate so clearly that belief follows the miracle in the signs material, that there was such a focus on such "signs belief"

---

[50]This miracle is explicitly identified as a sign in 4:54: "This was now the second sign that Jesus did when he had come from Judea to Galilee."

[51]The Greek text has *ha epoiēsen.* The modified translation is an attempt to reflect that the Greek relative is a neuter plural and therefore was undoubtedly intended to refer to "signs" which would also be neuter plural.

[52]The Greek is the same as in 11:45. I have modified the RSV as in the previous verse.

[53]Although this statement of belief originally was part of the signs material, it has undoubtedly been redacted to include the later crisis of synagogue exclusion. See the full discussion in chapter 3.

and they also show how "easy" such belief was considered to be. But they are also important from a form critical viewpoint because they demonstrate clearly that the stereotyped formulas were an integral part of the signs themselves. Several theories dealing with the signs material (notably those of Nicol and Schnackenburg) have suggested that the signs were not part of a narrative framework, but that the narrative framework was the result of the evangelist. The nature of these stereotyped expressions of belief makes this view unlikely.

It has long been recognized that the form of a miracle story consists of (1) the description of the illness, (2) the working of the miracle itself, (3) the reaction of the crowd/attestation of the miracle. Several examples of the stereotyped expressions of belief identified above (e.g., 2:11; 4:39, 53; 11:45) clearly constitute the third element of the miracle "form" and so cannot be considered simply as an appendage to the miracle. Thus we can see that the material we have identified is not distinct (at least at the literary level) from yet another signs source beneath it. The signs material we are discovering is the first edition of the gospel!

We have mentioned the theological importance of these stereotyped expressions. We will return in a later chapter[54] to a full discussion of these theological features.

6. TANDEM BELIEF

A second feature of the material is what could be called "tandem" (or "chain reaction") belief. That is, within the material of the first stratum of the gospel, belief is often pictured as being "passed on" from one to another. First, one person believes and then another person or group is also led to believe. Such tandem belief occurs in the story of the calling of the disciples (1:35-49), where Andrew gets Peter and where Philip gets Nathanael, and where, as we shall see below, it is possible that in the original sequence Peter had gotten Philip. It occurs in the story of the Samaritan woman where first the woman believes and then the townspeople believe on the basis of her report (cf 4:28-30, 39). It is also true of the official who believes—and also his whole household (cf 4:54). It occurs in the story of the Judeans who believe

---

[54]See chapter 4 below.

on the basis of the raising of Lazarus (11:45) and who then tell another group. This group also comes to Bethany to see both Jesus and Lazarus and also come to belief (12:9-11; cf 12:17-18).[55]

7. CONCERN FOR THE QUANTITY AND QUALITY OF JESUS' SIGNS

In those passages where the miracles of Jesus are referred to as signs, there is a particular emphasis on the number and the greatness of signs. But such concern is almost entirely absent from the material associated with the works. Let us look at the signs material first.

In 3:2 Nicodemus inquires about the signs saying, "No one can perform 'these signs' (*tauta ta sēmeia*) that you do unless God is with him." In 4:45 it is said that the Galileans had seen "all that he had done" (*panta heōraketes hosa epoiēsen*). In 7:32 the crowd asks whether, when the Christ appears, he will do "more signs" (*Me pleiona sēmeia poiēsei*) than this man. In 9:16 the signs are referred to as "such [great] signs" (*toiauta sēmeia*). In 10:40-42 we hear that John did "no" sign. This contrast also puts emphasis on the signs worked by Jesus. In 11:47 the authorities ask what they are to do since this man performs "many signs" (*polla sēmeia poiei*). In 12:37 the narrator, describing the unbelief of the authorities, says, "Though he had done 'so many signs' . . ." (*tosauta sēmeia*). In 20:30 the narrator states, "Now Jesus did 'many other signs' . . ." (*polla men oun kai alla sēmeia epoiēsen*) (RSV throughout).

In addition to these passages which are characterized by specific adjectives, there are other passages which focus on the magnitude of Jesus' signs but without such specific characteristics. These passages include, of course, the narratives of the (public) signs themselves (2:1-11; 4:4-42; 4:46-54; 5:1-9; 6:3-14; 6:16-21; 9:1-41; 11:1-45), where as we shall see in detail in chapter 4 there is constant emphasis on the greatness of the signs. Finally, there is the mention in the aftermath of the raising of Lazarus the fact that because of the greatness of that miracle, many others were coming to see Jesus (12:9, 18-19).

---

[55]It also occurs in 1:35-49 where the disciples, who first come to belief on the report of John the Baptist, later get other disciples to follow Jesus. See the discussion in chapter 3.

In material of the second edition, the picture is quite different. Jesus asks the Jews to consider his "works" (5:20; 10:32) and even predicts "greater works (*erga*) than these will he [the Father] show him [Jesus] that you may marvel" (RSV) (*meizona toutōn deiksei autō*). But there is no reaction to these "works." They are intended to witness to Jesus (5:36) but they have little effect. In 10:25 we read: "The works that I do in my Father's name, they bear witness to me; but you do not believe." In 10:31-33, when the "Jews" take up stones to stone Jesus, he says, "I have shown you many good works from the Father, for which of these do you stone me?" (RSV) "The Jews" answer, saying, "It is not for a good work that we stone you but for blasphemy..." (RSV). Later he says, "Even though you do not believe me, believe the works..." (RSV). In the material of the second edition, the miracles do not seem to have any effect at all; they do not lead to belief as they did in the first edition. Not only do the language and ideology differ in the two editions, but the overall conception of the miraculous is hardly the same.

8. EMPHASIS ON THE VARIETY OF GROUPS WHICH COME TO BELIEF IN JESUS

Within the signs material there is an evident interest in showing that the belief in Jesus was not something confined to a single segment of society but that this belief occurred in widely diverse groups. This is evidenced in two ways. First, in the stereotyped formulas of belief described above, there is a striking diversity of groups represented: his disciples (2:11) (*kai episteusan ... hoi mathētai autou*); the people in Jerusalem for the feast (2:23) (*polloi episteusan*); the Samaritans (4:39) (*ek de tēs poleōs ekeinēs polloi episteusan...*); the people in Jerusalem for the feast of Tabernacles (7:31) (*ek tou ochlou de polloi episteusan...*); people across the Jordan where John used to baptize (10:42) (*kai polloi episteusan ... ekei*); many of the Judeans who came to console Mary at the death of Lazarus and who saw the sign (11:45) (*polloi oun ek tōn Ioudaiōn hoi elthontes pros tēn Mariam kai theasamenoi ha epoiēsen, episteusan ...*); many of the Judeans who had heard about the sign and had come from Jerusalem (12:11) (*polloi hypēgon tōn Ioudaiōn kai episteuon ...* (see also 12:18). Even many of the authorities believed (12:42) (*ek tōn archontōn polloi episteusan ...*) although they did not confess their belief openly.

A second type of evidence for this concern for the variety of groups is more general but nevertheless clear. In 1:35-49 it is noteworthy that former disciples of John the Baptist come to belief in Jesus. In 3:26 we are told that "all" from the Judean countryside are "going to him." This is echoed in 4:1, where we hear that Jesus is making more disciples than John. 4:45 echoes the belief of the crowds in Jerusalem for the feast but tells us that some of these were Galileans and that they welcomed Jesus upon his return into Galilee (see also 6:2, 14). Certainly the official of 4:46-54 (whether he was a Roman military official or a Jewish synagogue official) and his household represent another sector of society professing belief in Jesus. At the end of the public ministry (12:20), the reference to the Greeks coming to Jesus is a final example of such a group—and this time it is a Gentile group—about to express their belief in him. It seems unlikely that the presentation of the belief of such diverse groups is accidental but intended to show the eminent reasonableness of such belief. Even the authorities come to such belief (12:42) but are afraid to express it. Finally, the author himself (20:30-31) expresses the hope that the signs will be the cause of belief for yet another group: the readers.

9. REACTION OF THE PHARISEES TO THE SIGNS

In the material of the first edition of the gospel, there is a repeated pattern whereby after an expression of belief by the common people, there is an immediate reaction on the part of the religious authorities. This is not present in the material of the second edition. The element in focus here is that the reaction follows *immediately* and is *directly* tied to the reaction of the people to the signs. There are other passages where the Pharisees, chief priests, and rulers discuss the meaning of the signs, but these passages do not exhibit the immediacy that the other passages do. We will look at those second.

a) Immediate Reaction by Authorities

Following the expression of belief in 2:23-25, there is a reaction in 3:1-2 by Nicodemus, identified as a ruler of the Jews, who inquires about the meaning of the signs and points out that Jesus must be from God.[56]

---

[56]The frequency and consistency of the pattern of belief followed by reaction of the

In 7:32, after we have heard that many of the common people believe in Jesus, we find an immediate reaction on the part of the Pharisees who are aware of this and react by sending soldiers to arrest Jesus.

After the healing of Lazarus, when the large crowd of Jews (i.e., Judeans) come to believe in Jesus, some go to the Pharisees and the chief priests (11:46-47). The Pharisees and chief priests convene the Sanhedrin, and discuss his signs (v47) and decide that if they allow him to continue "all will come to believe in him" (v48), and the Romans will come and destroy the Temple and the nation.

In 12:9-11, the chief priests react again to the Lazarus miracle and to the fact that many are coming to believe in Jesus because of Lazarus. As a result they decide to put Lazarus himself to death.

Finally in 12:18-19, after the comment that the reason the crowd had given Jesus acclaim was "that they heard he had done this sign, we hear immediately: "The Pharisees then said to one another, 'You see that you can do nothing; look, the world has gone after him.'"

b) Other Examples of Reaction by the Authorities

There are also several other passages in which the "Pharisees" discuss the meaning of Jesus' signs but the discussion does not follow so immediately upon the reaction of the people.

In 7:45-52 the authorities again engage in debate following the return of the attendants who have not arrested Jesus and who almost seem to have been "converted" also (cf their remark in 7:46: "No man ever spoke like this man!" They again discuss his claims and "what he does" (this time in entirely negative terms) and deny that he could be "the (Mosaic) prophet."

In 9:13, after the healing of the man born blind, the Pharisees again enter into a discussion of what Jesus' miracles mean. This time they discuss it with the man himself. After the intervention of 9:18-23 (which comes from the second stratum) the discussion becomes specific: this man is a sinner (v24) and because he is a sinner he cannot be from God (vv29, 31).

---

authorities in the early material is one of the indications that 2:24-25 did not belong to that early material but were a later addition. These verses will be discussed more fully in chapter 3.

The popularity of Jesus following the raising of Lazarus and the reaction of the authorities was noted above. However, yet again in 11:57 after the remark that the people coming to the Passover were looking for Jesus and asking one another whether he would come to the feast, the Pharisees finally give orders that anyone who knows where Jesus is is to inform the authorities so they might arrest him (11:57).

This repeated reaction of the Pharisees, as I indicated above, has two elements. First, it occurs in a pattern in which such reaction frequently follows immediately on indication of belief of the people. Second, and somewhat more generally, this reaction is always *to the signs of Jesus.*

In the second edition there is none of this. The miracles are not a concern for the authorities! Jesus himself has to call attention to them. In 5:20 he is presented as himself saying that they will see "greater [works] than these." In 10:25-39, when Jesus addresses the authorities (now of course identified as Jews) they say that they are not about to stone him because of his miracles (now of course identified as works) but because of the fact that he blasphemes. Clearly, the portrayal in the material of the middle edition is totally different in its orientation from that of the first.

10. THE INCREASING HOSTILITY OF THE PHARISEES[57]

In the material of the first edition of the gospel, the reaction of the authorities (Pharisees, etc.) grows in intensity throughout the gospel. In the material of the second edition, the hostility toward Jesus exhibits the same level of intensity from the beginning.

Within the signs material, we find at first the curiosity of Nicodemus. However, there is evidence of considerable skepticism by 4:1-4, where in reaction to the Pharisees Jesus withdraws to Galilee. The next time they appear on the scene (7:32, 45-52), the Pharisees are ready to arrest

[57]R. Fortna has spoken of a tension in John's portrayal of the authorities ("Locale" 90-91). Although his article was not intended to be a source-critical study, in the list he provides, the texts proposed as demonstrating "increasing hostility" match in almost every respect the listing given here. The same is true of the listing given regarding those passages which demonstrate "intense but level hostility" throughout.

him so that he can be questioned. But the enthusiasm of the crowds persuades even the attendants and so nothing is done.[58] In chapter 9, the Pharisees are still presented as divided in their assessment of Jesus (v16).[59]

However, after the raising of Lazarus the problem of Jesus becomes unbearable and they convene the Sanhedrin (v47-50)[60] and, on the basis of his signs, decide to put him to death. "If we let him go on thus, everyone will believe in him and the Romans will come and destroy both our holy place and our nation." 12:53 then makes the issue clear: "So from that day on they took counsel how to put him to death."

Even beyond this there is a portrayal of increasing intensity. In 11:54 we hear that Jesus no longer went openly among the Jews (i.e., Judeans). In 11:55-57 we hear of the speculation in the crowd whether Jesus will come to the feast, and we hear that the chief priests have given orders that anyone who knows where Jesus is should inform the authorities. In 12:9 we hear that the reaction to the Lazarus miracle is still growing and that many more Judeans are believing in Jesus and that this has caused the chief priests to decide to put even Lazarus to death! In 12:19 the Pharisees sense their helplessness in the face of this popular reaction. It then eventuates of course in the arrest of Jesus (18:1-3) (also narrated in the early material).

Thus, following the sequence of material in the early edition, we see not only a gradual increase in hostility but also the presentation of the details of the events from the decision of the Sanhedrin to put Jesus to death to the actual arrest.

In the material of the second edition, where the authorities are the Jews, there is no sense of building to a climax. From the first time they appear (2:18-22) the Jews exhibit an intense hostility which seems

[58]The comment in v30 that "no one laid hands on him because his hour had not yet come" is almost surely from the material of the second edition where the superiority of Jesus to all things human is stressed.

[59]This contrasts sharply with the addition of "Jews" material in vv18-23 where the authorities are presented not only as unanimous in their appraisal of Jesus but as having reached their conclusion so long ago that they had already issued a formal edict of communication which was now well known (cf. the reaction of the blind man's parents).

[60]V51-52 are almost surely later additions to the text. See the discussion in chapter 3.

designed to simply present typical Jewish objections to Jesus.[61] This impression is confirmed in 5:10-20 where they persecute Jesus because he acted on the Sabbath but all the more because "he called God his own Father, making himself equal with God." In this material as early as 5:18 we hear that they are seeking to kill Jesus. This is repeated in 7:1 where he is said to stay away from Judea (cf also 11:8). In 8:59, the Jews take up stones to stone Jesus and it is only by (an evidently miraculous) disappearance that Jesus escapes. In 10:31, the Jews again seek to stone him. All of this has little in common with the picture of the authorities' hostility presented in the early stratum.

We are undoubtedly on solid ground saying that in the first edition of the gospel, the narrative intended to portray a more historically plausible view of the authorities' hostility while in the second edition the authorities are simply the device for the presentation of Jewish objections to Johannine Christianity toward the end of the first century.

11. THE PEOPLE'S REACTION TO THE AUTHORITIES

In the early material there is a consistent portrayal of the authorities as fearing the reaction of the people, and the common people enter into debate with the authorities. In the second edition the reverse is true: the people consistently fear the authorities and indeed are afraid to talk back to them.

In 4:1-4, the Pharisees are concerned with the number of disciples that Jesus is making.[62] In 7:32, the Pharisees and chief priests hear the crowd talking about Jesus and evidently fear the people's acclaim of Jesus and so send attendants to arrest Jesus. In 7:45 the attendants return without arresting Jesus and when they are questioned they dare even to talk back to the authorities.

In chapter 9, the man born blind engages in extended debate with the Pharisees. They ask him what he thinks of Jesus, he in turn asks them if they wish to become disciples of Jesus![63]

---

[61]This feature of the "Jews" material is discussed at somewhat greater length in von Wahlde, "Jews" 47-54.

[62]Jesus is portrayed as moving from Judea to Galilee because of this but there is no indication of the abject fear characteristic of the material of the second edition.

[63]Compare the attitude of the parents in the material of the second edition inserted into 9:18-23, where the parents are afraid to respond "because of fear of the Jews."

In chapter 12, even though the chief priests have given orders to inform the authorities if anyone should know of the whereabouts of Jesus, the people ignore their orders and continue to come to Bethany and to give public acclaim to Jesus. In v19 the Pharisees confess their own helplessness in the face of the situation: "You see that you can do nothing; look, the world has gone after him." Such a remark on the lips of the Jews is inconceivable.

In the Jews passages, the presentation is the reverse of the earlier material. Now the people are fearful of the authorities and are afraid to react to Jesus because of the Jews.

The man in chapter 5, who had been paralyzed, informs the Jews of the identity of Jesus in an almost subservient way. In 7:13, it is said that no one spoke openly of Jesus "for fear of the Jews." In 9:18-23, in the addition to the healing of the man born blind, the parents of the man are said to be afraid to respond when questioned about their son "for fear of the Jews." In the Passion even Pilate is said to be afraid because of the Jews (19:7-8). Joseph of Arimathea is identified as a disciple in secret "for fear of the Jews" (19:38). The disciples are hidden in the upper room "for fear of the Jews" (20:19).

Once again the portrayal in the two editions is radically different yet at the same time consistent with the other ideological and linguistic features.

12. DIVISION OF OPINION REGARDING JESUS[64]

In the signs material, there are repeated references to divisions among both the people and the authorities regarding Jesus. The authorities in particular are not sure what to make of Jesus. This is not present in the material of the second edition. Rather the reverse is true: the authorities are presented as already set in their judgment about Jesus even before the events take place. We will see this in more detail in the next chapter but some examples may be noted here. For example, in the first edition there are two instances of debate among the Pharisees (7:45-52; 9:16). In these debates there is clear division among the authorities. Some are in favor of Jesus; others are not. Never is

---

[64]This feature of the material is also noticed by Fortna ("Locale" 91) but is described only as a "tension" in his thought.

there division among the Jews. In 9:18-23 for example, the Jews "*had already agreed* that if any one should confess him to be the Christ, he was to be put out of the synagogue." Not only is there unanimous agreement, it is so determined that a formal edict of excommunication has already been arrived at!

There is also division among the people even though the vast majority of them believe in Jesus (7:31, 40-44; 10:19-21;[65] 11:45-50). There is none of this in the material of the second edition.

13. THE PREDOMINANCE OF NARRATIVE IN THE EARLY EDITION

One of the most striking and obvious differences between the material of the early and middle strata of the gospel is the way in which narrative predominates, punctuated by brief exchanges either among the authorities themselves or with the common people. The authorities almost never debate directly with Jesus. In fact the brief exchanges of 3:1-2 and 9:40-41 are the only instances of dialogue between the authorities and Jesus in the entire public ministry as represented in the signs material.

However, in the second edition the material is almost exclusively dialogue and discourse material and it is consistently (almost exclusively) between the Jews and Jesus (2:18-22; 5:10-47; 6:30-59; 7:14-19, 33-36; 8:13-29, 48-59; 10:22-39). This confirms the earlier observations that the second edition was less concerned with historical plausibility and more with debate regarding the typical issues between Jews and Johannine Christians.[66]

The Theological Differences

Our purpose here is to indicate in outline form the theological

---

[65]Note the neutral use of "Jews" in the sense of "Judeans."

[66]This also confirms the observation of scholars (most notably Bultmann) who, without sufficiently objective criteria, nevertheless sensed a difference in authorship for the narrative and discourse material. Of course the criteria adduced here indicate that the discourse material was not a source but a second edition of the gospel. H.H. Wendt (*Gospel* 58) was the first to observe the association of the signs with the narrative and works with the discourse material of the gospel.

orientation of the first and second editions of the gospel. The discussion here will be relatively brief. A full discussion of the theological orientation of the signs material will take place in chapter four.

14. A BELIEF BASED ON SIGNS

The first of the theological features of the first edition of the gospel is its obvious concentration on the relationship between the miracles of Jesus and belief. Perhaps the most distinctive feature of this is the fact that in John, belief occurs consistently after the miracle rather than before it (as in the synoptics). Secondly, the only significant factor in belief is the performance of signs.[67]

Nevertheless, it is true that in the second edition, the theology of works is somewhat similar to that of the "signs" in that, repeatedly, Jesus points to his works as actions which should bring the "Jews" to belief (e.g., 5:36; 10:25-39). In this sense the theology of the middle edition takes up where the theology of the first leaves off. However, the difference between the two is that within the middle edition, the belief on the basis of works is cast within a different framework. In the middle edition, the works are one of four "witnesses" to Jesus. These witnesses are spelled out paradigmatically in 5:31-40 and are referred to again several times within the gospel.[68]

15. BELIEF PRESENTED AS AN EASY AFFAIR

The second theological element of the first edition is that belief is presented as an easy affair. This too should be clear from a review of

---

[67]This is true of the signs material that remains in the present edition of the gospel. Parts of that first edition are of course missing from the gospel as we now have it and so it is difficult to be sure that this was so clearly the case in the full version of the first edition. The orientation of the signs toward belief is universally recognized as a characteristic of the earliest material in the gospel (e.g., Bultmann, Fortna, Nicol, Schnackenburg, Wilkens, Boismard).

[68]For a detailed discussion of the witness theme in the gospel see my "The Witnesses to Jesus in John 5:31-40 and Belief in the Fourth Gospel," *CBQ* 43 (July 1981) 385-404. The discussion there is not conducted in terms of the various editions involved; however, when the material is examined in the light of the criteria presented here, it should be clear that the theme of the witnesses to Jesus structures much of the second edition of the gospel.

the many stereotyped formulas of belief. Although there are now elements in the immediate context of these formulas to show the insufficiency of the belief based only on signs, within the first edition such immediate and spontaneous belief was looked upon as the only appropriate response to the tremendous miracles of Jesus.

Although not all of the common people are presented as believing in Jesus, it clearly is the response of the overwhelming majority of the people, from various sectors of society. In contrast, among the religious authorities, although there are some indications that a few believed in or were at least favorably disposed to Jesus, the overwhelming majority do not believe. It is these that are referred to, in 12:37, where the narrator comments in dismay that, in the face of so many and so great signs, "they" did not believe. Their unbelief in the face of the signs is, in the eyes of the narrator, almost incredible.

16. A TRADITIONAL CHRISTOLOGY

The third major theological feature of the first edition is its presentation of belief within traditional Jewish messianic categories.

Repeatedly in the first edition there is a discussion of the meaning of the signs for the identity of Jesus. This circulates around the very basic question of whether Jesus can be "from God" (3:2; 9:16); whether he is a sinner (9:16, 24); whether he is "the Prophet" (6:14; 7:52[69]); whether he is "a" prophet (4:19; 9:17).[70]

In addition, the titles of "son of God" and "Christ" are applied to Jesus in the first edition; however, these titles are also used in the second edition and indeed are such universal titles within the New Testament that they cannot of themselves be used to indicate one or other christology. However, nowhere in the first edition is there evidence of a "high" christology.

Within the second edition there is a concentration precisely on such a high christology in passages such as those which speak explicitly of the identity of Jesus with God (e.g., the "I Am" statements, 8:58) or the

---

[69]As will be seen in the discussion in chapter 3, the textual evidence is strong for the presence of the definite article before *prophētēs*.

[70]There are also a number of traditional titles applied to Jesus in 1:37-42, 44-49. For the relation of this passage to the first edition see the discussion in chapter 3.

equality of Jesus with God (e.g., he calls "God his own Father, making himself equal with God" 5:18, see also 10:33).

17. THE SUPERNATURAL KNOWLEDGE OF JESUS

> NOTE: Several of the passages discussed here do not contain the primary linguistic characteristics identified previously. Nevertheless, it will become apparent in chapter three that the supernatural knowledge of Jesus functions in distinct ways within each of the first two editions of the gospel.This feature is presented here for the sake of completeness although its adequacy as a criterion cannot be fully judged until chapter three.

In the early edition, the supernatural knowledge of Jesus functions to bring about belief. For example, his knowledge of the whereabouts of Nathanael is clearly intended to be supernatural and is presented as affecting the belief of Nathanael (1:47-49). His knowledge of the marital history of the Samaritan woman (4:16-19, 25, 39) is also supernatural and brings her to belief. It may even be true that Jesus' knowledge that Peter was the "son of John" may also be intended to be of this sort (1:42) although this is less clear.

However, in the material of the second edition, the supernatural knowledge of Jesus functions only as an aside for the reader to indicate the sovereign superiority of Jesus to all things human. Examples of this are: 2:24-25, where Jesus is aware of the limitations of the crowd's belief; 6:15, where his knowledge allows him to escape from the crowd's attempt to make him king; 6:64, where Jesus is said to have known from the first who would betray him; 18:4-9, where Jesus is presented as knowing all that will befall him.

In the first edition, the supernatural knowledge of Jesus is one of his signs demonstrating his power before the people; in the second edition it is a christological statement indicating for the reader that Jesus was superior to everyone around him.

These theological differences will be elaborated at greater length in chapter four. However, for the present it should be clear that there are several major differences in orientation between the two editions.

Other Characteristics Useful in the Identification of the Signs Material

In addition to these major characteristics, in the course of the analysis other features will be mentioned. These are also mentioned here for the sake of completeness.

18. THE OCCURRENCE OF TERMS ONLY ONCE IN THE GOSPEL

This is a minor consideration in our analysis because it is so ambiguous. Nevertheless there are at times terms (e.g., "priests and Levites," 1:19) which are quite precise yet which do not figure in the argument of the passage nor in the remainder of the gospel. Dodd,[71] in his discussion of the so-called "transitional passages," spoke of, "small undigested scraps of different material." This material often contained names which "have no particular interest in themselves." As Dodd says "there seems to be no discernible reason why they should have been introduced except that they came down as an integral part of an historical tradition, and were preserved as such."[72] Earlier he had spoken of such material as being "out of relation to other topographical data and does not in any way contribute to the development of the thought of the gospel."[73]

Dodd's observations here are significant. It is difficult to affirm that all such instances stem from the early edition, but some are so idiosyncratic that there can be little doubt that they come from the first edition. I would apply Dodd's principle to other unique terms within the gospel particularly: "priests and Levites (*hiereis kai Levitas*) (1:19) and the discussion with "a Jew" (the only occurrence of the singular in the gospel) about "cleansing" (*katharizmos*) (3:25); "some of the Jerusalemites" (*tines ek tōn Ierosolymitōn*) (7:25); and finally the "some Greeks" (*Hellēnes tines*) (12:20). For a detailed discussion, the reader is directed to the specific passages.

---

[71] *Tradition* 243-44.
[72] *Ibid.*
[73] Dodd, *Tradition* 235.

19. REFERENCES TO EVENTS NARRATED ELSEWHERE IN THE SIGNS MATERIAL

This criterion is also quite ambiguous and should not be considered a major tool. Nevertheless there are times particularly in the passion when such consistency seems helpful as an indicator of authorship.

20. GEOGRAPHICAL REFERENCES WHICH ARE QUITE SPECIFIC AND ACCURATE

Attention was called above to the observations of Dodd regarding the peculiar geographical references in the gospel. In a gospel where anachronisms commonly appear, it is striking how many geographical (and other) references are quite specific and quite accurate.While not a major tool in the analysis, such specific references occur so consistently within the signs material that they can be said to be a characteristic of it, while the anachronisms are typical of the material of the second edition.

21. CONTRAST WITH THE SURROUNDING THEOLOGY

This is the most difficult of the criteria to apply in a purely objective way. It will be used only in the passion where the theological orientation of the two (three) bodies of material is quite evident.

22. QUESTIONS OR STATEMENTS WITH A RESPONSE THAT IS NOT CONSISTENT

It is commonly pointed out that the gospel of John contains a number of statements (usually by others than Jesus) to which Jesus responds. But in each case, the response of Jesus does not deal directly with the statement of the person. For example, Nicodemus comes to Jesus and asks about the signs and their meaning for understanding Jesus. However, in 3:3, Jesus responds but does not in any of the ensuing material address the question of the meaning of the signs. Rather he speaks about the necessity of having the Spirit. In another example, from the end of the public ministry, in 12:20-22, some Greeks come first to Philip who then in a somewhat elaborate way goes to

Andrew. Together they report to Jesus the desire of the Greeks to see him. However, in what follows there is no mention of any meeting between the Greeks and Jesus. Rather in the response by Jesus the topic changes almost completely and Jesus speaks of the coming of his hour. While it could be said that this inconsistency of narrative sequence is simply another form of the aporias which permeate the gospel text, it is such a frequent and consistent one that it seems to be a deliberate technique. Consequently it is listed separately here. Such "broken responses" occur in 3:3, 27; 4:15; 7:28, 33; 12:23; 18:30, 35.

Conclusions

We have now reviewed a total of seventeen major and an additional five minor features which will enable us to identify the material of the first and second editions of the gospel. It will be recalled that the discovery of all of these features began with a first sorting of material on the basis of the appearance of either of the two sets of terms for religious authorities. All of the subsequent features have been found to be associated consistently and exclusively with one or other set of terms for authorities throughout the gospel. In all cases the major features are sufficiently objective to avoid the charge of subjectivity. These major features (together with the minor features as appropriate) will be in chapter three our means for recovering the signs and their original context within the gospel.

In chapter three, then, our procedure will be to determine the literary seams by means of the aporias and to identify the material by means of the various features discussed above.

When we get to the Passion and Resurrection material, however, the features which characterize the signs material in the public ministry occur less frequently. This is to be expected since many of those features are associated with the signs themselves. In the Passion the signs are not at issue the way they were in the public ministry.

Nevertheless, the procedure for identifying material in the Passion and Resurrection material will be the same as in the earlier part of the gospel: to determine literary seams by means of aporias and to identify the material by means of the characteristics discussed above. But in this latter material we will rely more heavily on the presence of framing repetition, inconsistencies of sequence and shifts in theology as markers of editing (some of which were listed in the "other" category above). By the time the reader gets to the Passion and Resurrection material, he/she will have a fairly clear conception of the portrayal of Jesus in the signs material and how clearly this material contrasts with the portrayal in the material of the second edition marked by the term "Jews." In the Passion, those "Jews" passages continue in a clear and consistent portrayal and contrast starkly with the more "neutral" passages of the signs material. This is of no little help in the analysis.

It should be apparent from the references in footnotes that many of the features I have presented here have been noticed before by scholars. But one of the elements which distinguish the current approach is the interrelationship of these various features. These features can be shown to interrelate in a consistent way. Another of the major factors in the development of this new synthesis, as was mentioned before, is the recognition that differences in terminology should not be used uncritically. To simply use all instances of "Jews" or of "signs" or of "works" as a criterion for distinguishing editions is not sufficient. It should be clear from what has preceded that such terms are excellent indicators of changes in authorship only when it has been recognized that such terms may have different meanings. Only those instances which are used in the same way can be grouped together and used as a single criterion. Because of this, we will be able to delineate the signs material with a greater precision and clarity than was previously possible.

It will be seen in what follows that the approach taken here is considerably different from that taken by Fortna and other recent critics. While they sought (as I have) to base their analysis on the aporias, in order to identify the author of a particular stratum, they employed the criteria of style and ideology (theology). The criteria I have used are considerably different and seemingly more objective. In addition, Fortna's signs gospel begins with an analysis of the signs themselves on the basis of what might be called the prima facie case for such a source established by Bultmann's analysis.[74] He then includes a study of the passion and resurrection material on the basis of the common observation that some source was also used there.[75] Finally

[74]Fortna, *Signs* 22-25.
[75]Fortna, *Signs* 113-114.

he asks about the possibility of other pre-Johannine material on the basis of yet other aporias.[76] However, Fortna's criteria did not lead him to ask about the presence of source material in, for example, chapter 7. Nor did the criteria used in the analysis of the signs themselves figure as prominently in the analysis of the passion and resurrection material. As will be seen below in chapter 3, although Fortna continued to use the criteria determined earlier, he frequently identified (as did Bultmann before him) the source material of the passion and resurrection by comparing it with the synoptic accounts—a criterion which is at best indirectly related to those included among his original listing of criteria.

In contrast, the approach taken here identifies certain characteristics of the signs material at the beginning and then proceeds to see where they occur throughout the *entire* gospel (rather than in pre-selected groups of material). This means that the same criteria are applied consistently throughout the analysis. This approach then results in an identification of signs material which is more precise, consistent, and complete than that of previous studies.

[76]Fortna, *Signs* 161.

3

The Signs Material in John

In the previous chapter we saw the literary features of the gospel which enable us to identify and isolate the signs material. In this chapter we come to the heart of our endeavor: the recovery of the original edition of the gospel and the understanding of its theology.[1]

In what follows, the text is from the RSV, modified as noted. [ ] = Brief phrases belonging to a later edition. < > = My modifications of the RSV translation. The boldface represents many of the characteristics typical of the signs material. Not all of the characteristics could be so represented without making the text confusing. However, a full accounting of the characteristics can be found in the discussion which follows each passage.

1. The Interrogation of the Baptist (1:19-28)

[19]And this is the testimony of John, when the Jews sent priests and Levites from Jerusalem to ask him, "Who are you?" [20]He confessed, he did not deny, but confessed, "I am not **the Christ**." [21]And they

---

[1]Our primary concern will be the discussion of the major features of the signs material. As I have mentioned before, there are indications from time to time of minor modifications *within* the signs material. In most cases, their presence can be debated—and in any event they are less important theologically. It is more important to identify the major lines of the signs material and it is with this that the book is primarily concerned. Discussion of these minor elements as well as of alternate explanations will be confined to the footnotes.

asked him, "What then? Are you **Elijah?**" He said, "I am not." "Are you **the prophet?**" and he answered, "No." [22]They said to him then, "Who are you? Let us have an answer for those who sent us. What do you say about yourself?" [23]He said "I am the voice of one crying in the wilderness, 'Make straight the way of the Lord,' as the prophet Isaiah said."

[24]Now they had been sent from **the Pharisees.** [25]They asked him, "Then why are you baptizing, if you are neither **the Christ, nor Elijah, nor the prophet?**" [26]John answered them, "I baptize with water; but among you stands one whom you do not know, [27]even he who comes after me, the thong of whose sandal I am not worthy to untie." [28]This took place in Bethany beyond the Jordan where John was baptizing.

The first passage clearly associated with the signs material is the answer given to the Pharisees when they come to interrogate John the Baptist. It is identified as signs material by the presence of Jews in the sense of Judeans in 1:19[2] and by the term Pharisees in 1:24. In addition, the "priests and Levites" (*hiereis kai Levitas*) are mentioned only here in the entire gospel and are therefore more likely a part of the traditional material rather than a deliberate addition by an editor.[3] There is some repetition in the passage (compare the questioning in the final part of v19 with that in v22) which would suggest that there may have been editing, but there are plausible explanations of this (see below).[4] Finally, the geographical reference in 1:28 was probably the work of the author of the signs material since it occurs again in 10:40.[5]

---

[2]This is evidently the intended meaning of *Ioudaioi* in 1:19 since they are so closely associated with Jerusalem/Judea (cf the Jew in 3:22, the Jews in 11:45-46; 12:9). They are also the motivation for the action of other religious personnel (i.e., the priests and Levites) as in 11:45, where they are the reason the chief priests and Pharisees convene the Sanhedrin. This represents a change of my opinion since my article "Jews" (p42, 50). Fortna (*Signs* 170), however, would see it as the hostile "Johannine" sense.

[3]So also Dodd, *Tradition* 263.

[4]Some would see the peculiar verb "confess" (which is quite strong for this occasion) as an addition to the text. If so, it is a minor feature.

[5]The material of the second day with John's description of Jesus as "the Lamb of God who takes away the sin of the world" and as "a man who ranks before me, for he was before me" is clearly from a later edition and reflects a radically different theology, one more at home in the thought of 1 John. In any event, it shows none of the characteristics typical of the signs material.

The overall intention of the passage is the explicit and repeated denial of any eschatological role for John and the affirmation of his preparatory function. Many commentators see vv20-21 and 22-24 as doublets, giving two versions of the interrogation.[6] However, the repetition is explained when it is noticed that the verses answer first in a negative way (vv20-21) and then in a positive way (vv22-24) the question of who John is.[7] John, while rejecting any messianic claims for himself, describes himself as the Isaian voice of preparation in the desert.[8]

Vv25-28 answer the question why John is baptizing. John responds that he baptizes in water and that he is not worthy to untie the sandal laces of the one coming after him.[9] This theme of subordination of John to Jesus, which is to a certain extent present in all the gospels, is particularly evident in the signs material where Jesus is presented as himself conducting a baptismal ministry alongside that of John but as eventually winning over more disciples.[10]

---

[6]Perhaps the most famous treatment of these verses is that of Boismard ["Les traditions johanniques concernant le Baptiste," *RB* 70 (1963), 5-42] who proposed a complicated theory of multiple editions. The theory is discussed in Brown, *Gospel* 68-71.

Bultmann (*Gospel* 84-85) considered vv22-24 and 26-28 as additions by the Ecclesiastical Redactor. Thus he could see the references to the "Pharisees" here as stemming from the latest rather than the earliest stratum of material. On the passage see also G. Richter, "Zur Frage von Tradition und Redaktion in Joh 1:19-34," *Studien zum Johannesevangelium* (ed. J. Hainz; BU 13; Regensburg: F. Pustet, 1977) 288-314. All of these theories attempt to deal with the seeming repetitiousness of the text.

[7]The mention of the Pharisees in v24 is not a duplicate of v19 but further specifies them. It may be that the intention of the verse is to present a scene similar to that of 7:31-32, where the Pharisees send the attendants of the chief priests as their emissaries. Thus the Judeans would be the ones who initiated the process by approaching the Pharisees who in turn sent the priests and Levites.

[8]It is tempting to see the statement "whom you do not know" (1:26) as an editorial addition, but there is no evidence other than the theological similarity to other passages in the second edition (e.g., 8:28, 55; 14:7, 9; etc.).

[9]The mention of baptizing "in water" is intended to contrast with Jesus' baptism "in the Holy Spirit." It could be an addition since theologically it would appear to be more appropriate within the second edition. But there is no literary evidence of editing other than this slight awkwardness in thought.

[10]Other evidence of this subordination is evident in 1:35-50; 3:22-26; 4:1-4; and 10:40-42 (which refers back to this passage). However ,the theme of John's subordination is not confined to the first edition (see 3:27-30; 5:33-36a).

2. The First Disciples Come to Jesus
(1:35-49, without v43)

[35]The next day again John was standing with two of his disciples; [36]and he looked at Jesus as he walked, and said, ["Behold the Lamb of God!!"] [37]The two disciples heard him say this, and they followed Jesus. [38]Jesus turned, and saw them following, and said to them, "What do you seek?" And they said to him, **"Rabbi" (which means Teacher)**, "where are you staying?" [39]He said to them, "Come and see." They came and saw where he was staying; and they stayed with him that day, for it was about the tenth hour. [40]One of the two who heard John speak and followed him was Andrew, Simon Peter's brother, [41]He first found his brother Simon, and said to him, "We have found **the Messiah" (which means Christ)**. [42]He brought him to Jesus. Jesus looked at him, and said, "So you are Simon the son of John? You shall be called **Cephas" (which means Peter)**.
...[44]Now Philip was from Bethsaida, the city of Andrew and Peter. [45]Philip found Nathanael, and said to him, **"We have found him of whom Moses in the law and also the prophets wrote**, Jesus of Nazareth, the son of Joseph." [46]Nathanael said to him, "Can anything good come out of Nazareth?" Philip said to him, "Come and see." [47]Jesus saw Nathanael coming to him, and said of him, "Behold, an Israelite indeed, in whom is no guile!" [48]Nathanael said to him, "How do you know me?" Jesus answered him, "Before Philip called you, when you were under the fig tree, I saw you." [49]Nathanael answered him, "Rabbi, you are **the Son of God!** You are **the King of Israel!**

The third day of John's witness sets the stage for the call of the first disciples.[11] It is striking that these first disciples are identified as being followers of John the Baptist before they become disciples of Jesus. This is information not found in the synoptics.[12]

John's references to Jesus as the "Lamb of God" is one of the few references in the gospel to the death of Jesus as a sacrificial, atoning

---

[11]Because of limitations of space, it will not always be possible to speculate on the original sequence of the material nor to discuss in detail the nature or the purpose of the subsequent editing which has taken place. However, in many cases the reader will be able to perceive the intention of the subsequent editing simply by consulting the text of the omitted section. When the theology of the intervening material is grasped, the purpose of the addition frequently also becomes clear.

[12]The only reference to the disciples being fishermen in John is in chapter 21.

death and may well be a later modification.[13] Two of his disciples then respond to his words and follow Jesus. When Jesus asks them whom they seek, they ask him, "Rabbi (which is translated 'Teacher'), where are you staying?" Jesus tells them to come and see. They stay with him that day "for it was about the tenth hour." (RSV). Andrew, one of the two disciples[14] then finds his brother, Simon Peter, and announces that they have found the Messiah. Again the religious term is translated, as is Cephas, the new name given Peter by Jesus.

The next verse (v43) is probably not part of the original. The reasons for this judgment will be discussed below. However, the original probably depicted Peter (or Andrew) as the one who found Philip. Philip in turn finds Nathanael who also comes to Jesus. Jesus tells Nathanael that he had seen him under the fig tree. Nathanael in turn answers: "Rabbi, you are the Son of God! You are the King of Israel!"

The passage is marked as signs material by several features. First, there is the easy manner in which the disciples come to belief. Although there is evidence in the gospel (all of which occurs in strata later than the original one) that the disciples' belief is to be deepened,[15] and indeed that it did not even exist (at least in its fullest sense) until after the resurrection,[16] here the disciples immediately ascribe to Jesus several titles of traditional Jewish messianism, titles which in Mark come only at a great price, after considerable experience with Jesus. Such "easy belief" will be characteristic of the signs material throughout!

A second feature of the passage is the tandem aspect of the belief. One person believes and then another is led to belief on the basis of the

---

[13]Arguments for this cannot be given in the present study. The exact source of the imagery is disputed. For a summary see Brown, *Gospel* 58-63.

[14]The other disciple is not named, a fact which has led many scholars to think that it was the author of the gospel and perhaps the Beloved Disciple who appears later in the gospel. See the discussion of this possibility in Schnackenburg, *Gosepl* 1 97-100; 3 375-388.

[15]Although the references to the imperfection of the belief of the disciples are relatively infrequent, such references do exist. For example 6:60-71 speaks of a total departure of one group of disciples. See also 4:31-38 (where the disciples do not fully understand Jesus' reference to "food"); 14:7, 9-14, 28 (where the disciples do not fully comprehend Jesus' meaning).

[16]The post-resurrection fulfillment of the disciples' belief is stated explicitly in 2:17, 22; 12:16; 20:8. All of these texts come from material later than the signs material.

witness of the prior individual (Andrew gets Peter; Philip gets Nathanael; perhaps in the original Peter got Philip). There seem to be two purposes to this tandem form of belief which we will encounter throughout the gospel. First, it seems intended to demonstrate in another way that belief in Jesus should have been easy since it was so easy for so many during the ministry of Jesus. Second, this tandem aspect may well have been meant as a model for the missionary work of the members of John's community: their reports of faith were to draw others to belief in Jesus. The success of such efforts during the ministry would be a model for them.

A third feature, characteristic of the signs material, is the repeated translations of the Hebrew/Aramaic names into Greek: Rabbi; Messiah; Cephas. Fourth, there is the supernatural knowledge of Jesus regarding Nathanael's character and his presence under the fig tree. This foreknowledge is clearly meant to be a factor in Nathanael's belief. In this respect it is a parallel to the supernatural knowledge of the Samaritan woman's past in chapter 4. There also such foreknowledge is a factor in coming to belief.[17] Because of the parallel with the story of the Samaritan woman, I would take this incident too as a "sign" although not a public one.[18]

Finally, there is the clear emphasis on traditional titles given to Jesus. Although the titles are limited to traditional ones, there is a certain hierarchy in the titles as they are given to Jesus. The first disciples refer to him as "Teacher." On the basis of their stay with Jesus, Andrew gets his brother Simon and tells him that they have found the "Messiah." The third title, given by Philip, progresses to "him of whom Moses in the law and also the prophets wrote, Jesus of

---

[17]It is not common to title this knowledge of Nathanael a "sign" but it clearly functions as one, just as does the story of the Samaritan woman (See 4:54 and the discussion there). It is sometimes suggested that there are seven signs in the gospel, a number which is intended to be symbolic. This hardly was the intention in the original material where the number of signs (far more than seven) is constantly stressed. To show such a symbolism is intended, it would have to be shown that the editor did not consider this and the story of the Samaritan woman as signs but intended to include the walking on the water and exclude the miracle at the sea of Galilee following the resurrection. See Brown, *Gospel* cxxxix-cxlii; Schnackenburg, *Gospel* 1 515-517. In any event such symbolism would be "laid over" the original meaning and number of signs in the first edition.

[18]The first of the public signs is clearly labeled in 2:11.

Nazareth, the son of Joseph." (RSV).[19] Finally, Nathanael proclaims Jesus "Son of God" and "King of Israel."[20] The title "son of God" was given to the king in the coronation formulae of the Old Testament and is associated with kingship here. It indicated a special relationship with God. If so, it provides the climax and culmination of the series of titles that have been used during the passage.[21] Nevertheless, in comparison with the various other identifications of Jesus in the later strata ["he calls God his own Father, making himself equal with God" (5:18; cf 10:33); "I AM" (8:24, 48, 58; 13:19—all of which occur in passages identified with "Jews"], these titles clearly reflect a much less profound understanding of the reality of Jesus.

V43

This verse is probably not part of the signs material. There is considerable evidence to support this conclusion. First, such a sequence would certainly fit well with the sequence of the remainder of the passage where each disciple in turn finds another. Second, the statement of 1:43 that Jesus decided to go to Galilee and found Philip is awkward and intrusive. Third, the statement that Philip was from Bethsaida, "the city of Andrew and Peter" (1:44) fits well with the hypothesis of an original which ties his call to Peter. And it does not fit well with the later statement of Philip to Nathanael (v45) that "*We* have found him. . . ." J.M. Robinson points to a number of efforts to

---

[19]It is not certain whether a specific figure is intended by this description. A plausible candidate for "the one about whom Moses wrote" would be the Prophet like Moses described in Deuteronomy 18:15-18. The one about whom the prophets wrote is more difficult to identify. The Messiah? Elijah? The Son of Man? Jesus is identified by Philip simply as "the son of Joseph, the one from Nazareth."

[20]Nathanael himself is mentioned only here as a disciple; he appears in none of the lists of the Twelve. The term "Israelite" appears only here in the gospel. Nor is it clear what is meant by the "lack of guile."

[21]On the Old Testament use of "Son of God" to refer to the king, see, for example, 2 Sam 7:14; Ps 2:7; 89:28. It could also be attributed to the individual devout person, e.g., Ps 73:15. But this meaning is less likely here.

This progression in the insight, evident in the titles given to Jesus, is also evident in the story of the Samaritan woman and the story of the blind man, as we will see below. Yet it is important to see that in each case the final title given to Jesus does not come from the signs material.

orient Jesus toward Galilee in the early material of the gospel.[22] This may be the purpose of the insertion.

Vv50-51

Vv50-51 are not part of the signs material.[23] They extend the conversation awkwardly. They criticize Nathanael's faith and such criticism of miracle faith is not found elsewhere in the signs material although it is common in the material of the other editions (cf. 2:24-25; 3:3; 4:40-42; 4:44, etc.). The verses point to the need to extend and deepen the theology of the signs and (here) to show a more profound basis for the disciples' faith. V51 speaks suddenly to "you" [plural— rather than to "you" (singular) which has occurred to this point]. In addition v51 introduces the title of the Son of Man which occurs nowhere in the signs material. Together the verses represent the judgment of later editors that this level of belief which is based upon report and upon supernatural knowledge and which reveals only traditional understanding of Jesus is not complete.

3. Jesus Changes Water into Wine (2:1-11)

> [1]On the third day there was a marriage at Cana in Galilee, and the mother of Jesus was there; [2]Jesus also was invited to the marriage, with his disciples. [3]When the wine gave out, the mother of Jesus said to him, "They have no wine." . . . [5]His mother said to the servants, "Do whatever he tells you." [6]Now six stone jars were standing there, for the Jewish rites of purification, each holding twenty or thirty gallons. [7]Jesus said to them, "Fill the jars with water." And they

[22]J.M. Robinson, "The Johannine Trajectory" in *Trajectories Through Early Christianity,* J.M. Robinson and H. Koester (Philadelphia: Fortress, 1971) 243. See also Bultmann (*Gospel* 97-98) who discusses the issue at some length. The statement has attracted the attention of most commentators, as early as Wellhausen and as recent as Brown, Fortna, and Schnackenburg.

[23]The secondary nature of these verses has been frequently noted by various scholars (e.g., Bultmann, Boismard). However, many (e.g., Fortna, Brown, Nicol) would consider only v51 to be added. I am inclined to think that v50 is from the second edition and that v51 was a still later addition at the time of the final version of the gospel. Fortna (*Signs* 187) is correct in pointing to the inconsistency between the two verses themselves as well as with the previous context.

filled them up to the brim. [8]He said to them, "Now draw some out, and take it to the steward of the feast." So they took it. [9]When the steward of the feast tasted the water now become wine, and did not know where it came from (though the servants who had drawn the water knew), the steward of the feast called the bridegroom [10]and said to him, "Every man serves the good wine first; and when men have drunk freely, then the poor wine; but you have kept the good wine until now." [11]This, **the first of his signs,** Jesus did at Cana in Galilee, and manifested his glory; **and his disciples believed in him.**

This is the first of the (public) signs that Jesus performs in the gospel of John. The miracle itself which consists of changing six jars of water into wine, a wine which the steward testifies is the best yet served, would be classified as a "nature" miracle. It is clearly intended to illustrate that the power of Jesus is tremendous, for he produces one hundred and twenty gallons of wine![24] It is identified as a sign and indeed as the first of the signs of Jesus (2:11). We hear in the first of the formulaic statements of belief that because of this sign his disciples believed in him. In addition we are told that the disciples come to belief because of the glory of Jesus which they see within the sign. In the Old Testament description of the signs at Exodus, the signs are said to reveal the glory of God (cf Num 14:22).[25] This is the intention of the Johannine signs also.[26]

In its present form the sign is replete with symbolism.[27] First, there is

[24]The element of the magnitude of Jesus' signs will continue to be emphasized and is a major element of the theology of the signs, as we shall see (see especially chapter 4 below).

[25]Some (Bultmann, Fortna, Nicol) would see the mention of "glory" here as an addition by the Evangelist (i.e., part of the second edition). There is no literary evidence of editing and the close association of signs with glory in Exodus makes such a proposal unnecessary. Nevertheless, this use of glory in relation to the signs is distinct theologically from the use of the same word to refer to the death of Jesus. I would agree that the use of the term in this latter sense occurs only in the second edition.

[26]The sign is described as the "first" of the signs. This is evidently to be taken as meaning the first of the *public* signs—unless the supernatural knowledge of Nathanael's whereabouts did not appear prior to the Cana miracle in the original edition. Clearly, the knowledge of the character and whereabouts of Nathanael is intended to be miraculous, but it is not a public display nor even one intended for all the disciples.

[27]This symbolism is discussed in most commentaries. See, for example, Brown, *Gospel* 101-111; Schnackenburg, *Gospel* 323-340.

the wedding feast which was symbolic in Judaism of the coming eschatological age (cf Is 54:4-8; 62:4-5). Second is the Old Testament symbol of "abundant wine" which symbolized the blessings of the eschatological age (cf e.g., Amos 9:13-14; Hos 14:7; Jer 31:12).

Third, there is the symbolism of the jars used for purification. These could well be intended to symbolize all of Jewish ritual which is transformed by Jesus. The number six could also symbolize imperfection or incompletion. Thus Jesus would transform and bring to completion the prior dispensation of salvation.

Finally, there is the exchange between Jesus and his mother; this also may be intended to be symbolic. Two elements would seem to be of importance here. First is the role of his mother, a role which appears again at the scene of the crucifixion. Second is the meaning of the "hour" of Jesus which Jesus says is not yet present.

It is difficult to tell how much of this symbolism was intended by the original author and how much is the result of later editing, but it is likely that at least some of this symbolism was present in the original. Yet it would not be possible to settle the issue here without a lengthy exegesis of the passage. The symbolism here is different from most in the gospel in that it is not developed either by a separate discourse (as is done in 5:10-47; 6:30-59; 8:12-59 and 10:22-39) or by insertions into the discourse (as in 4:4-42 and 11:1-45). The original intent of the sign was probably a genuine concern to show the ministry of Jesus as the beginning of the eschatological age, just as Mark had chosen Jesus' exchange with the demons in the synagogue at Capernaum (cf Mk 1:23-28) as a public demonstration of Jesus' battle against the demonic at the beginning of his ministry.

I would judge only v4 (the exchange between Jesus and his mother) to be an addition. Even here the conclusion is somewhat speculative since the only real basis is the theological orientation which refers to the coming of the "hour" of Jesus, a theme which occurs typically in additions elsewhere in the gospel (e.g., 4:23; 5:25, 35; 7:6, 30; 8:20; 11:9; 12:23, etc.).[28]

---

[28]So also, for similar reasons, Fortna (*Signs* 31-32); Nicol (*Semeia* 30). Bultmann (*Gospel* 116 n 4) includes v4 in his signs source but points to the similarity with 4:48, where Jesus also refuses the request for a miracle at first. Most scholars today would see both verses as editorial additions. However, Wilkens (*Entstehungsgeschichte* 39-41) would consider the narrative to be without additions.

The public ministry in the signs material opens with the revelation of Jesus' glory and the belief of the disciples. It will close with the statement of the author in 12:37 that in spite of the many signs Jesus worked "they" (the religious authorities) did not believe. Thus the public ministry is bound together by a kind of inclusion.[29]

4. A Report of Jesus' Signs and the Reaction of Nicodemus (2:23-3:2, without vv24-25)

> [23]Now when he was in Jerusalem **at the Passover** <**at the**> **feast, many believed in his name when they saw the signs which he did;**. . . . Now there was a man **of the Pharisees,** named Nicodemus, **a ruler of the Jews.** [2]This man came to Jesus by night and said to him, "Rabbi, we know that you are **a teacher come from God; for no one can do these signs that you do, unless God is with him.**"

The next section of signs material concerns a report of the signs of Jesus at a Passover feast in Jerusalem and an exchange between Jesus and Nicodemus, one of the Jewish "rulers." This section is important for understanding the process by which the gospel has been edited. The characteristics of the signs material here are quite clear. But equally clear are the indications that the material has been edited. Studying the passage in some detail will make it easier to recognize the editing process and its theological purpose throughout the remainder of the gospel.

This passage is identified as belonging to the first edition by numerous characteristics: the formulaic belief, the terminology of signs, and (after the omission of vv24-25) the immediate reaction of the authorities to the belief of the people, and the emphasis on the quantity and quality of Jesus' signs. In addition Nicodemus is identified in the vocabulary of the first edition: a "ruler" and "a Pharisee." He reacts to the mention of belief among the people and is convinced that they mean that he is "from God" (in the terminology of traditional christology).

The purpose of this passage is to recount in summary fashion the effect of Jesus' trip to Jerusalem for the Passover.[30] In its formulaic

---

[29]The structure of the signs material will be discussed in chapter 4.

[30]That the intervening material has been from the later stratum is clear from the

presentation of belief, we see the first report of the considerable belief the signs of Jesus attracted among various groups. Later there will be similar statements about such belief among the Samaritans (4:39), the common people of Jerusalem at Tabernacles (7:31), the Judeans (11:45), and even among the Pharisees (12:42).

In 3:1-2, Nicodemus recognizes that no one is able to perform such signs unless God is with him. And this principle becomes, for the remainder of the first edition, the focal point of the theological assessment of Jesus. The conviction contained within the statement is also the chief evidence within the signs material of the Pharisees' hardness of heart. Beginning here and extending throughout the gospel, the Pharisees will focus on the meaning of the signs, repeating the theological principle that no one can work signs unless God is with him, yet failing to accept the conclusions which the signs by their own admission force upon them (12:37-43). For the present, the authorities (in the person of Nicodemus) are curious.

However, the signs material is cut off abruptly after Nicodemus' statement in v2 and Jesus' response is given in the material of the second edition. Jesus' response does not deal with the topic introduced by Nicodemus at all. This contextual aporia (the break in sequence of thought) will prove to be a common editorial device of the author of the second edition. A close reading of 3:3ff shows that Jesus does not discuss the meaning of signs but takes the discussion to a considerably deeper level than that occasioned by Nicodemus' question. Rather than dealing with the signs on a superficial level, Jesus explains the principle by which anyone is able to "see" the signs: the need for rebirth from the Spirit. If one is to see/enter the Kingdom of God, one must be born of the Spirit (3:5). This explanation involves a terminology and theology radically different from that of the proposed question. Only the Spirit which blows where it will can bring true belief (3:8). As was said above, this technique of retaining the material of the first edition where a topic is introduced but replacing the original answer with the theology of the second edition is a common one in the gospel. In all cases we will find both breaks in the thought sequence (contextual

identification of the authorities as "Jews" in vv18 and 20 and by the peculiar use of "sign" in 2:18. This use of sign distinctive of the second edition was discussed in chapter 2 above.

aporias), as well as differences in theological orientation, each of which indicates the presence of editing.[31]

Vv24-25

Up to this point the discussion of vv24-25 has been omitted. Like the answer to Nicodemus' question, which was given in the second edition, these verses introduce a sudden and unexpected change of thought. We are told that Jesus did not entrust himself to the Jerusalem crowds because he "knew everything" and because "he knew what was in man." In this statement (as in that of 1:50-51) we have a clear example of a qualification (in fact almost a rejection) of the theology of miracles in the earlier stratum. Coming as the verses do before the answer to Nicodemus, they provide a first warning that the editor of the second stratum finds the signs' belief inadequate.[32]

There are several indications that these verses are an addition and do not come from the signs material. First, there is the way the verses interrupt the sequence of signs-belief-followed-by-reaction-of-authorities typical of the signs material. In addition the verses are incompatible

---

[31]The same technique is clearly present in the editing of 3:22-26; 7:25-27, 31-32; 12:20. It is somewhat similar to the technique used in the insertion of material into the story of the Samaritan woman.

[32]These verses are a good example of the way scholars have attempted to come to grips with the signs and with the question of editing in general. Dodd says of the verses that they are "probably the Evangelist's introduction to the *pericope* of Nicodemus rather than a true transitional passage" [*Historical Tradition in the Fourth Gospel* (Cambridge: Cambridge University, 1963) 235], so also I. de la Potterie, "Ad dialogum Jesu cum Nicodemo" *VD* 47 (1969) 148. Brown calls 2:23-25 an "editorial transition to chapter 3" (*Gospel* 126-27, 524). Both point to "Johannine" vocabulary and phraseology as indicators of origin. However, our analysis is able to gain more precision by means of both the criteria used for identifying 2:23 and 3:1-2 as belonging to the signs gospel and also by means of the typical sequence which marks 3:1-2 as the original sequel to 2:23. It is commonly observed that the verses are introduced so casually that they were originally thought of as a unit with what precedes (e.g., Bultmann, *Gospel* 130 n. 2, 3 and p. 133; de la Potterie, "Dialogum" 148). Our analysis gives a clear explanation of all these features of the text.

It is curious that these verses which speak so clearly of miracle faith are attributed by Fortna to the Evangelist (on v 23, *Signs* 35, 56; on vv24-25, see p. 60). V23 speaks positively of miracle faith as would be typical of the first edition. In addition, v23 is to be distinguished from vv24-25 by the criticism of miracle faith in vv24-25. Thus the clear conflict in thought between v23 and vv24-25 would also argue against them being from the same author.

with the consistent theology of the signs material, where the signs are always by the author himself valued as leading to belief.[33] Finally, the supernatural knowledge of Jesus here does not function to bring about belief as it does in the signs material, rather it is intended for the reader to illustrate the superiority of Jesus and his supreme control of what is going on around him.[34]

Theologically the purpose of the verses is quite clear.The crowds' response to Jesus is not sufficient. Although the people seem to believe, they do not have the proper "inner" qualification. This lack of inner qualification is not specified in vv24-25 but in the light of 3:3ff, it is undoubtedly intended to be the crowds' failure to be reborn in the Spirit!

5. The Continued Success of Jesus and the Concern on the Part of John's Disciples (3:22-26)

> [22]After this Jesus and his disciples went into the land of Judea; there he remained with them and baptized. [23]John also was baptizing at Aenon near Salim, because there was much water there; and people came and were baptized. [24]For John had not yet been put in prison.
>
> [25]Now a discussion arose between John's disciples and **a Jew** over purifying. [26]And they came to John, and said to him, "Rabbi, he who was with you beyond the Jordan, to whom you bore witness, here he is, baptizing, and **all are going to him.**"

These verses provide a rich source of information about Jesus not found elsewhere in the gospel tradition. They chronicle the movement of Jesus into the Judean countryside, where he remains for a while in a ministry of baptism. In addition we are told that this ministry was being conducted *before* John the Baptist had been put in prison, and that the ministry of Jesus was gaining more converts than that of John the Baptist.

Several features indicate this material is from the signs edition. First, it uses the term "Jew" in the neutral sense to refer to a person from

---

[33]See especially 12:37; 20:30-31.

[34]This knowledge which indicates Jesus' superiority is also found at 6:4, 15, 64; 13:11; 18:4; 19:28.

Judea (cf the reference to Judea in 3:22).[35] Second, the verses continue
the theme of easy belief (v26). Third, the material here is consistent
with and is referred to in the signs material in 4:1-4. Fourth, there are a
number of features which occur only here and are not developed
theologically. In addition to the information listed above, there is the
identification of the specific location of John the Baptist's baptizing,
the obscure reference to a discussion "over purifying", and the further
mention of John the Baptist's disciples.[36]

Whether this material immediately followed the material about
Nicodemus is impossible to say, but when this material is joined with
that of 4:1-54 one gets the sense of being in contact with an extended
sequence of material which is relatively intact.[37]

The material of the early edition ends with v26. As was the case in
3:3ff, the editor of the second edition has supplied a "new" response to
the disciples of John the Baptist. In the present edition of the gospel,
the theological importance of the passage resides in this answer rather
than in the material of the signs edition which leads up to it. The
response of John the Baptist in vv27ff is somewhat more directly
related to what precedes than was Jesus' answer to Nicodemus in 3:3ff,

[35]This is the only instance of "Jew" in the singular in the gospel. For a detailed
discussion see von Wahlde, "Jews" 49-50.

[36]Although this is not a primary criterion as was explained in chapter 2, information
which is not the product of any particular interest on the part of the Evangelist is likely
to be traditional (i.e., signs material). The observation is closely related to the observation that the signs material focuses on narrative while the second edition focuses
upon dialogue. The obvious explanation is that the second edition was not done in
order to supplement the historical information supplied in the first but rather to
provide what was considered to be a more adequate theological explanation of the
ministry of Jesus.

The observation that material, which is not the product of any particular theological
interest is likely to be traditional, is used considerably by Dodd (*Tradition* 233-250) in
his attribution of the "transitional passages" to a tradition earlier than John's own
work. Dodd has been among a minority who saw the transitional passages as being
traditional. It is the more common practice to attribute these to the Evangelist on the
grounds that they were his means of linking together the traditional narrative units.

Many of the passages identified by Dodd as "traditional" and "transitional" are
among those identified by me as belonging to the signs material. The ability to identify
these transitional passages with greater accuracy is one of the gains of the criteria I
have employed. In addition, since the characteristics are the same as those appearing
in the signs themselves, it is clear that we are in contact with an entire narrative rather
than simply a "miracles source" without a narrative sequence.

[37]This does not deny the presence of editing within the sequence, but *the sequence
itself* appears to be intact.

but the relation of vv27ff to the discussion about purification is totally obscure. In addition, there is considerable difference in theology between what follows and the typical signs theology. This is evident particularly in the imagery of "being given from above"[38] For whether or not Jesus is making more disciples, and apart from the content of the discussion about "purification," John is made to testify that Jesus' success is given from above. Jesus utters the words of God because Jesus has the Spirit without measure![39]

As was the case in the editorial addition in 3:3ff, the focus of vv27ff is also on the (Holy) Spirit as the source of belief and success, thus pointing once again to the view of the second editor regarding the "critique of signs theology."

6. A Transition: Jesus Begins a Journey Through Samaria (4:1-4)

[1]Now when [the Lord] knew that **the Pharisees** had heard that **Jesus was making and baptizing more disciples than John**[2] (although Jesus himself did not baptize, but only his disciples), [3]he left Judea and departed again to Galilee. [4]He had to pass through Samaria.

These verses are closely linked with the material in 3:22-26. They portray Jesus' shift of his ministry from Judea to Galilee because of increasing hostility on the part of the Jewish religious authorities. This hostility was due to the fact that Jesus was making more disciples than John (4:1). Thus the passage is closely linked with what had preceded in 3:22-26. In what follows we evidently have most if not all of the original sequence of that journey. When Jesus passes through Samaria (4:4-6), he stops in the town of Sychar and meets with a Samaritan woman who comes to believe in him and who leads many of the townspeople to believe in him also (4:7-40). After that, Jesus comes

---

[38]The contrast between above and below occurs frequently in the gospel, first of all 3:3, but also 3:12-15; 3:27-35; etc.

[39]Bultmann (*Gospel* 167-68) provides a thoughtful consideration of the verses, concluding that the verses as a whole are probably Johannine except for v25 which he asserts must have come from a source since it is so puzzling and unrelated to what follows. Fortna (*Signs* 179-80) attributed v22 and v25ff to the Evangelist and vv23-24 to a tradition. Dodd (*Tradition* 236) considers vv22-23 as a pre-Johannine tradition. He bases himself on similarity to Marcan itinerary fragments, absence of Johannine phraseology, the content which portrays a period of ministry rather than to specific incidents. Nicol does not discuss the verses.

into Galilee and we find a brief summary of the reception he receives there (4:43, 45). He then continues on to Cana in Galilee and is met by an official from Capernaum whose son is ill. Jesus heals the son at a distance. At the close of this passage there is the statement that this was the "second sign which Jesus performed as he came from Judea to Galilee" (4:54).

The clearest indications that vv1-4 (except for v2) belong to the first edition are the characteristic term for religious authorities in v1 (Pharisees) and the emphasis on easy belief.[40] This is confirmed by the way these verses continue the interest in specific geographical locations (the town of Sychar, Jacob's well) we have found repeatedly in the signs material.[41] These features, together with the consistent narrative they create with 3:22-26 and with what follows, indicate without a doubt that the verses come from the first edition of the gospel.[42]

Verse 2 is a puzzle and undoubtedly a later addition. It directly contradicts 4:1 and 3:22.[43] Certainly it was added in an attempt to

---

[40]The reference to Jesus as "Lord" here is peculiar since it is not the normal secular use found in the gospel, but the more exalted religious sense found frequently in the New Testament, especially in Paul. It is certainly a redactional detail, perhaps added at the time of the addition of 4:2. See also at 6:23; 20:18, 20.

[41]It is particularly noteworthy that these various references to geographical locations have, where scholars have found evidence to check the information, proved to be quite accurate. Other examples of such specific information occur at 1:29; 3:22, 23; 5:2; 9:7; 10:40; 11:54; 12:1; 18:1; 19:13. The fact that such historically accurate features are confined *to the first edition* helps explain how the gospel could be known as a source of unique and quite detailed traditions about the ministry of Jesus and at the same time exhibit features (such as the term "Jews" for authorities and references to synagogue exclusion) which are at times vague and imprecise and even anachronistic. See also the discussion in chapter 2 above.

[42]Bultmann (*Gospel* 175), in keeping with the earlier tendency to attribute transitional passages to the evangelist/editor, considers vv1-3 as the Evangelist's introduction to the traditional material which begins in v5. He provides no criteria for the attribution. Dodd (*Tradition* 236-38) admits to the editing process demanded by v2 and, considering the remainder clumsy, suggests that the Evangelist modified traditional material here. Fortna (*Signs* 179) calls it "an obvious Johannine construct" yet seems to provide no evidence for the assertion. The difference of the present analysis and the criteria which found it will of course be evident. The present analysis also provides a much more consistent theology and sequence.

[43]The verse serves as a clear reminder of how different the Johannine community's standards for an acceptable form of the text were from contemporary standards. In the light of inconsistencies such as this, there seems to be little grounds for suggesting that editors were concerned to remove inconsistencies let alone to imitate the style of

make the Johannine account consistent with the synoptics.

7. Jesus Demonstrates His Knowledge of the Samaritan Woman's Past (4:5-42, without vv10-15, 20-24, 31-38, 40-42)

⁵So he came to a city of Samaria, called Sychar, near the field that Jacob gave to his son Joseph. ⁶Jacob's well was there, and so Jesus, wearied as he was with his journey, sat down beside the well. It was about the sixth hour. ⁷There came a woman of Samaria to draw water. Jesus said to her, "Give me a drink." ⁸For his disciples had gone away into the city to buy food. ⁹The Samaritan woman said to him, "How is it that you, a Jew, ask a drink of me, a woman of Samaria?" For Jews have no dealings with Samaritans....

¹⁶Jesus said to her, "Go, call your husband, and come here." ¹⁷The woman answered him, "I have no husband." Jesus said to her, "You are right in saying 'I have no husband'; ¹⁸for you have had five husbands, and he whom you now have is not your husband; this you said truly."...

²⁵The woman said to him, "I know that **Messiah is coming (he who is called Christ)**; when he comes, he will [tell] us all things." ²⁶Jesus said to her, "I who speak to you am he."

²⁷Just then his disciples came. They marveled that he was talking with a woman, but none said, "What do you wish?" or "Why are you talking with her?" ²⁸So the woman left her water jar, and went away into the city, and said to the people, ²⁹"Come, see a man who told me all that I ever did. **Can this be the Christ?**" ³⁰They went out of the city and were coming to him.... ³⁹**Many Samaritans from that city believed in him because of the woman's testimony, "He told me all that I ever did."**

The story of the Samaritan woman, one of the most famous and popular stories of the gospel, is a good example of how the later editors chose to edit the signs material. In this story, the signs material forms a clear and coherent whole when the additions are removed. Both the extent and the content of the editorial additions are generally

the other in order to disguise their work. Brown refers to it as "almost indisputable evidence of the presence of several hands in the composition of John" (*Gospel* 164).

quite clear and understandable. A clear understanding of the way the passage has been edited makes the story even more rich and fascinating.

The presence of signs material in the passage is indicated by numerous features. First, there is the presence of the stereotyped expression of belief on the part of the townspeople (4:39). Second, the belief comes about as a result of Jesus' demonstration of miraculous knowledge of the woman's past life. Third, there is an emphasis on the magnitude of the miracle in the woman's statement: "He told me *all* that I ever did." Fourth, there is the characteristic translation of terms (4:25). Fifth, the belief occurs in chain reaction form with the townspeople believing on the basis of the report of the woman (cf 1:35-49; 4:46-54; 11:45; 12:9-11). Sixth, the belief is an "easy belief" in which both the woman and the townspeople come immediately to full belief. Seventh, in 4:54 the episode is specifically identified as one of two signs performed by Jesus during his trip to Galilee. Eighth, the christology of the passage (with the editorial additions removed) does not rise above the traditional. Finally, in the mention of Sychar as the location of the well we may have another of the examples of specific and accurate geographical references typical of the first edition.

That the passage has been edited is evident, first, from the way the discussions of living water (vv10-15), worship (vv19-24) and food/harvest (vv31-38) interrupt the basic sequence of the narrative and introduce an entirely different literary technique and theology.[44] In

---

[44]Scholars are in general agreement about the extent of the editing within the story of the Samaritan woman. That is, they would see vv10-15, 20-24, 31-38 and some part of vv40-42 as added. Discussion continues about relatively minor matters. Bultmann would omit v8, would include v40. Fortna omits vv8, 27, and 41. Nicol omits vv25-27, 39. Boismard generally follows this pattern also, although his analysis is considerably more intricate. Wilkens (*Entstehungsgeschichte* 135-138) does not attribute the story of the Samaritan woman to the first edition although he would consider it to be the work of the same individual. In its primitive form it contained, according to Wilkens, vv5-7, 9-26, 28-30, 40 (p. 136).

The omission of v8 by Bultmann and Fortna is on the grounds that since vv31-38 are the only ones to deal with the theme of food, and, since they are secondary, this verse which prepares for that exchange must also be secondary. While this may be possible, there is no real literary evidence for omitting it, and it is not impossible that the original contained some explanation of the absence of the disciples. In any event the verse is not of great importance theologically. I will make further reference to the treatment of vv40-42 below. A peculiarity of the verses, however, is that they are treated by Bultmann, Fortna, Nicol and others, apart from the primary body of signs

addition, the fact that the belief of the Samaritans is (awkwardly) extended to include a third group and that the theological intention of the verses is so clear indicates that vv40-42 also are an editorial addition.

Vv5-9

The passage begins with the arrival of Jesus at Jacob's well near Sychar. The identification of the well is given together with the tradition of its naming.[45] A Samaritan woman comes to the well to draw water and Jesus asks her for a drink of water. The woman is surprised that Jesus, a Jew, would speak with a Samaritan. And the author adds an explanation that Jews have no dealings with Samaritans. At this point some details of the original account are not clear. It may be that the original version contained a request for a drink of water and then the conversation shifted to the request that she bring her husband to the well. At any rate, the request for a drink is of importance only in the addition; the focus in the original is on the woman's marital history.

Vv 10-15

These verses are an editorial addition by the author of the second edition. In it, the request for water is taken to a symbolic level in which the water becomes "living water." This is an offer by Jesus to give the woman the Holy Spirit[46]—a topic completely out of keeping with the theology of the original as evident even in the stereotyped formula of belief which concludes the passage. There the focus is still on the fact that Jesus told her everything she had done. However, the insertion continues the theme of the importance of the Spirit and the promise that Jesus will give it to her if she asks.

The woman, however, while excited about the possibility of getting

---

material, as "other possible traditional material." The analysis here shows that there can be no doubt that the material is an integral part of the main body of signs material.

[45]We have seen before that such accuracy with regard to details of geography, persons, titles, etc. is typical of the first edition.

[46]Living water as a symbol of the Spirit is described explicitly in 7:37-39. Water and the Spirit are connected also in 3:5—and perhaps at 19:30, 34.

living water, misunderstands Jesus, taking the phrase first to mean "spring water,"[47] and then after Jesus comments that she would never thirst, takes it as some miraculous water which would make the daily trips to the well unnecessary. Thus the woman misunderstands the same way Nicodemus had, mistaking Jesus' words as applying to physical reality rather than to the spiritual.

Vv 16-18

The original sequence resumes in v16. Jesus asks the woman to call her husband and to return to the well. The woman tells Jesus that she has no husband. But Jesus replies that she has had five husbands and so in that sense the one she has at the present time is not really hers.

Vv 19-24

On the basis of this supernatural knowledge exhibited by Jesus, the second author puts on the lips of the woman the acknowledgement of Jesus as a prophet.[48] Then, on the basis of Jesus' prophetic ability, the woman asks for his opinion on the correct place of worship. Jesus explains that neither Gerizim nor Jerusalem is the correct place, but that the time has arrived for those who worship truly to worship in spirit and in truth. "For God is Spirit and those who worship him must worship in spirit and truth."[49] (RSV) Again in the addition, the focus is on the importance of the Spirit!

Vv 25-30

In v25, we find another title given to Jesus—this time "Messiah, he who is called the Christ." When he comes, he will tell us all things ("show" (RSV) is incorrect). This second title given to Jesus parallels

---

[47]"Living" water would also be a common term for spring water.

[48]We shall show in the discussion of vv25-30 the reasons for not taking v19 as the acclamation of the woman in the first edition of the story.

[49]Both the topic and its elaboration are the work of the second author. This is significant because it gives lie to the theory that all symbolization was an elaboration of material already present in the first edition. That is not true. Clearly, the interest in symbolization is due to the author of the second edition.

the identification of him as a prophet in v19. However, this one has the claim to being the title used in the original version. First, in this title we find explicit mention of one who "will tell us all things." This is what Jesus has done in telling her she has had five husbands. Secondly, it, like the titles used elsewhere in the first edition, is given first in its Hebrew form and then translated into Greek. Finally, it is also the title used in the woman's remark in v29. The exchange ends with Jesus accepting the woman's identification of him.

At this point, the disciples of Jesus return from the town with food and express surprise that Jesus is speaking with a woman. The woman then leaves the water jar, returns to the town, and tells the people: "Come, see a man who has told me everything I have done! Is this not the Christ?" (RSV) The townspeople then leave the town and come to Jesus. Their arrival, however, is not mentioned until v39.

Vv 31-38

Interrupting the arrival of the townspeople are vv31-38. The verses contain two topics: the question of the food that Jesus has to eat, and the topic of the fields which are ripe for harvest. It is difficult to tell whether there had been any mention of food in the original version; there are really no literary features to clearly settle the issue. However, it seems quite certain that even if there was some mention of the disciples bringing food in the original, the present state of the text indicates a development of the topic by the author of the second edition.

The topic of food is developed in a way that is identical to the elaborations earlier in the chapter and in the gospel: some activity is spoken of by Jesus but is understood by the listener as being meant in a physical/material sense rather than in the spiritual sense intended by Jesus. We have seen this technique previously in the discussion with Nicodemus where rebirth was taken in a crass physical sense rather than as spiritual rebirth as intended by Jesus. Here, in the conversation with the Samaritan woman, "living water" had been spoken of by Jesus as a symbol of the Spirit (cf 7:37-39) but misunderstood by the woman. The question of worship is first cast by the woman in terms of the proper physical location (Gerizim or Jerusalem) but Jesus speaks of the necessity of the possession of the spirit for true worship ("in spirit and in truth"). Here in the discussion with the disciples, the statement by Jesus that he has food that they are not aware of is taken by them in a purely physical, material sense, but Jesus explains that it is a "spiritual" food, to do the will of the Father.

Given the similarity between the discussion regarding food and that regarding living water and regarding true worship, it is certain that the discussion regarding food comes from the second stratum also. The second part of the passage (dealing with the fields ripe for harvest) also betrays some similarity to the techniques of the second stratum in that it applies to the harvest of souls what is proper to the harvest of grain. But the passage is so brief and obscure that it is difficult to be sure.

V 39

V39 resumes the original version of the story by stating, in a typically stereotyped formula, that "many Samaritans from that city believed in him because of the woman's testimony, 'He told me all that I ever did ' (RSV).[50] This stereotyping, together with the easy belief, based on miracles, and the tandem belief (first the woman and then the townspeople) mark the verse as part of the original edition. Theologically, the story clearly intends to show another facet of the power of Jesus. Presumably Jesus' knowledge of *all five* husbands is a detail that is intended to illustrate the completeness of his knowledge. This is also reinforced by the woman's statement that the Messiah would tell us "all things" (v25) and her statement to the townspeople that "he told me all that I ever did."

Thus ends the original version of the miracle. In its original form it was undoubtedly intended to be another of the demonstrations of Jesus' marvelous power. He is able to perform all sorts of miracles (2:23) but also among the most varied groups of persons. Jesus' signs have caused belief not only among the disciples (2:1-11) but also among the people of Jerusalem (2:23), and now among the Samaritans (4:4-42). Soon we shall see a demonstration of it even among the Gentiles (4:46-54). The fact that the early Christian community had a mission to the Samaritans may also help explain the interest in this story.[51] But

---

[50]The stereotyping is even clearer in a more literal translation: "From that town, many of the Samaritans believed in him because of the word of the woman...."

[51]The mission to Samaria is described in Acts 8:1-25. The gospel of John is the only

in the present text of the gospel, the story is not finished.

Vv 40-42

Vv40-42, which are only awkwardly related to the previous material, take the signs material one step further and add a new dimension to the faith of the Samaritans. This is the first clear example within the signs material of the editorial technique known as the "repetitive resumptive." This technique was described in chapter two[52] as an editorial technique where an author repeats a brief section of material from before his editorial addition as a means of resuming the original sequence. In a previous discussion of this technique,[53] I showed that v40 is introduced by the phrase *hote oun* ("when therefore") but the phrase is not intended primarily in its temporal sense but rather in a resumptive sense returning to the context of v30. Thus the narrative sequence returns to the context of v30 where the townspeople are coming to Jesus rather than to v39 where they had arrived and believed.[54]

In addition to the resumptive phrase *hote oun*, the intervening material contains several aporias, confirming the presence of editing. In v40 the townspeople ask Jesus to stay with them, and he remains with them for two days. We are then told that yet a third group ("many more") come to believe in Jesus *because of his word*. The introduction of this third group as well as the new and deeper basis of belief and the criticism of the belief based just on the report of the woman indicates an important shift in the story. It is no longer the report of a miracle, nor even the miracle itself, which is the basis of belief but the *word of Jesus.*[55] V42 confirms this in the most explicit way. The townspeople

gospel to mention a mission of Jesus there. Mt 10:5 forbids the disciples to enter a Samaritan town.

[52]See above chapter 2 p. 27.

[53]von Wahlde, "A Redactional Technique," 530-32.

[54]The awkward relationship between vv30 and 40 is somewhat smoothed out in the RSV. In the original Greek there is a clear sense of "arrival" in v30 which then makes the statement of v40 awkward, especially after the statement of belief in v39.

[55]Fortna (*Signs* 192-93) claims that v39 is Johannine on stylistic grounds. He correctly points out that v40 resumes v30 but he does not consider it to be an addition. Rather he makes numerous minor excisions in order to remove "Johannine" style elements. I find these various minor omissions to be difficult to substantiate objectively.

tell the woman: "'No longer do we believe because of your report. For we ourselves have heard and we know that this is truly the Saviour of the World.'"

Thus in these verses, we find another clear example of the critique of faith based on the miraculous, like those of 1:50-51 and 2:24-25. However, although it is undoubtedly true that the verses are a "critique" of the miraculous, their intention is perhaps better said to be a desire to "relativize" such belief by indicating that it is a first stage, a belief that should lead to an interest in the word of Jesus, and that ultimately that word is the more solid basis for faith.

8. *Transition: Jesus Comes into Galilee* (4:43-45, without v44)

> [43]After the two days he departed to Galilee.... [45]So when he came to Galilee, **the Galileans welcomed him, having seen all that he had done** in Jerusalem at the feast, for they too had gone to the feast.

These verses provide a transition from the story of the Samaritan woman to the healing of the official's son. However, they also contain their own significance within the signs material. The arrival in Galilee is, it seems, the occasion for yet more popular acceptance of Jesus, again on the basis of his miracles at the Passover in Jerusalem.

Apart from the introductory words ("After the two days...") which may have been occasioned by the addition of vv40-42 to the previous episode, and apart from v44, which will be discussed below, the verses belong to the first edition. First, they indicate the "easy belief" of the

Fortna also claims, following J. Bowman ["Samaritan Studies," *BJRL* 40 (1957-58) 298-327] that the phrase "saviour of the world" is Samaritan usage for the Messiah and so may be pre-Johannine. However, the same phrase occurs in 1 Jn 4:14 and throughout the New Testament generally, and so should not be seen as reflecting a particularly Samaritan context. The verses reflect the same sort of expiatory role for Jesus which is found in the addition of 1:29 and elsewhere and probably reflect a view of the later (3rd edition?) tradition rather than an earlier one. Nicol (*Semeia* 40) limits the addition to vv41-42 but simply asserts his position rather than discuss the verse. The awareness of the repetitive resumptive here provides, in my view, a much more systematic and consistent explanation of such awkward additions throughout the gospel.

signs material in the statement that "the Galileans welcomed him." They echo the concern of the signs material for the quantity and quality of Jesus' signs. They are consistent with the surrounding context in that they continue the journey to Galilee that was begun in the signs material of 4:1-4, and they refer to the signs performed in Jerusalem at the time of the feast (2:23), also a part of the signs material.[56]

V 44

The only interruption is v44, a statement by Jesus also known from the synoptic tradition.[57] However, its placement here is awkward, making it difficult to tell the source of the rejection. From the context it would seem that it was either the Samaritans (whose town he has just left) or the Galileans (whose region he has just entered). But both have been described as believing in him. Some would say that it refers to the religious authorities in Judea, whose hostility has made this trip necessary. But then one would have expected it to be placed at the beginning of chapter 4, where the hostility which made the trip necessary is described. The most likely explanation is that it has been added by the editor to again qualify the belief based on the miraculous.

That the verse is not part of the original is indicated first of all by the fact that it is so awkward and difficult to interpret. Secondly, the peculiar repetition, even more clear in the Greek original than in the English, indicates that the editor has repeated part of v43 after making his addition, as a way of resuming the sequence after his interruption.[58] This repetition, when linked with the awkwardness of the intervening material, is another example of the editorial device known as the "repetitive resumptive," which occurred previously also at 4:40.[59] The

---

[56]These verses are attributed to the Evangelist by Fortna (*Signs* 184, 85) on the grounds that they are part of the artificial removal of Jesus from Judea to Galilee. Bultmann (*Gospel* 204 n. 1) and Wellhausen (*Evangelium* 23) also attribute them to the Evangelist paralleling them with 2:23-25. Dodd, however, observes that it is free of "distinctive marks of Johannine composition" and "the statement that Jesus was welcomed by the Galileans leads to nothing" (*Tradition* 238).

[57]Mt 13:57; Mk 6:4; Lk 4:24.

[58]The last phrase of v43 reads *ekselthen ekeithen eis tēn Galilaian*. V44 begins *hote oun elthen eis tēn Galilaian* ... thus repeating almost verbatim the end of v43.

[59]For a detailed discussion of its occurrence here, see von Wahlde, "A Redactional Technique" 527-29.

basic intention of the verse is to provide a critique of miracle faith by incorporating a synoptic-like assessment of the faith associated with that region. In addition to its similarity to the synoptics, it is similar to 4:2.

9. *Jesus Heals an Official's Son at Cana* (4:46-54, without v48)

> [46]So he came again to Cana in Galilee, where he had made the water wine. And at Capernaum there was an official whose son was ill. [47]When he heard that Jesus had come from Judea to Galilee, he went and begged him to come down and heal his son, for he was at the point of death. . . . [49]The official said to him, "Sir, come down before my child dies." [50]Jesus said to him, "Go; your son will live." The man believed the word that Jesus spoke to him and went his way. As he was going down, his servants met him and told him that his son was living. [52]So he asked them the hour when he began to mend, and they said to him, "Yesterday at the seventh hour the fever left him." [53]The father knew that was the hour when Jesus had said to him, "Your son will live"; **and he himself believed, and all his household.** [54]**This was now the second sign that Jesus did when he had come from Judea to Galilee.**

The healing of the official's son continues the sequence of the trip begun in 4:1.[60] It describes the healing at a distance of a young boy who was sick unto death. The official whose son is healed is not identified exactly, but it is generally assumed that the man is an officer of king Herod, possibly a soldier, and probably a gentile.[61]

---

[60]Fortna (*Signs* 39) claims that the healing did not take place at Cana (a locale invented by the Evangelist). Rather, in the source this episode followed 2:12a and the encounter with the nobleman took place either in Capernaum or on the road between Cana and Capernaum. This conjecture is occasioned by the "pointless character of 2:12a" and fits in well with Fortna's conviction that the healing of the official's son was originally the second episode in the signs source, occurring immediately after the first Cana miracle and now separated from it by 2:13-4:45 (*Signs* 39). Thus for Fortna, the first part of v46 is the work of the Evangelist. So also R. Schnackenburg "Zur Traditionsgeschichte von Joh 4, 46-54," *BZ* n.s. 8 (1964) 58-88, esp. 64. Wilkens (*Entstehungsgeschichte* 41-43) sees vv46b-54 as homogeneous and does not excise v48.

[61]See for example the discussion in Brown, *Gospel* 190.

The miracle is typical of the signs material. The belief is based on the working of a miracle, and therefore occurs after the miracle. It is an example of "easy belief" and contains the "chain reaction" belief (both the man and his household) typical of the signs material. It is identified as a sign specifically in v54, and in fact as the *second* sign within the return trip to Galilee thus confirming that the revelation of the Samaritan woman's past was also considered by the author to be a sign.

V 48

The peculiarity of the passage lies in v48: ("Jesus therefore said to him, 'Unless you (pl) see signs and wonders you will not believe.'"). The designation of miracles here as "signs and wonders" (*sēmeia kai terata*) is unique in the gospel and echoes the usage in Acts.[62] The theological *Tendenz* of the verse runs counter to the remainder of the story by its criticism of faith based on miracles. Finally, in Jesus' response to the man, there is an unexplained shift to the plural "you." This shift is identical to those within the additions in 1:51 and 3:11. These features strongly suggest that v48 has been added to the original signs material. That this is so is confirmed by the way much of v47 is repeated in v49 (the official states his request in both verses). This repetition may be yet another instance of the editorial use of "repetitive resumptive" to frame the insertion.[63] Given these various features, there can be little doubt that the verse is added as another critique of miracle faith.[64]

The miracle continues the theme of the signs material showing not only the variety of the powers of Jesus, manifest here in a healing of a person near death *at a distance,* but also the fact that this person was, evidently, not a Jew but a gentile.

[62]See for example Acts 2:22, 43; 4:30; 5:12; 6:8; 7:36; 14:3; 15:12.

[63]It is studied by J.M. Robinson "The Johannine Trajectory" in *Trajectories* 242-44. Robinson sees the repeated references to the movement to Galilee beginning with 1:43 and including 3:22; 4:1, 45 as all being redactional. Therefore he also includes the first half of v47 as also calling attention to the movement into Galilee. While the first part of v47 is somewhat repetitious, I do not think that it is sufficiently so to identify it as an addition to the signs material.

[64]It will be recalled that every instance of faith on the basis of miracles (even that of the disciples in 1:34-49) except that of 2:11 has been in some way criticized or made subordinate to other forms of faith: 2:24-25; 4:40-42; 4:44; 4:48. This is of course a

The sign is then identified in v54 as the "second" sign. In much of modern scholarship, this is taken to refer to the numbering of the signs within the source.[65] Those who understand it that way then take the phrase "coming from Judea into Galilee" to be the evangelist's attempt to make sense of the numbering in the present state of the text. But there is no literary evidence to suggest that the phrase is an addition. However, the fact that material such as 2:23-3:2; 3:22-26; 4:1-4; 4:43, 45, can now be demonstrated to belong to the signs material makes it much more likely that within its context the reference to "second" in v54 is simply what it appears to be, the description of the healing as the second sign performed during the trip from Judea.

10. *Jesus Heals a Man Ill for Thirty-Eight Years* (5:1-9)

[1]After this there was a feast of the Jews, and Jesus went up to Jerusalem. [2]Now there is in Jerusalem by **the Sheep Gate a pool, in Hebrew called Bethzatha,** which has five porticoes. [3]In these lay a multitude of invalids, blind, lame, paralyzed. [5]One man was there, who had been ill for thirty-eight years. [6]When Jesus saw him and knew that he had been lying there a long time, he said to him, "Do you want to be healed": [7]The sick man answered him, "Sir, I have no

---

clear indicator of one purpose of the redaction: to put miracle faith within a wider context and perspective. In 4:48, it would also seem that the faith of the official is somewhat "redeemed" by the fact that the text says he believed "the word" of Jesus before he departed. While this of course could refer simply to the trust the man puts in the statement of Jesus, it is possible that it was interpreted as referring at least on a verbal level to the "word" of Jesus in its deeper theological sense. Fortna would see this reference to the word as John's addition to the text and so excise it from the signs material. But there is little literary evidence for this.

[65]Fortna is certainly the most prominent proponent of this theory today. In addition to the numbering of the first and second miracles, Fortna associates the miraculous catch of fish in chapter 21 with this numbering because it is said there that it was the "third" (*Signs* 102-09). However, this is not convincing. First, it seems unlikely that such numbering would be retained if it was useless. Second, the numbering in 4:54 is at its face value, a reference to a second miracle in the sequence of the trip. Many commentators see the reference to the sign as the second one of the trip as an attempt to make an otherwise obscure numerical reference intelligible. This overcomplicates the situation. The reference is what it seems to be: a reference to the second sign performed during the trip!

man to put me into the pool when the water is troubled, and while I am going another steps down before me." 8Jesus said to him, "Rise, take up your pallet, and walk." 9And at once the man was healed and he took up his pallet and walked.

The next passage from the signs material is the healing of the man who had been ill for thirty-eight years. It takes place in Jerusalem at an unnamed feast.[66] Although in the final edition of the gospel the miracle follows the healing of the official's son, it is unlikely that this was the case in the first edition of the gospel. 6:1ff provides a much better sequence with the end of chapter 4. At the end of chapter 4, as we have seen, Jesus is in Cana of Galilee. According to the introductory notice of chapter 6, Jesus crosses to the other side of the sea of Galilee, a notice that presumes his presence already within Galilee. Further, it is said that the crowds were following Jesus because of the signs he was performing on the sick, a notice that is plausible in the light of the healing of the official's son in 4:46-54.[67]

[66]In the original version, the feast mentioned here could well have been the Passover mentioned as being near in 6:4. When the order of the miracles was reversed (see the discussion in the following note), the specific name of the feast then would presumably have been dropped. If that is the case, then we must postulate some editing here in order to provide a mention of the feast.

[67]The order of this miracle and the multiplication was probably reversed for theological reasons at the time of the second edition. In the second edition, the healing (5:1-9) serves as the basis for the discourse in which Jesus asserts his identity with God the Father. The discourse of 5:19-47 then provides several basic christological affirmations of the second edition: the two basic powers of Jesus (5:19-30), the four witnesses to him (5:31-40) and the only kind of glory he accepts (5:41-47).

The witnesses to Jesus in particular (5:31-40) provide the key to the organization of the major discourses in the second edition. The witness of scripture is presented in the multiplication/discourse on bread complex (6:1-59); the witness of the word is presented in the complex of the Tabernacles dispute (7:1-52) and its associated discourse (8:12-59) which interprets it; the witness of Jesus' works is presented in the complex of the healing of the blind man (9:1-41) and the discourse which interprets it (10:22-39).This organization is discussed in detail in the author's "Witnesses," esp 395-98.

Because the sign/discourse unit in chapter 5 (within the second edition) contains the paradigm of witnesses which is worked out in the following chapters and because of the appropriateness of the multiplication as a basis for the discussion of the witness value of scripture, the order of the two episodes was reversed by the author of the second edition.

The theological structure of the second edition is, of course, "laid over" the structure of the signs material. Yet the structure of the signs material is still considerably in evidence and will be discussed in chapter 4.

The healing of the cripple, although it is part of the signs material, lacks several of the more common features of the signs. There is no mention of it as a "sign" and there is no mention of "easy" belief. In fact it is the only one of the signs in the gospel to have no form of belief expressed after it. These peculiarities are explained by the fact that the author of the second edition has removed all material following the actual narration of the miracle itself and replaced it entirely by his own material in which the Jews are the main actors (cf "Jews" in the hostile Johannine sense in vv10, 15, 16, 18).[68] Nevertheless a number of elements characteristic of the signs material are still apparent. The narrative contains the precise and accurate geographical information characteristic of the early edition.[69] In addition the place is identified first in its Greek form and then in its Hebrew version, continuing the pattern found in the material of the first edition. Finally, the emphasis on the extent of the illness (a man ill for thirty-eight years) is typical of the signs material.

The working of the miracle is narrated very briefly.[70] After a dialogue with the man, Jesus simply commands him to get up, take his pallet and walk. Immediately the man is healed and does as Jesus commands. As was the case in all of the previous miracles, Jesus works the miracle simply by his verbal command.[71] The mention of the fact that it was a

[68]The theology of the addition is also clearly different from that of the first edition. Here in the Jews material of vv10-18, there is a clear shift to the hostility characteristic of the second edition as well as to the much higher christology which debates the claim of Jesus to equality with God—a topic nowhere found in the first edition.

[69]The discovery of the pool is narrated and discussed in J. Jeremias, *The Rediscovery of Bethesda* (Louisville: Southern Baptist Seminary, 1966). The Hebrew name is the object of several textual variations. There is also attestation of the pool in the copper scroll from Qumran. See J.T. Milik, *Discoveries in the Judean Desert,* III, (1962) 271.

[70]Most scholars agree that v1 has been modified by the Evangelist but see little evidence of editing elsewhere within the passage. Fortna (*Signs* 48-54) would see evidence of editing only in v1 and then in the identification of the day as a sabbath in v9b. So also Nicol, Schnackenburg, Wilkens, all of whom consider the mention of the Sabbath as a later addition. Bultmann extends the material of the sign to v15, but this can hardly be the case. Wilken (*Entstehungsgeschichte* 50-51) considers the original material to continue as far as v16 and parallels this development of the miracle with that of 9:8-41. However, this is hardly possible given the numerous linguistic, ideological and theological differences between 5:9b-16 and 9:8-41.

[71]The only miracle effected by means other than the word of Jesus is the healing of the man born blind in chapter 9, where Jesus applies mud to his eyes and orders the man to wash at the pool of Siloam.

Sabbath day when Jesus effected this cure is strange, occurring as it does almost as an afterthought. This had led most scholars to suppose that it is in fact an addition of the evangelist. This is very likely.[72]

11. A Transition: Jesus Crosses the Sea of Galilee (6:1-2)

[1]After this Jesus went to the other side of **the Sea of Galilee, which is the Sea of Tiberias.** [2]And a multitude followed him, because **they saw the signs which he did** on those who were diseased.

These verses serve as a transition between what preceded them in the original gospel (the material of 4:54) and the multiplication of the loaves which follows in 6:3-14. Again, features of the early stratum are clearly evident. The sea of Galilee is given two names: the sea of Galilee and its later secular name "the sea of Tiberias."[73] The term sign is used for miracle, and there is a consistent portrayal of the great popular response to Jesus.[74]

[72]For an indication of scholars who hold this position, see note 70 above.

[73]While not precisely a translation, the fact of the Jewish and secular names side by side has the same purpose as the provision of the Jewish and secular Greek versions of religious terminology and geography found elsewhere in the signs material. The various names for the lake are discussed in Brown, *Gospel* 232, and Schnackenburg, *Gospel* 2 13.

[74]This reference to a great popular following is paralleled in 2:23; 3:26; 4:1, 45—and later at 11:56; 12:9, 19. Such passages, in addition to the various stereotyped formulas of "easy belief," attest to a positive response to Jesus on the part of large numbers of people within the signs material.

The mention here of a large number of healings of sick is curious. These healings have of course not been mentioned in the current version of the gospel. We cannot tell whether they had been narrated in detail in any previous version of the signs material.

Scholars had previously tended to see indications of some traditional material in these verses but to base their analysis on criteria that seem to be somewhat weak. Fortna (*Signs* 55-56) basing himself on the awkward relation of v1 to its present context suggests that it may well have been in the source. He finds "synoptic-like" elements in v2 and concedes that this may also be traditional, but the similarities between v3 and 2:23; 4:45 lead him to attribute the verse in its present form to the Evangelist. Nicol (*Semeia* 33) takes a similar position, as do Bultmann (*Gospel* 211); Schnackenburg (*Gospel* 2 10-12); Dodd (*Tradition* 210-11). It is difficult to see, however, how the Evangelist who constantly criticizes (e.g., 2:24-25; 4:40-42, 44, 48) miracle faith would be considered the author of verses such as 2:23; 4:45; 6:1-3, where such

12. Jesus Multiplies the Loaves and Fishes (6:3-14, without vv6, 15)

[3]Jesus went up on the mountain, and there sat down with his disciples. [4]Now the Passover, the feast of the Jews, was at hand. [5]Lifting up his eyes, then, and seeing that a multitude was coming to him, Jesus said to Philip, "How are we to buy bread, so that these people may eat?". . . [7] Philip answered him, "Two hundred denarii would not buy enough bread for each of them to get a little." [8]One of his disciples, Andrew, Simon Peter's brother, said to him, [9]"There is a lad here who has five barley loaves and two fish; but what are they among so many?" [10]Jesus said, "Make the people sit down." Now there was much grass in the place; so the men sat down, in number about five thousand. Jesus then took the loaves, and when he had given thanks, he distributed them to those who were seated; so also the fish, as much as they wanted. [12]And when they had eaten their fill, he told his disciples, "Gather up the fragments left over that nothing may be lost." [13]So they gathered them up and filled twelve baskets with fragments from the five barley loaves, left by those who had eaten. [14]**When the people saw the sign which he had done**, they said, "This is indeed **the prophet who is to come into the world!**"

The multiplication of the loaves occurs in all of the gospels. However, some of the theological emphases of the synoptics are absent from the Johannine version. For example, there is no mention of a prior intention to teach (cf Mk 6:34; Lk 9:11) but only that the crowd has been following Jesus because of his signs (v2). Nor is there mention of a motive of compassion because of the hunger of the crowd (Mk 6:35-36; Mt 15:32). This, however, is the only version where any of the disciples present are mentioned by name.

Jesus asks the disciples how they are to buy bread to feed the crowds. The narrator then notes that Jesus said this to test them since he knew what he would do. Jesus is told that there is a boy with five barley loaves and two fishes. Jesus' action over the food is brief: he

"easy belief" is presented in a positive way. The attribution of these verses to the signs material on the basis of the more objective criteria we have suggested seems to explain the language usage itself more adequately but also to deal more effectively with the issue of miracle faith and the Evangelist's criticism of it.

gives thanks and distributes it. All of the people, who numbered five thousand, eat their fill. Thereupon the disciples gather up twelve baskets of fragments. In v14, we are told the reaction to the feeding: "When the people saw the sign which he had done, they said, 'This is indeed the prophet who is to come into the world.'" The narrator then tells us that Jesus, "perceiving they were about to try to make him king, withdrew again to the mountain."

There can be no doubt about the identification of the Johannine multiplication as part of the signs material. The miracle is identified as a "sign" in v14.[75] In addition, the absence of other motives for the miracle puts the focus on the event as a demonstration of Jesus' power. The people's identification of Jesus as the Prophet like Moses (low christology) and their spontaneous attempt to take Jesus by force to make him king ("easy" belief) also mark the passage as coming from the signs material.

Vv 6, 15

As is generally recognized, there are two significant instances of editing within the miracle;[76] both involve demonstrations of Jesus'

---

[75]There is a textual variant with considerable support from early manuscripts for a plural reading of "signs." The evidence is discussed at length in B.M. Metzger, et.al., *A Textual Commentary on the Greek New Testament* (London: United Bible Societies, 1971). It may be that the singular is an attempt to make the statement fit only this miracle rather than function as a more general reaction as is found frequently in the signs material.

[76]Many scholars suggest that the mention of the Passover in v4 is added. Bultmann (*Gospel* 210), Nicol (*Semeia* 33), Fortna (*Signs* 57), Schnackenburg (*Gospel* 2 22), and Wilkens (*Entstehungsgeschichte* 43-45) argue that the reference to Passover (v4) interrupts the narrative and is added by the Evangelist. However, Dodd (*Tradition* 209-210) argues correctly that the theme of Passover is not elaborated in what follows (the discourse of 6:30-59 elaborates the theme of manna in the desert.) There is a traditional Christian relation between the Eucharist and Passover but the reference is too brief to claim that such symbolism is intended here. It may well be simply one of the chronological and geographical references which seem to abound in the signs material; it has no theological importance for the narrative. In the original version of the signs material when chapter 5 *followed* chapter 6, it may have served to explain Jesus' trip to Jerusalem for the (now unnamed) feast where he heals the man at the pool of Bethesda.

There are also some other relatively minor instances of awkwardness in the passage that have been noted by scholars, but in my opinion no definite conclusions can be reached regarding them. In v8 the introduction of Andrew as "one of his disciples" is

knowledge. The evidence that they are added is based on ideological and theological grounds.

In the first instance (v6), the reader is told that Jesus knew what he would do and that he asked the disciples where they could buy food in order to test them. The second occurs at the end of the miracle (v15), where it is said that Jesus knew that the crowd was going to come to make him king. In the second, the reader is told that Jesus knew of the crowd's intention to make him king and so retreated to the mountain alone.[77] Like the foreknowledge evident in the addition of 2:24-25, this supernatural knowledge does not function to bring about belief. Rather, the comments are intended for the reader and are consistent with the high christology of the second edition in which the superiority of Jesus to human events and concerns is evident.[78] In additon, the second comment is correctly seen as a criticism of the miracle-faith of the crowd and consistent with the theology of the author of the second edition.[79]

13. Jesus Crosses the Sea of Galilee Miraculously (6:16-21)

[16]When evening came, his disciples went down to the sea, [17]got into a boat, and started across the sea to Capernaum. It was now

somewhat awkward since Philip has already been mentioned. Fortna (*Signs* 58), Schnackenburg (*Gospel* 2 22), Wellhausen (*Evangelium* 28) propose that no disciple was named in the *Grundschrift*. But there is not enough evidence to determine clearly that the mention of one or both of the disciples has been added. Dodd, Fortna, and Nicol suggest that the last four words of v12 "have a Johannine ring." I find this difficult to assess; it is minor in any case. There is also some discussion of the wording in v14 Fortna (*Signs* 60-62).

[77]That these two verses have been added in whole or in part is generally accepted: Fortna (*Signs* 58, 60-62); Bultmann (*Gospel* 210); Nicol (*Semeia* 34) although he proposes only v15 as added. Wellhausen (*Evangelium* 29) would keep both verses. Schnackenburg (*Gospel* 2 23) finds the evidence inconclusive.

[78]Although such supernatural knowledge would not be out of place within the signs material, within the signs material such knowledge is consistently shown as bringing about belief, never as an aside for the reader. See the discussion above in chapter 2 and on 2:23-25.

For a description of the historical verisimilitude of the passage and a discussion of the political implications of such an action, see Dodd, *Tradition* 214-216.

[79]So also, for example, Fortna (*Signs* 60); Nicol (*Semeia* 34).

dark, and Jesus had not yet come to them. [18]The sea rose because a strong wind was blowing. [19]When they had rowed about three or four miles, they saw Jesus walking on the sea and drawing near to the boat. They were frightened, [20]but he said to them, "It is I; do not be afraid." [21]Then they were glad to take him into the boat, and immediately the boat was at the land to which they were going.

The story of Jesus coming to the disciples upon the water is one of the more puzzling narratives of the gospel of John. Like the story of the multiplication, a variation of this story occurs in all the gospels. Jesus has gone to the mountain. The disciples have started across the lake in a boat toward Capernaum. When they had gone about four miles, and the wind had increased, the disciples see Jesus walking on the water near the boat. They become afraid but he identifies himself and they take him into the boat. The boat immediately arrives at the shore to which it was headed.

What makes the passage so puzzling is that in spite of the fact that three miraculous events are involved (the coming of Jesus to the disciples, the dying down of the wind, and the sudden arrival of the boat at the destination), there is no theological elaboration of the incident.[80] Nor is the incident identified as a sign nor is there any mention that it led somehow to further belief. It is generally included among the signs material and I would agree.[81] It is, in fact, another demonstration of the miraculous, and it shows no evidence of any of the theology characteristic of the later editions.

[80]Although the passage contains the *I am* formula which, in the later stratum of the gospel is used as a title of Jesus identifying him with Yahweh of the LXX (8:24, 28, 58), here the words are used simply as a means of self-identification.

[81]The majority of recent studies (Bultmann, Fortna, Nicol, Schnackenburg) include this episode within the signs material. Fortna (*Signs* 64-70) and Bultmann (*Gospel* 211) would extend the material to v25 without vv23-24. Wilkens (*Entstehungsgeschichte* 45-47) extends it to v27 but without v22 and parts of v23. However, the episode of the walking on the sea clearly ends in v21 and there are no features which could clearly identify vv22-25 as belonging to the signs material. Although parts of vv22-25 may be traditional, we cannot determine this on the basis of the present criteria. The next mention of one of the primary criteria is *semeia* in v26. This verse will be discussed in the following section.

13a. 6:26 [*Not Signs Material*]

This verse, although it contains the term signs, has been redacted to such an extent that it is not possible to recover its original meaning. Originally, it referred to the sign of the multiplication, but in the criticism of miracle-faith typical of the second edition, the verse has come to say that although they witnessed the sign, they have not fully "seen" (understood) the signs. Even the reference to the sign as being a symbol of something deeper indicates its revision by the author of the second edition. This mixing is itself evidence of a literary seam due to the transition from material of the one edition to that of another.[82]

14. A Fragment of a Discussion at Tabernacles (7:25-27)

> [25]Some of the people of Jerusalem therefore said, "Is not this the man whom they seek to kill? [26]And here he is, speaking openly, and they say nothing to him! Can it be that **the rulers** really know that **this is the Christ**? [27]Yet we know where this man comes from; and when **the Christ** appears, no one will know where he comes from." (RSV ,modified).

Overview of Chapter Seven

These verses constitute the first of four passages at the feast of Tabernacles which are part of the signs material.[83] The chapter as a

---

[82]This mixing is also evident in 7:25-26; 8:12-13; 9:35-41 and 12:42-43.

[83]7:1-13, dealing with material previous to the feast itself, are not from the signs material (contra Bultmann, *Gospel* 288-89), and Wilkens (*Entstehungsgeschichte* 48-49). The verses discuss the topic of "going up" in a physical and in a spiritual sense (i.e., crucifixion), a topic which we shall see dominating the chapter. However they contain the term Jews in the hostile sense (v1) and the term "works" for miracles (v3).

Curiously the only material that Bultmann (and Wilkens) would assign to the signs source in chapter 7 is vv1-13, although he does admit to several instances of material from the revelatory discourse source. Fortna and Nicol attribute no material here to their signs material. Boismard's analysis is not easy to summarize adequately; it is characterized, however, by the belief that much of the material that originally (i.e., at the level of Document C) occurred in the context of the feast of Tabernacles has now

whole provides perhaps the clearest instances of alternation between the two sets of terms for religious authorities. As was the case in the Nicodemus episode, the signs material throughout the chapter introduces various topics which are then taken up and answered by the material of the second edition.[84]

The overriding theme of the chapter *in the final edition of the gospel* is a discussion of the "whence and whither" of Jesus. The basic theme of vv14-24 is the "whence" of Jesus' ability to interpret the Law (from a human source/from God). In vv25-30 the topic is the whence of Jesus himself (earthly origin/heavenly origin). In vv31-36 the topic is his "whither" (the Diaspora/his return to the Father). In vv40-52, the topic returns to the question of the "whence" of Jesus (from Galilee). In each case, there is a contrast between the physical/earthly level of the topic and the spiritual level of understanding. The material, which is the basis of the misunderstanding, comes in all cases from the signs material and is reinterpreted by the material of the second edition. The one exception to this is vv14-19 where both the original topic and the discussion come from the second edition.

The presentation is completed by the discussion of the Spirit in vv37-39. As was the case with Nicodemus and with the Samaritan woman, the second editor affirms that living water (the Holy Spirit) is the basis for true understanding of Jesus and will be given to those who come to Jesus. With this arrangement in mind we are better able to see the plan of this dispute-filled chapter.

Vv 25-27

Vv 25-27 themselves are identified as signs material by the term "rulers" in v26b; by the characteristic division among the people; by

been moved to other parts of the gospel—and that vv31-32 and vv44-52 originally followed the healing of the man at the pool in chapter 5 (*Évangile* 218).

As can be seen, it is in the analysis of chapter 7 that my analysis would differ from most if not all recent theories. Yet it is in chapter 7 that we find some of the clearest examples of alternation in material from the first two editions. In addition the theological reasons for the editing are equally clear and follow the same pattern as elsewhere in the gospel.

[84]As we have seen in the case of Nicodemus and the Samaritan woman, the author of the second edition seems to be intent on providing a new set of answers to topics and questions that had already been dealt with in the first edition of the gospel.

the discussion which is confined to low christology (traditional Jewish expectations);[85] and by the occurrence only here of the term "Jerusalemite" (most likely a relic of early material not occurring elsewhere in the present edition.)

The issue within the verses is the origin of Jesus, which the speakers claim to know. The signs material breaks off abruptly at the end of v27, and the answer of Jesus is introduced equally abruptly and awkwardly.[86] Without previous indication of where Jesus or the crowd is, nor even of whether Jesus and the crowd were in the same place, it is said that Jesus begins "proclaiming as he taught in the temple." Yet he addresses the topic raised in the earlier material: his place of origin. However, in the material that follows, Jesus does not discuss this in earthly terms but in terms of his spiritual origin with the Father implying that they do not really know his true origin and that he has not come of his own will but that the Father has sent him. This discussion continues until v30 where there is further mention of his superiority evident in the inability of others to arrest him "because his hour had not yet come."[87] Then the signs material resumes in 7:31.

[85]The mention of "some of the people of Jerusalem" in v25 would parallel the use of this phrase constantly within the formulaic statements of belief. However, the reference to the desire to kill Jesus this early in the ministry is not characteristic of the signs material although it appears frequently in the second edition (cf 5:18; 7:1; 8:37, 59; 11:8). This feature is discussed in detail in chapter 2 above. The mixing of terminology (see also "work" for miracle in vv20-24) is an indication of a literary seam between material of different editions. It occurs also in 6:26; 8:12-13; 9:35-41 and 12:42-43.

[86]So also Bultmann (*Gospel* 297) with discussion. Bultmann recognized a change of authorship here attributing vv28-29 to his revelatory discourse source. Wilkens (*Entstehungsgeschichte* 99), following Wellhausen (*Evangelium* 38), suggested that these verses were a doublet of 7:40-44 but does not attribute them to the first edition of the gospel.

[87]This verse clearly comes from the second edition. It makes reference to Jesus' "hour"—a theme which appears secondary in the Cana miracle (2:4) and which occurs consistently in additions elsewhere (see the list in the discussion of 2:4 above). In addition, it conflicts with the report in 7:46 that the arresting officers were won over by Jesus' speaking and echoes the theme of superiority of Jesus typical of the second edition. Bultmann (*Gospel* 287) rightly points to the difficult sequence between v30 and the verse which follows. This aporia indicates the literary seam leading to the signs material which follows in v31.

15. The Belief of the Crowds and the Reaction of the Pharisees (7:31-32)

[31]Yet **many of the people believed in him**; they said, "When **the Christ** appears, **will he do more signs than this man has done?**" [32]**The Pharisees heard the crowd** thus muttering about him, and **the chief priests and Pharisees** sent officers to arrest him.

These verses are identified as signs material by numerous characteristics. There is the stereotyped formula of belief, a concern for traditional titles, the term signs, the emphasis on the quantity and quality of the signs, the characteristic terms for religious authorities three times, and the characteristic response on the part of the authorities immediately following a statement of the people's belief.

The content of the verses is quite simple. They appear to be a continuation of the original left off in v27. There, many of the common people,[88] debating the identity of the Messiah, thought Jesus was the Messiah but could not explain the fact that they knew where Jesus came from in the light of the tradition that the origin of the Messiah would be unknown.[89] Yet the majority of the crowd affirm their belief in Jesus as Messiah on the basis of his signs. Hearing reports of the common people's discussion, the chief priests and Pharisees send their attendants to arrest Jesus.

This attempt to arrest Jesus then becomes the occasion for a reinterpretation by the author of the second stratum. The present form of the text, as is typical in such editing, contains contextual aporias, for the addition of the second editor does not follow precisely on the context of the previous material.[90] The authorities will attempt to arrest him,

[88]The word *ochlos* is the usual word used to describe the common people as opposed to the religious authorities. The authorities express their disdain for the common people clearly in 7:48-49.

[89]M. de Jonge gives the background of this in his "Jewish Expectations About the 'Messiah' According to the Fourth Gospel" chapter 4 of *Jesus: Stranger from Heaven and Son of God* (ed. and trans., J. Steely, SBLSBS 11; Missoula: Scholars Press, 1977) 77-116.

[90]This awkwardness itself is the indication of a literary break and the shift to the second stratum. The aporia is noticed by Wellhausen (*Evangelium* 39) and by Bultmann (*Gospel* 297 n 1, 307) who again attributes Jesus' words to the revelation discourse source.

but Jesus indicates that he will be with them only a short time longer. Vv33-39 are identified as belonging to the second edition by several characteristics. Once again his supreme indifference and superiority to the plans of men become apparent: he is going away, but not because they will arrest him. Then in v35, the authorities, now identified in the terminology of the second edition as Jews, indicate their mis-understanding of Jesus by thinking of his departure on a physical rather than on a spiritual level. The material of this second stratum continues through v39, the promise of the Spirit.

16. The Debate Among the People (7:40-44)

[40]When they heard these words, **some of the people** said, **"This is really the prophet."** [41]Others said, **"This is the Christ."** But **some said, "Is the Christ to come from Galilee?** [42]Has not the scripture said that **the Christ is descended from David and comes from Bethlehem**, the village where David was?" [43]**So there was a division among the people** over him. [44]**Some of them** wanted to arrest him, but no one laid hands on him.

The debate over the various messianic figures ("the Prophet," "the Christ") continues in v40. It is not possible to tell their original context although presumably it was the same general one as the remainder of the signs material here. The debate focuses on two issues: Is Jesus the Prophet? Is he the Christ? But as an argument against his being the Christ is the fact that he comes from Galilee and the Messiah is to come from Bethlehem.[91]

The evidence for identifying these verses as the signs material is not totally certain, but several features suggest that this is the case. First, there is the repeated division within the crowds. Second, they are similar to vv25-27 both in the topic and type of debate.[92] Finally, the

---

[91]These verses are puzzling and it is impossible to tell whether they are meant in irony (Jesus has come from Bethlehem and the people are unaware of this fact) or whether they indicate that the Johannine community itself was not aware of the tradition of Jesus' birth in Bethlehem. See the discussion in Schnackenburg, *Gospel* 157-59; Brown, *Gosepl* 330.

[92]It will be recalled that the second edition is concerned with a much higher chris-

fact that there is no arrest fits well with the reports of popular acclaim evident within the previous signs material (vv25-27, 31-32) and with the sequence of the arrest attempts (vv32, 45-46).

17. The Debate Among the Religious Authorities (7:45-52)

> [45]The officers then went back to **the chief priests and Pharisees,** who said to them, "Why did you not bring him?" [46]The officers answered, "No man ever spoke like this man!" [47]The Pharisees answered them, "Are you led astray, you also? [48]Have **any of the rulers or of the Pharisees** believed in him? [49]But this crowd, who do not know the law, are accursed." [50]Nicodemus, who had gone to him before, and who was one of them, said to them, [51]Does our law judge a man without first giving him a hearing and learning what he does?" They replied, "Are you from Galilee too? Search and you will see that < **the**> **prophet is** <not> **to rise from Galilee.**" (RSV, modified)

These verses are the longest sequence of signs material not immediately joined to the narration of a miracle.[93] The verses are clearly marked as signs material by the terms for authorities in vv45, 47, 48 and by the way others talk back to the religious authorities.[94] Everything within the passage is consistent with what we have seen elsewhere

tology and different types of argumentation than are present here.

[93]This is even more true if vv40-44 form the original sequence with vv45-52. Bultmann (*Gospel* 287) points out the difficulty involved in having the attendants return on the last day of the feast (cf v37) when they had set out when the feast was half over (cf v14). He rightly concludes that the chronology here interrupts what has been another sequence in which the attendants were sent and returned on the same day. I would agree and would identify this interruption as the work of the author of the second edition. In order to achieve a proper chronology, Bultmann excises vv37-44. This is not necessary. In order to provide the proper chronology, only vv37-39 need be accounted for. That the interrupting material stems from the second edition is clear from the terminology in v14ff (cf the term Jews there) and from v37 which is, on theological grounds, to be identified as a continuation of the material of the second edition which began in v33.

[94]It will be recalled that, in the material of the second edition, the people are constantly said to fear the Jews and refuse to talk back to them. Texts and discussion are given in chapter 2.

in the early stratum: concern for the geographical origin of Jesus, concern for traditional titles, even the reappearance of the figure of Nicodemus.

The passage concludes the discussions of chapter 7. These discussions have taken place within two groups, the common people and the religious authorities. The passage here intends to contrast the belief of the common people with the unbelief of the authorities. The attendants, while not precisely "believing," sense the power of Jesus and report that they have not followed the orders of the authorities because "No one has ever spoken as this man does." The authorities then insult the attendants by associating them with the common people "who know nothing of the Law" and who are "accursed." But Nicodemus, one of their own, also speaks up not precisely in Jesus' behalf but on behalf of a proper hearing for Jesus. But the authorities ridicule Nicodemus by suggesting that perhaps he too is from Galilee. "Search [the Scriptures]," they say, "and you will see that the prophet is not to come from Galilee."[95]

17a. 8:12-13 *Not Signs Material*

This brief section contains the term Pharisees in 8:13 but the theology throughout is that associated with a later stratum. In addition, this is the only time in chapter 8 that the authorities are referred to as Pharisees, while they are referred to five other times (8:22, 32, 48, 52, 57) as "Jews." Although Jesus begins with the important statement "I am the light of the world" etc., the theme of light figures nowhere else in the chapter. Elsewhere in the gospel the imagery of Jesus as "light of the world" is associated with material of a later (second or third) edition.[96] It is very likely that vv 12-13 in their present form are a mixture of a fragment of the early stratum (perhaps carried over from 7:45-52) which has later been edited, probably by the author of the

---

[95]The manuscript evidence is strong for reading the definite article before "prophet" in v52. See Metzger, *A Textual Commentary* on 7:52. The discussion is not whether any prophet will come from Galilee but whether "the prophet" (like Moses) is to come from there.

[96]For example 1:7-9; 3:19-21; 11:9-10; 12:35-36; also the related concepts of "day/night" in 9:4-5; 11:9-10.

second edition.[97] This is one of several brief passages in the gospel where the material from two strata is mixed (see also at 6:26, and 12:42).

18. *Jesus Heals a Man Born Blind* (9:1-41, without vv2-5, 18-23, 35-41)

[1]As he passed by, he saw a man blind from his birth.... [6][As he said this] he spat on the ground and made clay of the spittle and anointed the man's eyes with the clay, saying to him, "Go, wash in **the pool of Siloam" (which means Sent).** So he went and washed and came back seeing.

[8]The neighbors and those who had seen him before as a beggar, said, "Is not this the man who used to sit and beg?" [9]Some said, "It is he"; others said, "No, but he is like him." He said, "I am the man." [10]They said to him, "Then how were your eyes opened?" [11]He answered, "The man called Jesus made clay and anointed my eyes and said to me, 'Go to Siloam and wash'; so I went and washed and received my sight." [12]They said to him, "Where is he?" He said, "I do not know."

[13]They brought to **the Pharisees** the man who had formerly been blind. [14]Now it was a sabbath day when Jesus made the clay and opened his eyes. [15]**The Pharisees** again asked him how he had received his sight. And he said to them, "He put clay on my eyes, and I washed, and I see." [16]**Some of the Pharisees** said, "**This man is not from God, for he does not keep the sabbath.**" But others said, "**How can a man who is a sinner do such signs?**" **There was a division among them.** [17]So they again said to the blind man, "What do you say about him, since he has opened your eyes? He said, "**He is a prophet.**"

...[24][So for the second time they called the man who had been blind, and] said to him, "Give God the praise; **we know that this man is a sinner.**" [25]He answered, "**Whether he is a sinner, I do not know;**

---

[97]The material of 7:53-8:11, the story of the woman taken in adultery, is a later addition to the text of the gospel. Consequently it is possible (although there is no way to be certain) that 8:12 was originally the immediate sequel to 7:52.

one thing I know, that though I was blind, now I see." [26]They said to him, "What did he do to you? How did he open your eyes?" [27]He answered them, "I have told you already, and you would not listen. Why do you want to hear it again? Do you too want to become his disciples?" [28]And they reviled him, saying, "You are his disciple, but we are disciples of Moses. [29]We know that **God has spoken to Moses, but as for this man, we do not know where he comes from.**" [30]The man answered, "Why, this is a marvel! You do not know where he comes from, and yet he opened my eyes. [31]We know that **God does not listen to sinners, but if any one is a worshipper of God and does his will, God listens to him.** [32]Never since the world began has it been heard that any one opened the eyes of a man born blind. [33]**If this man were not from God, he could do nothing.**" [34]They answered him, "You were born in utter sin, and would you teach us?" And they cast him out.

The story of the man born blind provides us with a long sequence of material from the early stratum which illustrates clearly and in considerable detail how such a miracle was developed within the signs material.

Throughout the passage[98] we see the characteristics typical of the early material: identification of the authorities as "Pharisees" (vv13, 15, 16); identification of the miracles as "signs" (v16); the reaction of the authorities to the signs (v13ff); division among the authorities (v16); emphasis on the greatness of the signs ("such signs"—*toiauta semeia*); the translation of the name of the pool (v7); the way the man is not afraid to argue and debate with the authorities; the concern with low christology [whether this man is from God (vv16, 33), and whether a sinner could perform such signs (vv24-25, 31), and whether he might be a prophet (v17)[99]]; finally in the mention of Siloam we see another of the specific and accurate geographical references frequent in the signs material.

---

[98]Except for the additions as noted below.

[99]Bultmann (*Gospel* 329-30) extends the signs material from v1-38, excluding vv4-5, 22, 23, 29-30, 34a, 39-41. Wilkens (*Entstehungsgeschichte* 51-55, 63-64) considers vv1-41 as belonging to the original edition with the exception of vv4-5, 17-23, although he believes that the later verses (vv8-41) were added to the sign. Fortna (*Signs* 70-74) includes vv2-3a in his source but ends the section after v8. Nicol (*Semeia* 35-36) ends the source at v7. Boismard (*Evangile* 246-262) sees extensive editing involving material from all four editions of the gospel.

V 1

The miracle begins with the abrupt notice that as he walked along, "he" (Jesus' name is not even given) saw a man blind from birth. This awkward transition indicates that material of 8:59 does not constitute the original sequence with this miracle, something confirmed by the repeated occurrences of "Jews" in that prior material.

VV 2-5

Immediately, there begins an addition by an editor containing an interchange between Jesus and his disciples about the cause of the man's blindness. Jesus explains that the man's blindness is not a result of personal or parental sin but that the "works" (miracles) of God might be made manifest. Jesus then explains that he is to "work the works of God" while it is day, that night is coming when no one is able to work, and that while he is in the world he is the light of the world.

The material is marked as coming from a later edition by the use of the word "works" for miracle (contrast the use of "signs" in the remainder of the narrative). In addition, the theology (cf especially the emphasis on "light" as in 8:13) is intrusive within the early stratum and echoes the thought of the Prologue, which is not part of the original edition of the gospel. In addition, the passage is marked off by the peculiar phrase "having said these things..." (*tauta eipōn*) at the beginning of v6, a brief but definite indication of editing.[100]

VV 6-17

Once the material of vv2-5 has been removed from consideration, the narrative of the signs material continues smoothly through v17. Jesus spits and, making mud from the saliva, applies the mud to the eyes of the blind man. Jesus then sends the man to the pool of Siloam to wash. The man then receives his sight. Immediately, a discussion begins among those who knew the man whether he was in fact the one who had been blind. The man affirms that he is the one and recounts

---

[100]Fortna (*Signs* 72) sees this phrase as a redactional marker; so also others. The phrase (with some variation) occurs consistently in such a function (11:7, 11, 28; 18:1, 38; 20:20, 22).

to them how he was healed. When asked the name of the person who healed him, he replies that it was Jesus, but that he does not know where he is now.

In the following verses, the man is taken to the Pharisees and is forced to explain again how he was healed. We are now told that it was a Sabbath when he was healed and this becomes the occasion for the accusation against Jesus. The debate contrasts the reaction of the religious authorities with that of the man. The authorities are split in their assessment of Jesus and debate whether he could be "from God," the same issue which Nicodemus had raised in chapter 3 and which again comes to the fore in vv30-33.

This debate more than any other characterizes the reaction of the authorities within the signs material. In the eyes of the author of the first edition of the gospel, signs such as Jesus had performed could mean only one thing: that he was from God. The unlearned man could see this clearly, but the Pharisees schooled in the Law could not. It becomes clear that the debate has not moved forward since the discussion with Nicodemus in chapter 3.

VV 18-23

These verses interrupt the original story. The evidence of editing is considerable. The religious authorities are identified as "the Jews" three times (vv18, 22 [twice]). The common people are said to "fear the Jews" (contrast this with the way the man talks back to the authorities in the surrounding material—as well as elsewhere in the signs material.) There is also the evident contradiction in that in the surrounding material the authorities are divided and attempting to discern the meaning of Jesus' signs, while in vv18-22 it is said that the authorities had *already determined* that if anyone would confess Jesus as the Christ, that person would be formally expelled from the synagogue. Finally, there is the peculiar shift in that in the early stratum there is no doubt that the man has in fact been born blind, while in vv18-22 even that is called into question.[101]

---

[101] Wellhausen (*Evangelium* 46) was the first to suggest that the change in terminology here is an indication of a change in authorship. The suggestion was not followed by Bultmann (*Gospel* 329-30) who removed only vv22-23. He does so on theological grounds only. Of course the linguistic indications show that the addition is larger.

This addition from the second edition attempted to make the story of the blind man relevant to the circumstances of the community at the time of the second edition. It gives clear evidence the community was undergoing persecution and expulsion from the synagogue. The man is an example of one who is firm enough in his faith to affirm it in the face of such persecution.

VV 24-34

The signs material and the discussion of the meaning of the signs continue in vv24-34. The authorities first attempt to proclaim Jesus a sinner, then they question the man again about the occurrence of the miracle. Finally, they revile the man who had been blind for his claim to know that Jesus is from God, and affirm that they do not know where Jesus comes from. The man then speaks back to them saying that it was amazing that they did not know where Jesus came from since God does not listen to sinners and since the miracle itself had been such a great one ("Never since the world began has it been heard that any one opened the eyes of a man born blind"). Finally, the Pharisees "throw him out."[102]

VV 35-41

With v35 we begin the final scene of the episode, the second meeting between Jesus and the man followed by another brief exchange between Jesus and the Pharisees. Although at first glance the material would seem to come from the first edition, (cf "Pharisees" v40[103]), this is unlikely. The title Son of Man occurs only here associated with signs material. Elsewhere it occurs in secondary material.[104] Nor is the signs

---

[102]In the signs material this action would not have referred to the act of synagogue expulsion but only to removing him from his presence. Its presence in the original story would have been a catalyst for the addition of the theme of synagogue exclusion in the second edition.

[103]The use of Pharisees in v40 may be similar to the use in 8:12-13 where it is simply a "relic." These few atypical instances, however, do not disprove the consistent use elsewhere.

[104]The secondary nature of the title is clear also in 1:50-51.

material apocalyptic in its orientation as is implied by this title.[105] This is also the only instance in the gospel where someone is asked to (or said to) believe in the Son of Man and to "worship" Jesus. Finally, in these verses the symbolic meaning of the man's physical blindness is brought out. The man who had been physically blind now is able to see spiritually (as well as physically), and the Pharisees who see physically are blind spiritually. This theology (contrast between the physical and the spiritual) is typical of the later editions.

The purpose of the material is to take the affirmations made by the man in the previous material (he is Jesus of Nazareth; he is from God; he is a prophet) to a still higher level: he is the Son of Man.[106] This mix of features itself strongly suggests editing, probably by the editor of the third edition.

19. Division Among the People (10:19-21)

[19]There was again a **division** among **the Jews** because of these words. [20]**Many of them** said, "He has a demon, and he is mad; why listen to him?" [21]**Others** said, "These are not the sayings of one who has a demon. Can a demon open the eyes of the blind?"

These verses comprise another of the short transitional passages of the gospel. Although there are ambiguities associated with the evidence here, I am inclined to think the verses come originally from the signs material. First, "Jews" seems to refer to "Judeans" (i.e., common people) since there is evidence of some rudimentary belief in the words of 10:21. Secondly, that this is the meaning of "Jews" is confirmed by the mention of division among the Jews. Such division is absent from those passages where "Jews" refers to religious authorities, but present in the signs material where "Jews" refers to people of Judea (cf esp 11:45). Finally, the fact that there is a reference to the healing of the man born blind and that the passage expresses continuing amazement

[105]Some of the later material in the gospel is clearly apocalyptic, e.g., 3:13-21; 5:27-29.

[106]This progression in recognition of Jesus is quite similar to that present in the titles given to Jesus by the first disciples and by the Samaritan woman.

at that healing would suggest that both bodies of material are from the first edition.

The peculiarity of the verses is that they occur as a reaction to the parable of the gate/shepherd. However, the parable itself shows none of the primary criteria for being part of the signs material. Therefore it is likely that the verses have been placed here by an editor who altered them somewhat to fit the context of the parable. In content, the verses simply reflect the discussion and uncertainty of the people in their assessment of the "evidence" for Jesus: the meaning of his words and his signs.

The most that can be said for the verses is that the usage within them is consistent with the usage in the signs material but not with the usage within the second edition. But the evidence is not as clear as might be wished.

20. Still Others Believe in Jesus (10:40-42)

[40]He went away again across the Jordan to the place where John at first baptized, and there he remained. [41]And **many came to him;** and they said, "John did **no sign,** but everything that John said about this man was true." [42]**And many believed in him there.**

After a long hiatus,[107] the material of the first edition resumes with a brief summary transition. It is clearly identified as signs material by the characteristic term for miracle (v41), the easy belief (v42), and the formulaic statement of this belief (v42).[108]

[107]Some of the material associated with the parable of the Shepherd may come from the signs material but its recovery is not possible without a discussion of the entire gospel.

[108]Brown had suggested that this was the ending of the ministry in the original version of the gospel and that chapters 11 and 12 had been added later (*Gospel* 414-15). The occurrence of the "neutral" use of Jews in chapters 11 and 12 was one of the major factors that led Brown to this conclusion. However it is clear that all of the characteristics of the first edition continue well beyond chapter 11. It is equally clear that the neutral use of Jews as well as the other characteristics associated with it occur long before chapter 11. It is most likely that 12:37 contains the ending of the public ministry (see below) and that 20:30-31 contains the ending of the first edition as a whole.

The passage reports the movement of Jesus across the Jordan to the place where John had first baptized. His popularity continues to be evident and to increase. Many come to him and see in his signs a clear indication of his superiority to John and at the same time they recognize that what John said about Jesus was correct. Once again many come to believe in Jesus. At this point there remains only one major incident in the public ministry before the religious authorities take final action for the death of Jesus: the raising of Lazarus.

21. Jesus Raises Lazarus from the Dead (11:1-45, without vv 2, 4-5, 7-10, 15b-16, 21-27, 40-42)

[1]Now a certain man was ill, Lazarus of Bethany, the village of Mary and her sister Martha. . . . [3]So the sisters sent to him, saying, "Lord, he whom you love is ill.". . . [6]So when he heard that he was ill, he stayed two days longer in the place where he was. . . .

[11][Thus he spoke, and then] he said to them, "Our friend Lazarus has fallen asleep, but I go to awake him out of sleep." [12]The disciples said to him, "Lord, if he has fallen asleep, he will recover." [13]Now Jesus had spoken of his death, but they thought that he meant taking rest in sleep. [14]Then Jesus told them plainly, "Lazarus is dead; [15]and for your sake I am glad that I was not there, so that you may believe. But let us go to him.". . .

[17]Now when Jesus came, he found that Lazarus had already been

Fortna (*Signs* 195, but also 106, 197, 169 n. 3) proposes that this is an artificial Johannine introduction to the raising of Lazarus. However, the language, the stereotyped expression of belief and various elements of theology are so consistent with the other signs material that it is very unlikely that it is Johannine (i.e., belonging to the second edition of the gospel).

Although Dodd (*Tradition* 241) considers some of the features as Johannine, he groups the passage with his transitional passages which provide the framework for the gospel and so suggests that it is "possible, or slightly probable, that we have a fragment of 'itinerary' material from tradition, worked over by the Evangelist."

Wellhausen (*Evangelium* 50) attributed the passage to his *Grundschrift*. However, he based his judgment on synoptic parallels rather than more objective criteria. Bultmann (*Gospel* 393) characterizes it as a fragment of the signs material but does not give arguments. Wilkens (*Entstehungsgeschichte* 55) attributes it to the *Grundevangelium*.

in the tomb about four days. [18]Bethany was near Jerusalem, about two miles off, [19]and **many of the Jews** had come to Martha and Mary to console them concerning their brother. [20]When Martha heard that Jesus was coming, she went and met him, while Mary sat in the house. . . .

[28][When she had said this,] she went and called her sister Mary, saying quietly, "**The Teacher is here and is calling for you.**" [29]And when she heard it, she rose quickly and went to him. [30]Now Jesus had not yet come to the village, but was still in the place where Martha had met him. [31]When **the Jews** who were with her in the house, consoling her, saw Mary rise quickly and go out, they followed her, supposing that she was going to the tomb to weep there. [25]Then Mary, when she came where Jesus was and saw him, fell at his feet, saying to him, "Lord, if you had been here, my brother would not have died."

[33]When Jesus saw her weeping, and **the Jews** who came with her also weeping, he was deeply moved in spirit and troubled; [34]and he said, "Where have you laid him?" They said to him, "Lord, come and see." [35]Jesus wept. [36]So **the Jews** said, "See how he loved him!" [37]But **some of them** said, "Could not he who opened the eyes of the blind man have kept this man from dying?"

[38]Then Jesus, deeply moved again, came to the tomb; it was a cave, and a stone lay upon it. [39]Jesus said, "Take away the stone." Martha, the sister of the dead man, said to him, "Lord, by this time there will be an odor, for he has been dead four days.". . . So they took away the stone . . . [43][When he had said this], he cried with a loud voice, "Lazarus, come out." The dead man came out, his hands and feet bound with bandages, and his face wrapped with a cloth. Jesus said to them, "Unbind him, and let him go." [45]**Many of the Jews therefore, who had come with Mary and had seen what he did, believed in him.**

Overview of the Lazarus Miracle

The raising of Lazarus is the final and climatic miracle of the public ministry in the signs material. It comprises part of a longer sequence of signs material which runs from 11:1-12:11.[109] This sequence contains

[109]There are some modifications as noted in the discussion which follows, but the

the raising of Lazarus, the decision of the Sanhedrin to put Jesus to death, the return of Jesus to Bethany, his anointing by Mary, the return of the crowds to Bethany to see Jesus and Lazarus, the decision of the chief priests to put Lazarus to death, and, finally, the coming of Jesus into Jerusalem. For convenience, the material will be divided into smaller sections in the following analysis. The first of these sections is the raising of Lazarus itself (11:1-45).

Although the analysis of the Lazarus miracle tends at first to give the appearance of a complicated sequence, the simplicity of the original narrative appears clearly once the additions have been removed. It is because of the importance of the miracle both in terms of its symbolic value and in terms of its relation to the following passion that several additions have been made. These additions focus on the reinterpretation of the miracle from the level of giving physical life to the level of symbolism for Jesus' ability to give spiritual life. Once the additions have been identified and their purpose understood, the reader is prepared for a richer reading of the narrative.

The characteristics which identify the Lazarus miracle as signs material are numerous.[110] The authorities are identified as Pharisees in 11:46. Although the word sign does not occur until 11:47, the people in 11:45 are described as having "seen what he did." The Greek (*theasamenoi ha epoiēsen*) speaks literally of "those things" which is almost surely intended as a substitute for *sēmeia* (signs) as is the same expression in v46. Except for its occurrence in 11:7,[111] the word Jews occurs in the neutral sense as "Judeans" (vv19, 31, 33, 45).[112] The belief of the

sequence of signs material seems to be relatively intact.

[110]Bultmann (*Gospel* 395 n 3, 4) proposes that vv1-44 come from the signs source except for vv4, 7-10, 16, 20-32, 40-42 where the Evangelist makes additions using material from the revelatory discourse source. He sees v2 as from the redactor. Fortna (*Signs* 74-87) attributes vv1-45 to the signs source except for vv5-6, 8-10, 12-14, 16, 21-27, 29-31, 35-37, 40, 42 and parts of several other verses. Nicol (*Semeia* 37-39) would include vv1-44 except vv4-5, 7-10, 16, 20-27, 40-42. Schnackenburg (*Gospel* 2 318-321) attributes much more of the passage to the Evangelist (vv2, 4-5, 7-16, 19-32, 35-38, 39b-42). Wilkens (*Entstehungsgeschichte* 55-60) would attribute the episode to the *Grundschrift* except for vv2, 5-10, 16, 18-32a, 35-37, 39b-40, 44. See also his "Die Erweckung des Lazarus," *TZ* 15 (1959) 22-39. Dodd (*Tradition* 228-232, esp 232) despairs of being able to reconstruct a pre-canonical form for the story: "John has worked it over too thoroughly."

[111]This occurrence will be discussed below.

[112]That this is the neutral, non-hostile sense is clear from the fact that these Jews are

people (v45) is the "easy belief" characteristic of the signs material. The statement of belief in v45 occurs in its characteristic stereotyped form. There is the division of opinion common to the signs material. Finally, as will be seen in the following passage, there is the characteristic reaction of the Pharisees to the people's belief (vv46-50).

Vv 1-3

Vv1 and 3 most likely come from the signs material; they state the illness and the request made of Jesus. Both are direct and theologically neutral.[113] However, v2, by all estimates, is a later addition identifying Mary with the Mary of the anointing in chapter 12.

Vv 4-5

Vv4-5 speak of the purpose of the miracle and probably come from the second edition. The death of Lazarus is not "unto death" but for the glorification of Jesus. In addition, they contain the comment that Jesus loved Martha, her sister and Lazarus. There is some literary evidence of editing. The words "so when he heard that he was ill" at the beginning of v6 harken back to v3 and repeat awkwardly much of what is said at the beginning of v4. The repetition is sufficiently awkward to suggest that this is the editorial use of repetition and in fact marks the boundaries of the insertion.[114] "Glorification" here refers to the coming death of Jesus.[115] In addition, the fact that Jesus is pre-

always associated with Jerusalem (cf 11:18, see also 12:9, 11) and they are said to believe (cf 11:45) in Jesus with the same easy belief characteristic of the signs material. See von Wahlde, "Jews" 46.

[113]These characteristics are not conclusive. However, there seems little reason to exclude them from the signs material since certainly there was some such report. Such a report could not be more direct and unadorned than this. As can be seen from the summary in the previous note, the analysis suggested here is accepted by almost all scholars.

[114]This repetitive resumptive has been seen earlier at 4:40, 43. This particular instance is studied in some detail by M.-E. Boismard, "Un procédé rédactionnel."

[115]The association of "glory" with the signs material occurred in 2:11 where there is a clear parallel to its occurrence with the signs in Num 14:22. However, here, glorification, referring to the death of Jesus, raises that use of glory to a more symbolic level, typical of the second editor.

sented here as knowing that Lazarus would die but that he would also be raised is typical of the "superiority" of Jesus present in the second edition. Finally, the verses are a repetition in more theological language of vv11-14 where the death of Lazarus is described as a "falling asleep."[116]

V 6

The statement that Jesus stayed two days where he was rather than going up immediately to help Lazarus is puzzling. It would seem to come from the original narration. Its purpose is evidently to remove any doubt that Lazarus was in fact truly dead.[117]

Vv 7-10

Vv7-10 are also an insertion into the signs material. They are introduced by the awkward "Thereupon after this..." (*epeita meta touto*), almost surely an informal marker of the beginning of an insertion. Jesus says that he and the disciples should return to Judea, but the disciples then remind Jesus that "the Jews" are seeking to kill him. This use of Jews is clearly in the hostile sense and should be associated with those other instances in the gospel where as early as chapter 5, the Jews had been attempting to kill Jesus.[118] Jesus then responds in terms of his superiority to all human intentions and refers to his ministry in terms of light and darkness, the same theme previously found in the inserted material of 9:2-5.

[116]As can be seen from note 110 above, this analysis is generally accepted by scholars.

[117]There was a traditional Jewish belief that the spirit of the dead person could remain with the body for three days (see the references in Strack-Billerbeck 544). Jesus' delay would then raise to three the days before Jesus actually raises Lazarus (cf v17, 39). Some have suggested that these two days are in fact the two days mentioned at the end of the story of the Samaritan woman, esp Fortna (*Signs* 194-195). But the narrative there gives no reason to think that Jesus went anywhere except back to Galilee, a fact which was indeed confirmed by 4:54.

[118]See 5:16-18; 7:1, 19, 25; 8:37, 59; 10:31-33. See further my article "Jews" esp 47-49.

Vv11-20 (with the exception of vv15b-16)

V11 begins with the repetitious "Thus he spoke and then he said,..."
(*Tauta eipen, kai meta touto legei autois,...*), another of the awkward
expressions which seem to indicate literary seams. Here it marks the
end of the insertion and the resumption of the original narrative. Jesus
then speaks of the death of Lazarus as falling asleep, an image that is
not understood by the disciples.

It may be that v16 has been added since it refers back to the theme
of the danger for Jesus in vv7-10.[119] Vv17-20 continue the signs narrative and describe the coming of Jesus to Bethany. Bethany is identified as a town close to Jerusalem and this is said to account for the
fact that many of the Jews (neutral sense) came to Martha and Mary
to grieve with them. When Jesus arrives, Martha meets Jesus while
Mary is said to be in the house.

Vv 21-27

Vv21-27 are an addition by a later editor. When they are viewed in
the context of what follows, their awkwardness and theological motivation are clearly evident. First, the awkwardness of the meeting of
Jesus with both Martha and Mary is evident. Jesus meets Martha
outside of the village. After his theological discussion with Martha,
Martha goes to get Mary. Mary then also comes out of the village to
the place where Jesus was. Both make the same statement to Jesus: "If
you had been here my brother would not have died" (vv21, 32). Yet
only the first contains a significant theological discussion. Finally, we
see that v28 begins with "Having said this...", the same redactional
phrase that marked the resumption of sequence in v11.

The theological motivation of the insertion is evident. It takes the
themes of the raising from the dead and of life and applies them to the
theological topics of the final resurrection and of Jesus as the "resurrection and the life." It ends with the theological affirmation by Martha
that Jesus is the Christ, the Son of God, he who is coming into the
world.

---

[119]Almost all scholars would agree that it has been added. See the listing in note 110
above.

Vv 27-45 (with the exception of vv40-42)

After the above insertion, the original miracle continues to v45, with the exception of vv40-42. Throughout the section, the bystanders are identified as Jews in the sense of Judeans. Jesus is then described as seeing Mary, and the Jews who came with her, weeping and he is "deeply moved in spirit and troubled."[120] The material continues by narrating the coming of Jesus to the tomb, the demonstration of Jesus' affection for Lazarus and the comment of the Jews that perhaps Jesus who opened the eyes of the blind man could have kept Lazarus from dying.[121] When Jesus comes to the tomb, Martha comments that there would be an odor for Lazarus had been dead for four days.

Vv40-42 are awkward and are also additions by the author of the second edition. They are the only verses in the gospel which speak of a miracle simply in terms of "seeing the glory of God." In addition they are the only ones which speak of belief as a prior necessity for the working of a miracle. The narration of the removal of the stone undoubtedly appeared in the original in some form, but then the elaborate gesture of raised eyes and the prayer to the Father "for the

---

[120]Schnackenburg (*Gospel* 2 337) takes the expression of being moved in spirit and troubled as an expression of anger and concludes after some discussion that it is an expression of anger at the unbelief of the Jews because of their lamentation. This is unlikely. First, it can hardly be the lamentation itself which would cause anger since Mary is also described as weeping. Second, it is not clear that the expression of emotion is one of anger. Given the fact that he is reacting as much to the sight of Mary weeping as he is to the others, it is more likely intended as a sense of sorrow at the death itself.

[121]Some scholars (Fortna, Schnackenburg, Wilkens) suggest that these verses have been added. Fortna (*Signs* 83) points to the repetition of the references to being deeply moved (vv33 and 38). This repetition is striking. There is, in addition, the third mention of emotion in the weeping attributed to Jesus in v35. There are in fact numerous mentions of mourning (vv19, 31) and weeping (vv31, 33 [twice], 35) being shaken (vv33, 38) throughout the story and this may be deliberate in order to emphasize the sadness of Lazarus' death. Consequently the repetition may be dramatic rather than redactional here.

The Jews in the neutral sense appear both in v33 and in v35. I can find no reason to think that these Jews are representatives of unbelief (they in fact do believe that Jesus has the power to prevent death, and not even Mary expresses the conviction that Jesus has the power to raise Lazarus once he has died—cf Mary's expression in v39). Nor is there a theological motivation within vv34-37 that would mark it as coming from the third edition. Finally, the reference to the healing of the blind man ties it to the signs material. As a result, although the repetition remains somewhat problematic, I would attribute the verses to the signs material as do Bultmann and Nicol.

sake of those standing around" is clearly from an editor. And, once again, the resumption of the original narrative in v43 is marked by the awkward and somewhat repetitious "When he said this. . ." (*Tauta eipōn*. . .) which we have seen previously in vv11 and 28.

In v43, the signs material resumes with the working of the miracle itself, which is narrated quite simply. Jesus cries out for Lazarus to come forth. Lazarus comes out, is unbound, and is allowed to go.

V45 then provides the customary reaction of "easy belief." In response to the miracle, "many of the Judeans" believe in Jesus. This is presented in the customary stereotyped formula. In v46 we are told that some of the Judeans went to the Pharisees (another indication of the early stratum) and told them "those things" (i.e., the "signs") which he had performed. This then leads into the convening of the Sanhedrin which continues in the following section.

22. The Sanhedrin's Decision to Put Jesus to Death (11:46-53, without vv51-52)

[46]. . .but **some of them went to the Pharisees and told them what Jesus had done.** [47]So **the chief priests and the Pharisees** gathered the council, and said, "What are we to do? For **this man performs many signs.** [48]If we let him go on thus, **every one will believe in him,** and the Romans will come and destroy both our holy place and our nation." [49]But one of them, Caiaphas, who was high priest that year, said to them, "You know nothing at all; [50]you do not understand that it is expedient for you that one man should die for the people, and that the whole nation should not perish.". . . [53]So from that day on they took counsel how to put him to death.

That this passage comes from the signs material can be seen in the mention of "Pharisees" (vv46, 47), "chief priests" (v47), the implicit (v46) and explicit (v47) mention of "signs," the easy belief based on signs, the stress on the quantity of Jesus' signs (v47), the authorities' fear of the people, and their concern for the belief of the people (v48). The verses describe the convening of the Sanhedrin (RSV: council) and articulate the problem created by the signs of Jesus and the decision of the Sanhedrin to put Jesus to death.[122] Their reason is that the increasing belief in Jesus will provoke the Romans to see in him a threat to the empire and so "destroy our holy place and our nation." The statement here is also significant because it represents an official declaration tied to a specific event.

In addition, the reason given here for the condemnation of Jesus is that the political authorities (the Romans) will see Jesus as a threat and that they will come and destroy the temple and the nation. This contrasts with the motive given in the later material where the reasons for wanting to kill Jesus are always religious (as is clear from 5:18; 8:59, etc.).

Vv 51-52

Vv51-52 give the theological significance of Caiaphas' words. According to the verses, the words of Caiaphas were an unconscious prophecy that "Jesus should die for the nation, and not for the nation only, but to gather into one the children of God who are scattered abroad." (RSV) The verses are almost certainly an addition to the signs material although this cannot be determined with certainty on the basis of the primary criteria. However they are quite incompatible with the remainder of the section on theological grounds.[123] The verses parallel very closely 10:15b-16:

> ... and I lay down my life for my sheep. And I have other sheep
> that are not of this fold; I must bring them also and they will heed
> my voice. So there shall be one flock and one shepherd.

---

[122]Bultmann (*Gospel* 409 n 8) attributes these verses to the Evangelist, citing stylistic criteria. Fortna (*Signs* 147-148) attributes only v47a and v53 to the source. Nicol finds no evidence of signs in the gospel after 11:44 except for the conclusion of the gospel at 20:30-31. Wilkens (*Entstehungsgeschichte* 57-58, 63-64) attributes the verses to the *Grundschrift*. As can be seen, scholars are quite divided in their assessment of these verses. It would seem that our more objective criteria permit a more definite identification of the episode as belonging to the signs material.

[123]So also Dodd, "The Prophecy of Caiaphas: John xi. 47-53," chapter 5 of *More New Testament Studies* (Grand Rapids: Wm. B. Eerdmans, 1968) 58-68. Dodd, commenting on v52, says: "He [the Evangelist] must be supposed to have received, from some source or other, the account of the prophecy of Caiaphas, and to have turned it adroitly to account by the introduction of the words of verse 52." He goes on to point out that it is exceptional that the pregnant saying is not uttered by Jesus.

In both passages (10:15b-16 and 11:51-52), the same two themes are joined: that Jesus dies for the people and that his death brings scattered groups of Christians together. These motifs are nowhere a part of the signs material and seem to reflect a level of theology more appropriate to the later editions.

V 53

V53, on the other hand, makes perfect sense as a continuation of the signs material. It links the decision to kill Jesus to this specific meeting of the Sanhedrin, and by so doing contradicts all the earlier mentions of attempting to kill Jesus, which come from the second edition and are closely associated with the term "Jews" in the hostile sense (e.g., 5:18, where the "Jews" are said to want to kill Jesus, see also 7:1—cf Jews in the same verse; 7:19—cf Jews in 7:15; 8:37—cf Jews in 8:31; 10:31-33—cf Jews in vv 31, 33; 11:8—cf Jews in v8).

23. The Aftermath of the Sanhedrin's Decision (11:54-57)

[54]Jesus therefore no longer went about openly among **the Jews,** but went from there to the country near the wilderness, to a town called Ephraim; and there he stayed with the disciples.
[55]Now the Passover of the Jews was at hand, and many went up from the country to Jerusalem before the Passover, to purify themselves. [56]They were looking for Jesus and saying to one another as they stood in the temple, "What do you think? That he will not come to the feast?" [57]Now **the chief priests and the Pharisees** had given orders that if any one knew where he was, he should let them know, so that they might arrest him.

These verses stem entirely from the signs material. This is evident from the use of "Jews" in the neutral sense (v54) and the references to the chief priests and Pharisees (v57). The intervening material involves a simple narrative and there is no reason to think that it has been edited. The chief priests and the Pharisees are presented as still operating in the background, just as in chapter 7 when they sent out the attendants to arrest Jesus, in chapter 9 where they question the man born blind about Jesus but do not enter into dialogue with Jesus himself, and as in 11:45 when the informants come to them. In content the verses indicate for the first time within the signs material the fact that the decision of the Sanhedrin makes it impossible for Jesus to go about publicly among the people. Here alone in the gospels we hear of a period spent in Ephraim together with the disciples.[124] It is also said that the Passover was near and that the crowds, which went up for the feast, inquired whether Jesus might attend the feast. Finally, we are told that the chief priests and the Pharisees had given orders that if anyone knew the whereabouts of Jesus that they should inform the authorities in order that they might arrest him.[125]

24. Jesus in Bethany (12:1-8)

[1]Six days before the Passover Jesus came to Bethany, where Lazarus was, whom Jesus had raised from the dead. [2]There they made him a supper; Martha served, and Lazarus was one of those at table with him. [3]Mary took a pound of costly ointment of pure nard and anointed the feet of Jesus and wiped his feet with her hair; and the house was filled with the fragrance of the ointment. [4]But Judas Iscariot, one of his disciples (he who was to betray him), said, [5]"Why was this ointment not sold for three hundred denarii and given to the poor?" [6]This he said, not that he cared for the poor but because he was a thief, and as he had the money box he used to take what was put into it. [7]Jesus said, "Let her alone, let her keep it for the day of

[124]Dodd (*Tradition* 242-243) lists v54 among the "framework" or "transitional" material. Although he would see the opening words as being from the Evangelist, Dodd ascribes the remainder to tradition. He points to the typical geographical notice, the fact that it does not describe a specific incident but a "period" of the ministry and the fact that Ephraim is nowhere else mentioned in the New Testament. It is the last of what Dodd calls the "small undigested scraps" of material, which have "no discernible reason why they should have been introduced except that they came down as an integral part of an historical tradition..." (p. 243). Bultmann (*Gospel* 413) considers them the work of the Evangelist on stylistic grounds, so also Fortna (*Signs* 152) without discussion.

[125]Vv55-57 are quite similar in content to 7:10-13 and almost seem to be a variant version. Bultmann (*Gospel* 413) notes the similarity but draws no literary critical conclusions from it.

my burial. ⁸The poor you always have with you, but you do not always have me."

Vv1-8 narrate Jesus coming to Bethany, the home of Lazarus. There, at a supper, Mary anoints the feet of Jesus with ointment. The action is symbolic of the anointing which will be performed on Jesus' body. The material is tied in closely with what follows and is evidently part of the signs material although there are no clear characteristics.¹²⁶ It certainly is consistent with the signs material in that it occurs at the home of Lazarus and therefore sets the stage for the people to come to see both Lazarus and Jesus.

25. *Crowds of Judeans Come to Bethany* (12:9-11)

⁹When **the great crowd of the Jews** learned that he was there, they came, not only on account of Jesus but also to see Lazarus, whom he had raised from the dead. ¹⁰So **the chief priests** planned to put Lazarus also to death, ¹¹because on account of him **many of the Jews were going away and believing in Jesus.**

Vv9-11 are marked as signs material by numerous characteristics: the mention of Jews in the neutral sense (vv9, 11), the mention of chief priests (v10), by the stereotyped formula of belief "many of the (Jews) were believing . . . ," the emphasis on "easy belief," and the fear of the people by the authorities. Finally, there is the chain reaction belief by which this group comes to belief on the basis of the report of the earlier group which had witnessed the miracle. In addition there is the peculiar feature of the authorities' desire to put Lazarus to death also, a detail which vividly portrays the extent of the fear the authorities have of Jesus.¹²⁷

---

¹²⁶It is considered traditional, but not signs, material by Bultmann (*Gospel* 414), Dodd (*Tradition* 162-173 esp 172) and Schnackenburg (*Gospel* 2 372). Fortna (*Signs* 149-152) attributes it to his signs gospel with only minor modifications.

¹²⁷Bultmann (*Gospel* 416), Fortna (*Signs* 152), Schnackenburg (*Gospel* 2, 370), Dodd (*Tradition* 158) attribute it to the Evangelist as do most other commentators. However, the overwhelming number of similarities to other signs material make it much more likely that it is in fact signs material.

The verses continue the heightening of the effect of the miraculous by showing the extent to which the people react to it. Nor is this the last reference to the tremendous impact of the Lazarus miracle among the people (cf 12:18-19). The reaction of the authorities is almost frantic as indicated by the striking statement that they planned to put Lazarus to death also!

26. The Action of the Crowd and the Reaction of the Pharisees (12:18-19)

[18]The reason why the crowd went to meet him was that they heard **he had done this sign.** [19]**The Pharisees** then said to one another, **"You see that you can do nothing; look, the world has gone after him."**

These two verses are also identified as signs material by the presence of sign for miracle (v18), and by Pharisees (v19), and by the authorities' fear of the people (v19), by the fact that belief is based on signs, and by the implied "easy" character of the belief. However, it is unlikely that the preceding verses (vv12-16) stem from the same stratum of material. There are several reasons for excluding them.[128]

The introduction of another crowd in v12 is awkward. The first group mentioned were the people who witnessed the raising of Lazarus itself (11:45), then there were others who came to Bethany later to see Jesus and Lazarus (12:9), then in v12 yet a third crowd hears that Jesus is coming now to Jerusalem and so goes forth to meet him. In order to properly understand what must have been the original sequence, a few words must be said about the intervening verses (12:12-16).

Vv12-16, which come from the second edition, describe the entry of Jesus into Jerusalem. In the passage we learn that as Jesus comes to Jerusalem a large crowd meets him, proclaiming him as coming in the name of the Lord, in a quote from Ps 118:25-26. Jesus in turn finds a

---

[128]Here again I would differ from earlier critics who tend to assign transition passages to the Evangelist and other units to the tradition. For example, Bultmann (*Gospel* 417) attributes this to "a" (non-signs) source. Fortna (*Signs* 152-155) includes it with some modifications in his signs gospel. However, Wilkens (*Entstehungsgeschichte* 64-67) would include the entirety of vv12-19 within the first edition of the gospel.

young ass and rides it into the city. Then we are told that this fulfilled the prophecy of Zechariah 9:9. Then in v16 we are told the meaning of the event.

The verses are quite similar in structure and purpose to 2:18-22 and undoubtedly are editorial additions as was 2:18-22. Both episodes are constructed of two parts and both parts are said to influence the belief of the disciples after the glorification/resurrection of Jesus.[129]

As was pointed out above, 12:12-16 raise the number of crowds spoken of to an awkward three. I would propose that v17 is another example of the editorial use of the repetitive resumptive. It attempts to explain the relationship between vv12-16 and what has gone before. When vv18-19 are read by themselves it can be seen that they make no reference to the crowd of 12:12 (which witnesses the entry into Jerusalem) but explain only how the crowd of 12:9-11 heard about the raising of Lazarus (the crowd which had witnessed it reported it to them) and why they came out to meet Jesus (because they heard that he [Jesus] had done this sign).

However, when these latter verses (vv17-19) are read in their present context (together with vv12-16), this difficulty is not immediately apparent. It would seem therefore that the second editor intended for the reader to identify the crowd of 12:12 with that of 12:9, something that is done only with difficulty.

Finally, the Pharisees make a telling comment in the light of all their efforts against Jesus: "You see that you can do nothing; look, the world has gone after him" (RSV). It is inconceivable that the authorities identified as "Jews" would ever make such a statement in the gospel. This is one of the clearest examples of the difference in portrayal of the authorities in the two editions.

---

[129]In 2:22, the disciples believe in the Scripture and in the word of Jesus but not until after the resurrection. Here, the disciples are said to remember these things (both in fulfillment of Scripture) after the glorification. Although it is not a widespread characteristic, it is true that in the signs material there is every indication that correct belief is possible on the basis of the signs themselves. However, throughout the other material and particularly within the 2:18-22 and 12:12-16, even the belief of the disciples is presented as not being adequate until after the glorification/resurrection, a view that is in keeping with the statement regarding the Spirit in 7:37-39.

27. The Greeks Want to See Jesus (12:20-22)

[20]Now among those who went up to worship at the feast were some Greeks. [21]So these came to Philip, who was from Bethsaida in Galilee, and said to him, "Sir, we wish to see Jesus." [22]Philip went and told Andrew; Andrew went with Philip and they told Jesus.

These verses narrate the request of some Greeks to see Jesus. The Greeks approach Philip, who then approaches Andrew and together they approach Jesus and tell him of the Greeks' request. In spite of the fact that there are none of the primary characteristics of the signs material here, it is very likely that this brief section does stem from the signs material. First, there seems to be an interest that these were Greeks who were coming to Jesus now. This ties in closely with the emphasis elsewhere in the signs material on the variety of groups which believe in Jesus. Second, there is the peculiar way in which one disciple then gets the other and then goes to Jesus. This is somewhat reminiscent of the way each disciple approached the other at the beginning of their relationship with Jesus. Thirdly, it is significant, I think, that the narrative breaks off suddenly, after the scene has been set and a response is given by Jesus which has little to do with the topic of the introductory material. We have seen this technique repeatedly (cf also 3:3; 7:28, 33; etc.) and in all cases it marked a break between the signs material and the material of the second edition. Finally, there is the unique mention of "the Greeks" here, a feature I would judge to be not specifically taken up in what follows and so in the present text is simply a "relic" from the first edition.

The meaning of these introductory verses is puzzled over in all of the commentaries. The most likely explanation is that they were meant to represent the scene of Zech 8:20-23, esp v23: "In those days ten men from the nations of every tongue shall take hold of the robe of a Jew, saying, 'Let us go with you, for we have heard that God is with you.'" Thus they demonstrate the recognition by the gentiles that Jesus is the eschatological agent of God.[130]

---

[130]Bultmann (*Gospel* 420) describes vv20-22 saying that "to outward appearance it is a fragment lacking a continuation." He finds it impossible to decide whether it is

28. The Conclusion of the Public Ministry (12:37-42)

³⁷**Though he had done so many signs** before them, yet **they did not believe in him;** ³⁸it was that the word spoken by the prophet Isaiah might be fulfilled: "Lord, who has believed our report, and to whom has the arm of the Lord been revealed?" ³⁹Therefore they could not believe. For Isaiah again said, ⁴⁰"He has blinded their eyes and hardened their heart, lest they should see with their eyes and perceive with their heart, and turn for me to heal them." ⁴¹Isaiah said this because he saw his glory and spoke of him. ⁴²Nevertheless **many even of the authorities believed in him,. . . .**

The next bit of signs material becomes evident in 12:37-42.[131] The material is identified as signs material by the characteristic term for miracle (v37), by the emphasis on the quantity and quality of those signs, by the "reverse" of the typical "easy belief," by the presence of the term "rulers" and "Pharisees" (v42), by the formulaic statement of belief in v42. However, the reference to being excluded from the synagogue (v42) can hardly have come from the first edition and once again [132] we find the mixing which indicates that the material has been edited.[133]

traditional or from the Evangelist. Fortna (*Signs* 155) points to similarities with 1:35ff but ends by attributing the verses to the Evangelist. Schnackenburg (*Gospel* 2 380) attributes the entire passage from vv20-36 to the Evangelist and sees no need for a literary critical solution to the verses.

[131]The change of scene after v36 and the reintroduction of Jesus in v44 define the present material as a distinct unit. Bultmann (*Gospel* 452, also 113) concludes that vv37-38 (but not the remainder) probably came from the signs source. Wilkens (*Entstehungsgeschichte* 66) attributes them to the first edition. Fortna (*Signs* 199) argues against Bultmann saying that such a saying is strange in the gospel as a whole but the thought of it being in the signs document is even stranger. I would argue that it is only strange if it is taken as referring to everyone. I would see it as referring only to the authorities. D.M. Smith ["The Setting and Shape of a Johannine Narrative Source," *JBL* 95 (1976), 231-241] proposes that this section is "a primitive transition from sign source to the passion, whereby the seemingly contradictory narrative of the Messiah's mighty works, already understood as *sēmeia*, and his suffering and death are brought together and the latter are made understandable in the light of the former."

[132]See also at 7:25-27, 8:12-13.

[133]The RSV creates the impression with its rendering of v42b ("but 'for fear of the

The passage is difficult to interpret. There is no subject expressed for the "they" who did not believe. Although some would take the plural as a reference to the people as a whole, I am inclined to think that it refers to the religious authorities. To take the verb as referring to the people forces the author of the first edition to change his opinion of the belief of the people after such a thorough buildup of signs faith not only on the part of the people but in his own narrative comment, including 20:30-31 as we shall see. But the statement is tempered somewhat by v42 which states that many even of the Pharisees believed but did not confess it.

The fact that the authorities are referred to in the proximate context would seem to indicate that they were the ones the author had in mind.[134] This would present a consistent picture of the authorities, for we have seen throughout that the people have believed and the authorities have not.

The unbelief of the authorities is explained by a quote from Is 53:1 which confirms their unbelief. Then a quote from Is 6:10 is added (somewhat awkwardly) and this attributes their unbelief to the hardening of the hearts by God.[135] It is then explained that Isaiah said what he did because he saw "his" (Jesus') glory. Thus Isaiah is like the disciples, who see the glory of Jesus, and thus come to full belief.

Immediately, however, the author appends a passage which is clear in its present form but which betrays editing. Two elements of these verses are awkward. First, the resumption itself is awkward, coming as it does as an afterthought to what had evidently already been a con-

---

Pharisees' they did not confess...") that this is a phrase close to the typical one, "for fear of the Jews," which occurs in the second stratum. Although the verse is the only one in the early material which mentions fear of the religious authorities, its phrasing is quite different. A more literal rendering would be: "Nevertheless, many even of the rulers believed in him, but because of the Pharisees they did not confess [their belief] lest they be put out of the synagogue."

[134]This must of course be distinguished from the view of the second editor, who undoubtedly did have the view that no one—neither common people nor religious authorities—came to true belief in Jesus on the basis of his signs. There is no evidence for such a position in the original version of the material however. This second editor may of course be the one responsible for omitting the subject of the verb in 12:37, but there is no way to be sure.

[135]This text which also occurs in Matthew (13:15) and Mark (4:12) occurs here in one of its strongest forms, attributing the hardening to God directly and without disguise.

clusion. Second, the association of signs material with synagogue exclusion is particularly awkward since there can be little doubt that such exclusion was a feature of the later history of the community rather than its early history. Finally, the contrast of the glory of God with the glory of men is not found elsewhere in the early material.

The mention of glory in v41 agrees well with the idea expressed in 2:11, where the disciples saw the glory of Jesus manifest within his sign and so believed in him.

In its present form the verses are not difficult to understand. They speak of belief on the part of the religious authorities, but this belief never becomes public because of fear of the Pharisees. Their failure, expressed in a play on words, is due to a desire to receive the glory which comes from men rather than to recognize the glory of God manifest in Jesus. Other than to point out that the mention of both the synagogue exclusion and the play on the word glory are later incorporations into the story, I do not think it is possible to determine the nature of the editing with complete precision.

The passage as a whole, however, forms the conclusion to the public ministry in the signs material. It forms an inclusion with the material of the first of his public signs: in contrast with the disciples who saw the signs, saw his glory and believed, the religious authorities have seen the signs but have neither seen the glory manifest in them nor believed in Jesus. This becomes the author's final judgment on the public ministry: the failure of the leaders of Jesus' own Jewish nation to see in all the great signs that Jesus had performed the glory that was present. The author could only reflect on the way this echoed the words of scripture from times past and echoed the historic unbelief of the nation previously. It was because their eyes had been blinded and their hearts had been hardened. And as a result they will not be healed!

29. Jesus Is Arrested (18:1-11, without vv4-6, 9)

[1]When Jesus had spoken these words, he went forth with his disciples across the Kidron valley, where there was a garden, which he and his disciples entered. [2]Now Judas, who betrayed him, also knew the place; for Jesus often met there with his disciples. [3]So Judas, procuring a band of soldiers and some officers from **the chief**

priests and the Pharisees, went there with lanterns and torches and weapons.... 7[Again] he asked them, "Whom do you seek?" And they said, "Jesus of Nazareth." 8Jesus answered, "I told you that I am he; so if you seek me, let these men go.".... 10Then Simon Peter, having a sword, drew it and struck the high priest's slave and cut off his right ear. The slave's name was Malchus. 11Jesus said to Peter, "Put your sword into its sheath; shall I not drink the cup which the Father has given me?"

Overview of the Passion Material

Because the passion material of the gospel is largely involved with narrative interspersed with sections of dialogue, it is suggested that the reader refer to the text of the entire passion as he/she works through the analysis of the signs material, for it is only in comparison with the final text of the passion that the character of the signs material, as well as the character of the later editing, becomes fully apparent.

The next body of material, clearly identified as part of the signs material, is a fragment of the arrest scene in the garden.136 The material

---

136According to the criteria that have been discussed in chapter 2, there is no evidence of signs material associated with the Last Supper. Bultmann (*Gospel* 462-464) would argue that a source lies behind 13:1-11, although it has been modified considerably by the Evangelist. Fortna (*Signs* 155-158) finds fragmentary evidence of a source in chapter 13 but not sufficient to reconstruct a continuous narrative, so also Wilkens (*Entstehungsgeschichte* 68-72).

On the arrest scene itself see Bultmann, *Gospel* 632-636. Bultmann attributes the verses to the Passion Source (which is met for the first time here and which, it should be recalled, is not in Bultmann's view the same source as the signs source.) As was seen in the case of Dodd's description of "traditional material" earlier, Bultmann here uses such criteria as the details and statements within the material "which are no use to the Evangelist theologically" (Smith, *Composition* 44). Bultmann, who is less confident of his ability to correctly separate source from redaction in all cases, summarizes his criteria for analysis of the passion on pp 635-636. Consequently in the analysis of the individual passages below we will not discuss the individual criteria. As Smith (p. 45) points out, in the analysis of the passion, many of the stylistic criteria claimed for the source also turn up in the work of the Evangelist, "therefore stylistic criteria cannot be decisive for source criticism" (p. 45). Nevertheless, there are points at which Bultmann would use contextual inconsistencies as his criterion for identification of material. See further Smith, *Composition* 45-47 for a discussion of Bultmann's criteria.

is identified by the terms "Pharisees" and "chief priests" in v3. There is no reason to doubt that the material of vv1-2 comes from the same source. V1 is introduced by the peculiar "Having said these things . . ."

Fortna (*Signs* 114-133) also discusses the passion and finds in it traditional material which he assigns to his signs gospel. His criteria remain similar to those used in the analysis of the public ministry. Specifically, Fortna would assign vv1-12 to the signs gospel except for vv6-9 and minor modifications elsewhere. His criteria are a combination of style, synoptic comparison, and theological tendencies.

Dodd (*Tradition* 65-81) discusses the arrest in some detail. He is, however, of less help since he focuses on the relation between the Johannine account and the gospel of Mark. However, both he and Fortna would attribute the first scene (vv4-6) to the source and the second to the Evangelist. This is unlikely since after the first mention of the *ego eimi*, it is said that the listeners fall to the ground. Clearly this is intended as a reaction to the power of the words intended in the divine sense.

A. Dauer, *Die Passionsgeschichte im Johannesevangelium. Eine traditonsgeschichtliche und theologische Untersuchung zu Joh 18, 1-19, 30* (SANT 30; München: Kösel, 1972) has also provided a detailed treatment of this material from a source critical perspective. As was the case with Dodd, Dauer seeks to address not only the question of sources, but also the possibility of reliance upon the synoptics. Dauer would see a source underlying this passage with the exception of vv4-9 and slight modifications elsewhere. See also the critique of Dauer in M. Sabbe, "The Arrest of Jesus in Jn 18, 1-11 and Its Relation to the Synoptic Gospels," *L'Evangile de Jean* 203-234. Wilkens (*Entstehungsgeschichte* 77-78) would attribute 18:1-11 to the first edition with the exception of v9.

F. Hahn, "Der Prozess Jesu nach dem Johannesevangelium. Eine redaktionsgeschichtliche Untersuchung." *EKK* 2 (1970) 23-96, studies only the hearing before Annas and the trial before Pilate. He proceeds by means of synoptic comparison in order to determine the unique Johannine editing. Although Hahn provides some very useful insights, this one-sided reliance on synoptic comparison is unsatisfactory.

Schnackenburg does not always deal with the text in sufficient detail to be helpful in our study. As with the other scholars surveyed here, Schnackenburg finds the analysis of the passion much more difficult than the previous signs material (p. 219) but would attribute in general considerably more material to the source than I would. With regard to 18:1-11, Schnackenburg (*Gospel* 3 221-227) proposes that the material comes from the source except for the mention of the Romans in the arrest scene (v3), the demonstration of superhuman knowledge (vv4-6), and the statement of the fulfillment of the word of Jesus (v9).

As this selective overview demonstrates, in the past, one of the primary means of determining the source used by John has been to do a comparison with the synoptics. In spite of this, it is the common assessment of scholars that such analysis is very difficult and the results somewhat tentative. The reader will notice that in my reconstruction there will be no reference to synoptic comparison as a criterion. I will restrict myself to the redactional and literary techniques which have been operative in the previous parts of the gospel and to the linguistic, ideological and theological criteria determined in chapter 2. It is my opinion that this thorough-going analysis based on internal criteria provides a more secure and objective means of determining the source.

(*Tauta eipōn* ...) which has consistently been evidence of editorial seams.[137] This therefore marks the beginning of the passage.

Vv 4-6

Another indication of editing is the fact that there are in effect two versions of the dialogue with Judas and those who accompany him. The first (vv4-6) betrays the characteristics of the second edition while the second (vv7-8) is much simpler and probably was the original version. The material of vv4-6 displays the supreme foreknowledge of Jesus which places him above human designs. It also contains the high christology characteristic of the second edition (*Ego eimi*—"I Am"—in the divine sense). Finally the resulting demonstration of power when the arresting party falls to the ground also demonstrates the superior power of Jesus even at this moment.

Vv 7-8

The second version of the scene (vv7-8) probably stems from the signs material since it is less developed theologically.

V 9

However, it is likely that v9 is an addition. Although fulfillment texts are consistent with the signs material, the word of Jesus as fulfilled is a topic in 2:22 and 7:39, both of which come from the second edition. The theology of the verse is also consistent with and refers to 6:39 (without the last phrase) and 10:28, 30.[138] The signs material continues in vv10-11 with the theme of the fulfillment of scripture and the incident of Peter cutting off the ear of Malchus.

The content of the original version is quite clear. Judas arrives at the garden with soldiers and attendants of the chief priests. Jesus identifies

---

[137]See at 9:6 and 11:11, 28; 18:1, 38; 20:20, 22.

[138]All of these texts (except 7:39) are clearly identified as belonging to the second edition by the occurrence of the term Jews in the immediate context. Cf 2:18, 20; 6:41; 10:24, 31, 33.

himself.[139] He asks that his disciples be allowed to depart (in fulfillment of scripture.) But Peter draws his sword and cuts off the ear of the high priest's slave. Jesus then tells Peter to return his sword to its sheath so that Jesus might drink of the cup the Father has sent him.

30. The Hearing Before Annas (18:19-24)

[19]The high priest then questioned Jesus about his disciples and his teaching. [20]Jesus answered him, "I have spoken openly to the world; I have always taught in synagogues and in the temple, where all Jews come together; I have said nothing secretly. [21]Why do you ask me? Ask those who have heard me, what I said to them; they know what I said." [22]When he had said this, one of the officers standing by struck Jesus with his hand, saying, "Is that how you answer the high priest?" [23]Jesus answered him, "If I have spoken wrongly, bear witness to the wrong; but if I have spoken rightly, why do you strike me?" [24]Annas then sent him bound to Caiaphas the high priest.

The next passage from the first edition concerns the hearing of Jesus before the high priest.[140] In the present edition of the gospel, the

---

[139]The statement, "I told you that I am he," has been of course modified by the addition of the first four words.

[140]The report of the taking of Jesus to Caiaphas (vv12-14) is from the second edition as indicated by the term Jews in vv12, 14. The passage, however, indicates a knowledge of the original sequence of the signs material in which there was a hearing before both Annas and Caiaphas. In the present text the actual narrative of the hearing before Caiaphas has been suppressed although references to it (v13["first"], v24, v28) remain. Dauer (*Passionsgeschichte* 83) makes the very interesting and plausible suggestion that the trial before Caiaphas has been dropped out of the signs material for theological reasons. In several prominent passages (all stemming from the third edition) Jesus speaks of his ministry in terms of a period of light during which it will be possible to become "sons of light" (12:35-36). After that time it will not be possible, the Jews will no longer have access to the light. Dauer suggests that the omission of the trial before Caiaphas is an example of this end of Jesus' dealings with the Jews. It will be noticed that in the hearing before Annas, Jesus gives no defense but only refers to his previous teaching. While I would attribute that statement to the signs material, it is possible that it was retained simply because it fit the theological conception of the refusal of Jesus to deal further with the objections of the Jews after the period of light. While this cannot be proven, it does reflect accurately the fact that the Johannine trial scenes focus on the hearing before Pilate and that within that trial, the Jews deal with Pilate rather than with Jesus and that Jesus' direct dealings with the Jews are very minimal.

material covering the events from the arrest to his arraignment are narrated in material of the later edition(s).

The hearing before Annas is clearly and neatly marked off by the editorial use of framing repetition in which v18c is repeated almost verbatim in v25.[141] The material surrounding the passage probably comes from the third edition of the gospel. I would judge the passage prior to v19 as referring to the Beloved Disciple, and I would consider the following passage to be a continuation of the prior one. This would help explain the various aporias associated with the verses of our passage (vv19-24).

The high priest in question is identified in v24 as Annas. In v24 we also hear that after this hearing was finished, Annas sent Jesus bound to Caiaphas. There are two problems here. First, it is unusual to designate as "high priest" a person such as Annas, who had been high priest formerly but who was not high priest at that time. One would think of Caiaphas as high priest here since he had been designated as

---

The report of Peter's admittance into the courtyard at the request of the unnamed disciple and of his first denial of Jesus comes from the third edition. There is considerable discussion whether the unnamed disciple here is the Beloved Disciple. I am of the opinion that he is. For a detailed discussion leading to the same conclusion, see F. Neirynck, "The 'Other Disciple' in Jn 18, 15-16," *ETL* 51 (1975) 113-141. Schnackenburg (*Gospel* 3 234-235) comes to the opposite conclusion. On the relation of the Beloved Disciple passages to the gospel, see also the article by M. de Jonge, "The Beloved Disciple and the Date of the Gospel of John," *Text and Interpretation. Festschrift für M. Black* (ed. E. Best and R.McL. Wilson; Cambridge: University Press, 1979) 99-114, and H.Thyen, "Entwicklungen innerhalb der johanneischen Theologie und Kirche im Spiegel von Joh 21 und der Lieblingsjuengertexte des Evangeliums," in *L'Évangile de Jean* 259-299. For a very useful survey of the discussion dealing with the Beloved Disciple; see Schnackenburg, *Gospel* 3 375-388. But the narrative of vv15-18 remains somewhat awkward since it does not distinguish *which* high priest was being referred to, nor does it take into account the change of locale implied in v24. Dauer would postulate a still earlier stage of the tradition in which this was joined to an account which contained two hearings.

Bultmann (*Gospel* 643-644) suggests that vv12-24 come from the source with additions in vv13-14 and 24 with shorter additions in v12 and v20. Fortna (*Signs* 117-122) considers vv13-28a to be from the source but transposes v24 to the position after v13 and omits the latter parts of v24. He omits v14, 16b, parts of 21 which is then followed by 16b, 17-18 and 25b-28.

Dauer (*Passionsgeschichte* 62-90) finds a source underlying vv12-24 with the exception of v14, 20-21, 22b-23 and minor modifications in vv17-18.

[141]Within the passion this use of framing repetition also occurs at 18:38 and 19:6 where it again clearly frames signs material.

such twice previously (11:49 and 18:13).[142] The second problem is that there is no report (at least in the current version of the gospel) of the hearing before the actual high priest, Caiaphas.[143]

That the passage comes from the signs material is suggested (but not proved) by the fact that the use of "Jews" here is not the hostile sense typical of the second edition (as it is elsewhere in the Passion) as well as by the neutral tone of the entire passage. The only questions posed to Jesus concern his disciples and his teaching. These charges are notably less specific than those raised in the synoptics—and those raised by the "Jews" (hostile sense) in the trial before Pilate.[144] On a theological level, the charges would seem to reflect the suspicion that Jesus was a false prophet. On a political level, the question about his disciples may indicate the fear of an insurrection.[145] Both concerns are very much consistent with the presentation of the signs material and totally lacking in the theological interests of the second edition.[146]

31. The Transfer of Jesus from Caiaphas to Pilate and Pilate's First Questioning of Jesus (18:28-29, 33-35)

[28]Then they led Jesus from the house of Caiaphas to the praetorium. It was early. They themselves did not enter the praetorium,

---

[142]It is not unheard of, however. It may be simply a title that was preserved for former high priests out of courtesy. See the discussion in Brown, *Gospel* 821.

[143]As early as the time of Augustine, there were suggestions that perhaps v24 was out of order and was intended to precede v19. While this would solve the problems, there is no manuscript evidence that this was ever the case. A solution based on the editorial history is much more plausible.

[144]See, for example, 19:6 where the Jews charge that "We have a law, and by that law he ought to die, because he has made himself the Son of God." (RSV). In 19:12 the Jews also intimidate Pilate (instead of fearing him as do the "Pharisees" in 11:47-48) by reminding him that "If you release this man, you are not Caesar's friend; every one who makes himself a king sets himself against Caesar." (RSV).

[145]So also Brown, *Gospel* 835.

[146]The concern for the disciples and the teaching of Jesus may reflect the statement of the religious authorities in 11:48 where there is fear that his following will cause the Romans to think that he is a political threat. Or, alternatively, the references to disciples and to his teaching might well be intended to refer to such discussions as that of 9:13-34 (signs material) where the man born blind is called a disciple of that one

so that they might not be defiled, but might eat the passover. [29]So Pilate went out to them and said, "What accusation do you bring against this man?"...

[33]Pilate entered the praetorium again and called Jesus, and said to him, "Are you the King of the Jews?" [34]Jesus answered, "Do you say this of your own accord, or did others say it to you about me?" [35]Pilate answered, "Am I a Jew? Your own nation and **the chief priests** have handed you over to me; what have you done?"

After the intervention of material from the third edition which resumes the narrative of Peter's denial (vv25-27),[147] we find the transfer of Jesus from Caiaphas to the praetorium. The narrative is straightforward, including the note that the crowd did not enter the praetorium so that they might not be defiled but eat the Passover. Therefore Pilate comes out to the crowd and asks about the accusation they bring regarding Jesus.[148]

There is no definitive indication that vv28-29 come from the signs material but this seems the most plausible explanation. After the intervention of vv30-32, which come from the second edition, the signs material resumes with the statement of Pilate that the Jews accuse Jesus of claiming to be king of the Jews—an accusation that does not appear in the previous text. It is most likely that the original answer to vv28-29 has been suppressed and a "new" answer has been provided by the author of the second edition (vv30-32).

Thus in this passage we find another example of the technique, which has occurred previously with considerable frequency, whereby questions or leading statements posed in the signs material are in the

(9:28) and is said to teach the Pharisees (v34). Both Schnackenburg (*Gospel* 3 236-237) and Dauer (*Passionsgeschichte* 80-82) find elements of Johannine theology in the references to the "world" but I would not consider this instance to be intended in the typical Johannine theological sense.

[147]Specific characteristics which would identify the material are lacking but on the basis of its relation to vv13-18, I would suggest that they come, at least in their present form, from the third edition. This is one of the most difficult passages to identify within the passion narrative.

[148]The division of the trial scene into two "scenes" or "stages" is frequently noted (Dodd, Brown, Dauer, etc.). See particularly Dauer, *Passionsgeschichte* 101-105. This very effective rendering of the trial scene is ultimately the work of the second author editing the signs material.

present state of the text answered or reacted to in material of the second edition.[149] This same technique will occur below in v36-37b.

That vv28-29 are signs material is likely, given their "neutral" tone, the evident suppression of the original accusation that Jesus is king of the Jews, the clear indications that vv30-32 come from the second edition, and, finally, the presence of the technique whereby a question or other introductory material from the signs gospel is combined with a response from the material of the second edition.

Vv 30-32

Vv30-32 provide a "new" answer to the question of the accusation brought against Jesus: he is an evildoer and should be put to death. The evidence that these verses belong to the second edition is significant. The accusation is not consistent with that of v33 (which is clearly signs material), the religious authorities are identified as Jews (hostile sense) in v31, and the theme of the fulfillment of the word of Jesus is theologically typical of the second edition.[150]

Vv 33-35

Vv33-35 awkwardly resume the signs material. Evidently in the original version, now supplanted by vv30-32, the authorities had accused Jesus of being "King of the Jews" because in v33 Pilate enters the praetorium and asks Jesus whether he is in fact King of the Jews. Yet in the present state of the text, there is no evidence that such a charge has been made.[151] Jesus asks Pilate in return whether he says this of himself or whether it is at the suggestion of others. Pilate answers in terms characteristic of the signs material: "Am I a Jew? Your own nation and the chief priests have handed you over to me."

[149]We have previously encountered this technique in 3:3; 4:10; 7:28, 33; 12:22.

[150]There is evidence that the Jews were able to put persons to death although the exact circumstances and the manner of execution are debated. The implication of the statement in vv31-32 is that because of their bringing Jesus before Pilate, Jesus will die by crucifixion (and thus fulfill his prediction [cf 12:32] of the manner of his death).

[151]So also Bultmann, *Gospel* 653; Fortna, *Signs* 123. Most commentators attribute these verses to the "source."

The signs material then breaks off at the end of v35 and the answer is given in terms of the second edition.

Vv 36-38

The material in vv36-38 is identified as coming from the second edition by the term "Jews" (vv36, 38) and by the way the issue of kingship is handled. Jesus' kingship is not "of this world" and his purpose is to "testify to the truth." Both of these theological themes are prominent in the gospel outside of the signs material.[152]

There are also two contextual features of importance here. The first problem is the appearance of the statement "I find no crime in him." This statement is repeated almost verbatim in 19:4, 6, and 15. Although the repetition can be accounted for partly by a desire to emphasize the statement, the fact that it appears *four* times is certainly due partly to editing. The instances of the statement in 18:38 and 19:6 neatly bracket the scene involving the release of Barabbas and the scourging, passages which give indications of being from the signs material as we shall see below. Thus the repetition of "I find no guilt in him" in these instances is probably an example of the same editorial framing evident in 18:18c and 25.[153] It is mentioned here because the first instance indicates a literary seam at the end of 18:38.

The second feature is the awkward way in which Pilate enters and exits the praetorium throughout the scene. Pilate had gone out to meet the Jews (18:29) and then questioned Jesus inside the praetorium (18:33). He then goes out in 18:38; and without mention of re-entry he departs again in 19:4; enters the praetorium in 19:8; and exits in 19:13. Undoubtedly part of this complicated sequence is due to editing also.[154]

---

[152]1:14, 17; 3:21; 4:23, 24; 5:33; 8:32, 40, 44, 45, 46; 14:6; 16:7; 17:17, 19.

[153]See the discussion in the following section.

[154]Bultmann (*Gospel* 648-651) attributes 18:28-38 to the source with the exception of vv28b, 30-38a. Fortna (*Signs* 22-124) would see the source here as nearly unrecoverable. As does Bultmann, Fortna uses comparison with the synoptics as a criterion repeatedly throughout the analysis. He would see a source in vv28b-38b with additions by the Evangelist in vv28d, 30-32, 34-36 and modifications in v33 and v37. Fortna, however, recognizes the difficulty of reconciling the religious charges with the more traditional charge of being "King of the Jews." Other than this, Fortna and Bultmann provide little detailed discussion of the verses.

32. The Release of Barabbas, the Scourging, Mockery, and the Cry for Crucifixion (18:39-19:6a)

[39]"But you have a custom that I should release one man for you at the Passover; will you have me release for you the King of the Jews?" [40]They cried out again, "Not this man, but Barabbas!" Now Barabbas was a robber.

19[1]Then Pilate took Jesus and scrouged him. [2]And the soldiers plaited a crown of thorns, and put it on his head, and arrayed him in a purple robe; they came up to him, saying, "Hail, King of the Jews!" and struck him with their hands.

[4]Pilate went out again, and said to them, "See, I am bringing him out to you, that you may know that I find no crime in him." [5]So Jesus came out, wearing the crown of thorns and the purple robe. Pilate said to them, "Behold the man!" [6]When **the chief priests** and the officers saw him, they cried out, "Crucify him, crucify him!"

The signs material resumes in v39.[155] Two features mark 18:39-19:6 as a unit. First, its beginning and end are marked by the framing repetition of the statement by Pilate (18:38 and 19:6) as mentioned above. Second, the material itself forms a unit which is consistent with the orientation of the previous signs material and which can be con-

Dodd (*Tradition* 95-96) sees the interrogation as drawn from an oral source. See also Dauer for a detailed treatment of this and the following section in *Passionsgeschichte* 100-164.

[155]Bultmann (*Gospel* 650-651) proposes an underlying source with additions in vv4-6. "A source narrative analogous to the Synoptic account therefore lies at the base of John's report; the Evangelist has cleverly set it forth and organized it through the repeated change of scenes" (p. 650). Fortna (*Signs* 124-126) considers vv4-7 to be "wholly John's creation"; otherwise he sees the section as stemming from the source except for minor modifications. Fortna, too, relies heavily on comparison with the synoptics for determining the character of his source here. I can find no "Johannine elements" in vv4-7. Rather the verses seem quite consistent theologically with the signs material throughout, which has dealt with the issue of whether Jesus was in fact a threat to the Romans and seriously to be considered a king as was proposed by the Jewish authorities in 11:48. In the light of this, the statement in vv4-7 seems designed to illustrate how little a threat Jesus was considered by Pilate. In addition to this consistency, we are able to show both editorial techniques and linguistic characteristics which identify the material well.

trasted with the theology of the second edition, which immediately precedes and follows it. Let us look at each of these more closely.

The repetition of Pilate's statement that he finds no guilt in Jesus in 18:38 and 19:6 is yet another example of the framing repetition which occurs in various forms throughout the gospel and most recently at 18:18c and 25.[156] The same statement in 19:4 was probably not an editorial device but simply the reaffirmation of his original statement following the questioning which ended in 18:38.[157]

The intervening material is identified as signs material by the reappearance of the term "chief priests" in v6. V40 also is marked as coming from a source by its mention of the crowd crying out "again" when in the present state of the text it is the first time they have done so.[158] Both the scene of the release of Barabbas and the scourging and mockery are all consistent with the portrayal in the previous signs material and center on the accusation of Jesus as "King of the Jews." The crowd then cries out "Crucify him; crucify him!" Pilate in turn says to them, "Take him yourselves and crucify him, for I find no crime in him."

The material of this passage ends in 19:6. In 19:7, however, the material of the second edition resumes in reaction to the statement of Pilate. This passage fits well with the previous passage from the second edition (18:36-38) and provides a consistent portrayal. Both of these surrounding passages are clearly marked as belonging to the second edition by the term for religious authorities and also by their characteristic theology.

In the previous passage from the second edition (vv36-38), the authorities were identified as Jews (vv36, 38) and the topic was truth. In 19:7 the response to Pilate is provided in the material of the second edition. Once again the authorities are identified as Jews (v7). In addition, the issue suddenly becomes a theological one phrased in terms of the high christology ("he made himself son of God") rather than the kingship which had previously been the charge. This concern

---

[156]I would judge its appearance in 18:38 to be the work of the second author and the appearance in 19:4-6 to be part of the signs material.

[157]The first statement would express the results of the questioning and the second would reaffirm it and, after the scourging, indicate Pilate's desire to have no part in Jesus' death.

[158]This was pointed out by Bultmann, *Gospel* 649.

with high christology is of course one of the most striking features of the second edition (cf esp 5:15-18; 8:21-27; 10:31-39). Thus we have several features which reinforce one another and together lead to the firm conclusion that 18:39-19:6 is signs material, bounded on both sides by material from the second edition, as we have said. Undoubtedly, some of the intervening signs material has been supplanted because 18:39 does not follow smoothly on 18:35.

The release of Barabbas, the mocking of Jesus as King, and the exhibition of Jesus before the crowd are all told in a quite straightforward manner. After Jesus has been tortured and humiliated, he is brought before the chief priests, and, rather than being softened by the appearance of Jesus, they cry out for his crucifixion. But Pilate, the one that the chief priests and Pharisees had allegedly thought would find Jesus a threat (11:47-50), pronounces him innocent.

33. The Final Questioning and Judgment by Pilate (19:13-16, without vv14b-15a)

[13]When Pilate heard these words, he brought Jesus out and sat down on the judgment seat at a place **called The Pavement, and in Hebrew, Gabbatha.** [14]Now it was the day of Preparation of the Passover; it was about the sixth hour. He said to the Jews, "Behold your King!"... [15]Pilate said to them, "Shall I crucify your King?" **The chief priests** answered, "We have no King but Caesar."

[16]Then he handed him over to them to be crucified.

The material of the second edition which began in v7 ends in v12 (cf Jews in the hostile sense there). These verses concluded the accusations of the "Jews" before Pilate. The presence of vv6b-12 here have created several problems of sequence as well as theological consistency. In v8, Pilate talks to Jesus inside the Praetorium without mention of the fact that he has led Jesus back into the building (cf v5). In addition, in v12 there is no mention that Pilate has come out again (or that the Jews had "gone in"—something they would of course not do for fear of defilement), yet the two groups talk together. Finally, in v13 (signs material) Jesus is now out again without mention of an exit. Finally as we have noted, the theology of vv6b-12 is clearly that of the second edition.

The signs material resumes in vv13-14a. It is identified by the characteristic way in which the name for the Stone Pavement is given in both Greek (first) and Hebrew.[159] In addition, the passage has the specificity and accuracy with regard to geography that is typical of the signs material.

The part of v13 which speaks of Jesus being led out again may be an editorial transition, but the remainder of the verse which deals with bringing Jesus to the judgment seat does not pursue the same theological interests as the previous section.[160]

After a brief passage from the second edition (vv14b-15a), in which

---

[159]Bultmann (*Gospel* 605-651) attributes these verses to the Evangelist who uses motifs found in the source. Fortna (*Signs* 126-127) attributes vv13-14b to the source and vv14c-15 to the Evangelist. Fortna would rearrange the text, however, putting 19:15a after 18:38c in the source. Fortna bases his conclusions here on a comparison with Luke and on stylistic traits.

[160]I have relegated the discussion of the original sequence to a note because of its complexity.

There is also a contextual difficulty created here by the exit of Pilate from the Praetorium. It is impossible to account for this with certainty but two possibilities present themselves. First, there may have been additional signs material in the original edition which necessitated Jesus being led back into the praetorium and then out again in v13. Alternatively, v13 originally followed immediately on v6a resulting in the following original sequence: After scourging Jesus, Pilate brings him out wearing the crown and robe (19:4-6a). When the religious authorities see him they cry out for his crucifixion (v16a).When he hears these words (v13a), Pilate sits on the judgment seat (v14a) and addresses the chief priests again: Shall I crucify your King?" They then respond, "We have no king but Caesar" (v15b).

This hypothesis is simple and accounts for all of the signs material. It presumes the omission of 19:6b-12 and 19:14b-15, material clearly marked as being from the second edition. Its uncertainty lies in the lack of clear evidence as to exactly where the signs material leaves off (in the middle or at the end of 19:6) and in the postulation of editing at the beginning of v13 (removing the notice that Jesus was led out—since he was already out in v6). But I am inclined to this second alternative in spite of this uncertainty. It provides not only a smooth and consistent sequence, it also results in a consistent portrayal of Jesus as being accused of being a king, mocked and scourged as a "king," condemned as a king, and finally crucified as a king.

The only significant concern in the second edition with kingship is in 19:12 where the "Jews" (hostile sense) who had intimidated everyone throughout the gospel now intimidate even Pilate, threatening him with the possible consequences of not condemning Jesus. Yet even here the Jews are not charging Jesus with kingship but only using the charge to intimidate Pilate. The mention of kingship in v14b is necessary only to provide the context for the cry, "Away with him, away with him, crucify him!" which had to be repeated from v6 after the insertion of vv7-12 by the author of the second edition.

the Jews (in the hostile sense) once more cry out for Jesus' crucifixion, the signs material resumes with vv15b-16.[161] For the last time the signs material raises the issue of the kingship of Jesus, and the chief priests declare their loyalty to Caesar. On hearing this Jesus is condemned by Pilate to death.

34. The Crucifixion of Jesus (19:17-25a)

[17]So they took Jesus, and he went out, bearing his own cross to **the place called the place of a skull, which is called in Hebrew Golgatha.** [18]There they crucified him, and with him two others, one on either side, and Jesus between them.

[19]Pilate also wrote a title and put it on the cross; it read, "Jesus of Nazareth, the King of the Jews." [20]**Many of the Jews** read this title, for the place where Jesus was crucified was near the city; and it was written in Hebrew, in Latin and in Greek. [21]**The chief priests of the Jews** then said to Pilate, "Do not write, 'The King of the Jews,' but, 'This man said, I am King of the Jews.'" [22]Pilate answered, "What I have written, I have written."

[23]When the soldiers had crucified Jesus they took his garments and made four parts, one for each soldier; also his tunic. But the tunic was without seam, woven from top to bottom; [24]so they said to one another, "Let us not tear it, but cast lots for it to see whose it shall be." This was to fulfill the scripture, "They parted my garments among them, and for my clothing they cast lots." [25]So the soldiers did this.

This material concerns the journey of Jesus to the place of crucifixion, the crucifixion itself and, finally, the division of Jesus' garments among the soldiers. The passage is identified as signs material by a number of characteristics. The authorities are identified as chief priests (vv15, 21). In vv20, 21, the word Jews is not used in the hostile sense as it is in the second edition. The phrase "chief priests of the

---

[161]It may well be that the author of the second edition inserted this brief exchange simply to reaffirm the intensity of the religious authorities' desire to have Jesus crucified. The surrounding material is clearly from the signs material.

Jews" echoes the similar phrase used in the signs material in 3:1 to identify Nicodemus.[162] The place of the crucifixion is given first in Greek and then in Hebrew (v17). In addition the material is straight-forward narrative as is the other signs material in the passion.[163]

It is noted that two others are crucified with Jesus. Next, Pilate puts a title on the cross which occasions some debate with the chief priests who again focus on the issue of kingship. Pilate's statement, in their eyes, becomes an unconscious prophecy of who Jesus truly is. The chief priests want it made clear that this was Jesus' claim and not Pilate's judgment. However, Pilate refuses to change the title.

The final scene of the section is the division of the garments of Jesus among the soldiers. They cast lots for Jesus' tunic, since it was without seam. This is seen as a fulfillment of scripture.

The signs material continues to the end of v25a. At that point there begins a scene from the third edition involving the Beloved Disciple and the mother of Jesus.[164]

35. Nicodemus Removes the Body of Jesus for Burial (19:39-42)

[39]Nicodemus also, who had at first come to him by night, came bringing a mixture of myrrh and aloes, about a hundred pounds' weight. [40][They] took the body of Jesus and bound it in linen cloths with the spices, as is the burial custom of the Jews. [41]Now in the place where he was crucified there was a garden, and in the garden a new tomb where no one had ever been laid. [42]So because of the Jewish day of Preparation, as the tomb was close at hand, they laid Jesus there.

In the intervening material (from the second and third editions)

---

[162]There Nicodemus was identified as a Pharisee and a "ruler of the Jews."

[163]Bultmann (Gospel 666-668) sees additions to the synoptic-like source in vv20-22. Fortna (Signs 128-134) attributes the majority of the text to the source with additions in vv20a, 21-22. Dauer (Passionsgeschichte 165-211) attributes the material to the source except for vv19-22. See also Wilkens (Entstehungsgeschichte 84-86).

[164]On the attribution of the Beloved Disciple passage to the third edition, see note 140 above.

there have been several events narrated. Jesus entrusts his mother to the Beloved Disciple for his care and entrusts the disciple to his mother. The actual death of Jesus is narrated, and the side of Jesus is pierced with a lance, allowing blood and water to emerge. Each of these incidents is extremely important for the theology of the second and third editions, drawing out the meaning of the event of the crucifixion. However, what had been narrated in the original edition is not clear, for the signs material does not resume until 19:39.

In v39 Nicodemus arrives to bury the body of Jesus.[165] However, in order to understand this passage we must begin at v38 with a verse that is clearly identified with the second edition by the use of Jews in the hostile sense and particularly by the characteristic "fear of the Jews." In v38 we are told that Joseph of Arimathea was a disciple of Jesus secretly "for fear of the Jews" and that he went to Pilate to ask for the body of Jesus. Pilate gives him permission and, we are told,". . . he came and took away his body." A careful reading of this verse reveals that Joseph alone is responsible for the removal of the body and that the removal is complete by the end of v38.[166] Yet in v39 the signs material begins again with the reappearance of Nicodemus who is, according to v39, also involved in the removal of the body.

[165]Bultmann (*Gospel* 666-667) sees a source underlying vv25-42 but attributes vv26-27 and part of v28 to the Evangelist. Vv34b, 35 come from the Ecclesiastical Redactor. Bultmann sees two motivations for the statement of Jesus that he thirsts. The first, he claims, is contained in the words "knowing that all was now finished" and the second is contained in the statement that he said this in order to fulfill the Scriptures. This is overly precise.

Fortna (*Signs* 128-133) includes much more material in the source at this point than I would. He attributes vv25-38 to the source except for vv26-27, parts of v28, v30, v34, all of v35, and parts of v40 and v42. See also Wilkens (*Entstehungsgeschichte* 84-87).

Although this is not the place for a detailed analysis of the material of vv25b-37 (since they show no characteristics of the signs material), some comment on their character may be in order. I would see vv25b-27, which concern the Beloved Disciple, as belonging to the third edition. Vv28-30 belong to the second edition on the basis of the supreme foreknowledge of Jesus demonstrated in v28 and on the theologically important v30 where, in my view, Jesus gives the Spirit promised in 7:37-39. V31 is marked as belonging to the second edition by the presence of Jews as the designation of the religious authorities. Vv32-37 belong to the third edition as evidenced by the presence of the Beloved Disciple's witness.

[166]Some see in this context yet another duplication. The Jews (19:31) had already asked that the bodies might be taken away and not remain on the cross for the Sabbath. Yet much the same is said of Joseph of Arimathea in v38. Bultmann (*Gospel* 666) thought these were duplicate versions and that both stood side by side in the

Nicodemus is identified as the one who had come to Jesus previously by night (3:1ff). He brought "a mixture of myrrh and aloes, about a hundred pounds' weight." In the original the narrative continued but with Nicodemus as subject rather than the plural which was added by the author of the second edition. Nicodemus took the body of Jesus, bound it in linen with the spices "as is the custom of the Jews." Because it was the Jewish day of Preparation they laid the body of Jesus in a tomb close at hand in the garden.

Although the evidence internal to the verses (vv39-42) is not probative, when the verses are compared with the surrounding context, it seems likely that the verses do come from the first edition. Internal features which would tend to confirm this are: the appearance of Nicodemus (and the cross-reference to his earlier appearance within the signs material), also the aporia which is created with v38. Undoubtedly, the signs material (v39) simply contained a notice of Nicodemus as the one responsible for the removal of the body. However, in the second edition, Joseph of Arimathea is added, evidently to bring the account into agreement with the synoptics (Mt 27:57-60; Mk 15:42-46; Lk 23:50-53) thus creating the awkward grammar as well as the increase in numbers of people involved in the process (much as had occurred for example in the editorial additions of 4:40-42 and 12:12-16).

36. The Appearance of the Risen Jesus to Mary in the Garden (20:1, 11, 14-16)

[1]Now on the first day of the week Mary Magdalene came to the tomb early, while it was still dark, and saw that the stone had been taken away from the tomb.

[11]But Mary stood weeping outside the tomb, and as she wept she

source. Both verses contain "Jews" in the hostile sense. On the basis of this, there can be no doubt that the two passages come from the same edition. It seems more likely that v31 simply indicates the wish of the Jews that the body be removed. The soldiers then break the legs of Jesus and remove the body from the cross. V38 then specifies Joseph of Arimathea as the one by whom the body was actually taken away and buried.

stooped to look into the tomb. . . . ¹⁴[Saying this,] she turned round and saw Jesus standing, but she did not know that it was Jesus. ¹⁵Jesus said to her, "Woman, why are you weeping? Whom do you seek?" Supposing him to be the gardener, she said to him, "Sir, if you have carried him away, tell me where you have laid him, and I will take him away." ¹⁶Jesus said to her, "Mary." She turned and said to him **in Hebrew, ""Rabboni!" (which means Teacher).**

Following on the scene of the burial in the signs material is the arrival of Mary Magdalene at the tomb early on the first day of the week to anoint the body. She discovers the stone rolled away from the tomb. However the account of what happens at the tomb has been clearly edited.

The discovery of the empty tomb was first narrated in the signs material and was comprised of 20:1, 11, 14-16. In this version Mary came to the tomb, found the stone rolled back and then, as she stood there weeping, was addressed by a voice from the rear. Mary, thinking it was the gardener, turned and asked where he had put the body. As she saw Jesus, she then recognized him and addressed him as "Rabboni."

However, in the present text, the appearance of Jesus to Mary is postponed and a passage is inserted by the author of the third edition. In this passage, Mary first goes to get Peter and the Beloved Disciple who come and inspect the tomb. The Beloved Disciple comes to belief and both disciples leave and return to their homes. Then another brief passage is inserted in which Mary sees two angels at the tomb and is asked by them why she is weeping. She tells them that it is because the body of Jesus has been taken away. Then the original text resumes, to be cut off finally by vv17-18.

In the original, v11 must have followed immediately after v1 since from a literary point of view the verse is awkward as a sequel to v10. As is the case in all of the passages involving the Beloved Disciple, the material of vv2-10 has no effect on the surrounding context.¹⁶⁷ In addition the commission which Mary receives from the risen Jesus is superfluous if the two disciples have already come to belief. Finally,

---

¹⁶⁷This has been pointed out by M. de Jonge in his very insightful article, "The Beloved Disciple," esp 107-108.

when Mary looks into the grave, she sees two angels which the disciples did not see and which certainly would have been there to see.[168]

Immediately after the notice of Mary weeping in v11a, the text is interrupted by the addition of vv11b-13. The account here which involves angels is a parallel to the following account (vv14-16) involving Jesus. In both Mary is asked why she is weeping; in both she explains that it is because the body has been taken away. In addition to this duplication, the two bodies of material can be distinguished by their characteristic linguistic and theological features, by the way the second set of verses fits with the surrounding context and by the presence of a clear redactional marker at the beginning of v14.

The first set of verses which narrates the appearance of two angels is relatively insignificant theologically and may simply be intended to bring the account more in line with the synoptic accounts which consistently speak of the appearance of angels at the tomb (Mt 28:2-7, Mk 16:5, Lk 24:4). These verses are marked as belonging to the third edition by the term "Lord" (in the religious sense) as referring to Jesus, a term which appears consistently in material from the third edition but never appears in the signs material.[169] In addition the angels do not figure in the remainder of the narrative.

The second set of verses, however, resumes the sequence well. These verses are marked as signs material by the characteristic translation of religious terms from Hebrew to Greek and by the typical low christology. In addition, that a literary seam exists after v13 and that the

---

[168]See the discussion in Bultmann (*Gospel* 681). Bultmann attributes vv2-8 to the Evangelist. It is generally recognized now, however, that the passages involving the Beloved Disciple are not the work of the Evangelist himself but of a later hand. Bultmann and Fortna (*Signs* 137) suggest that v9 cannot follow on v8. However, I would see v9 as simply echoing the conception typical of the second edition but, here, presented also by the author of the third edition, that true belief did not occur until after the glorification of Jesus (cf 2:22; 12:16).

Fortna (*Signs* 134-144) departs radically from the analysis of Bultmann here and follows that of G. Hartmann, "Die Vorlage der Osterberichte in John 20," *ZNW 55* (1964) 197-220. According to Fortna, vv1-16 come from a source except for vv4, 6, 13, 15 and parts of vv3, 5, 8, 11, 14, 16. I do not see a need to fragment the text to such an extent.

[169]It will be noticed that the use of "Lord" in the religious sense to refer to Jesus has occurred in editorial additions throughout (cf 4:1; 6:23; 11:2; 20:2, 13, 18, 20, 25; 21:7, 12). It is likely that the verses come from the third edition. However, detailed discussion of this material is beyond the scope of the current study.

signs material resumes in v14, is clearly marked by the redactional phrase "Saying this. . ." (Gk: *Tauta eipousa* . . .).[170] Mary, who has been standing at the open tomb weeping, turns around and sees a man. Mary thinks the man is the gardener and tells him that if he has taken the body to tell her and she will remove it. Jesus then addresses her as Mary. She turns around and, recognizing him, addresses him as "Rabboni" (which is characteristically translated into Greek).[171] Note the different term of address from the much more exalted "Lord" in the previous v13 and the following v18.

After this, the signs material breaks off and, in the material of the third edition, Jesus tells Mary not to "hold" him, but to go to the "brothers" (a new term for the disciples)[172] and to tell them that he is ascending to God. Mary then does as Jesus says and informs the disciples that she has seen the "Lord" (again in the religious sense).

Although in the signs edition of the gospel there was undoubtedly more material which dealt with the post-resurrection period, none of it remains in the final edition of the gospel. It has been replaced by material from the later two editions dealing with theological topics appropriate to those editions. In the present state of the gospel, the only passage from the first edition remaining is its concluding summary (20:30-31).

37. The Conclusion of the Signs Material (20:30-31)

[30]Now **Jesus did many other signs** in the presence of the disciples, which are not written in this book; [31]but **these are written that you may believe** that Jesus is **the Christ, the Son of God,** and that believing you may have life in his name.

The final passage of signs material in our analysis is the passage that

---

[170]This phrase in its verbal and participial forms occurred previously in 9:6; 11:11, 28, 43; 18:1. See also the similar phrase in 11:7.

[171]In its current form this first Easter scene is interrupted by three additions from a later (probably the third) edition of the gospel (20:2-10; 11b-13; 17-18).

[172]See also at 21:3 and throughout the first epistle where the term in now used to refer to fellow members of the community.

in all likelihood ended the signs gospel and which is referred to by most commentators as the "first" ending to the gospel.[173]

Once again the characteristics of the signs material are unmistakable: the use of sign for miracle, the emphasis on the quantity of the signs, and the conviction that the signs should lead to belief. The statement is quite straightforward, indicating that the signs narrated here are a selected number. However, as an ending to the gospel the verses are quite abrupt. They indicate only that the signs are intended to lead to belief and that this belief consists in the conviction that Jesus is the Christ and the Son of God. Thus here again, in the simplest of terms, the major theology of the signs material is evident: they were designed to bring about belief in Jesus. Only the final clause, "and that believing you may have life in his name," would give any indication of being an addition by the author of the second edition. Although this is proposed by most scholars, there is no definitive evidence that it is so.[174]

A Note on the Miracle of Chapter 21

There are some scholars who would include the miracle of chapter 21 within the material of the signs gospel (e.g., Fortna). But the material contains various idiosyncracies which set it apart from the remainder of the signs material. Among these is the fact that this is the only post-resurrection story set in Galilee; in addition it is the only material of the gospel to identify the disciples as fishermen. This suggests that the narrative did not stem from the same tradition as the remainder of the signs material. In addition, the chapter contains none of the

[173]For example, Brown, *Gospel* 1055-1061; Bultmann, *Gospel* 697-699; Fortna, *Signs* 197-198; Nicol, *Semeia* 39; Schnackenburg, *Gospel* 335-340; Wellhausen, *Johannesevangelium* 95; Wilkens, *Entstehungsgeschichte* 90-91. Nevertheless, there is discussion whether the verses have been retouched. Schnackenburg suggests that the phrase "in the presence of his disciples" in v30 has been added by the Evangelist; Bultmann would argue the reverse. A majority of scholars (e.g., Bultmann, Fortna, Nicol, Schnackenburg) would attribute the final clause "that believing you may have life in his name" in v31 to the Evangelist. I am inclined to agree, although the issue cannot be decided definitively without a complete examination of the theology of the second and third editions.

Bultmann proposed that these verses were immediately preceded in the source by 12:37-38. This is unlikely.

[174]See the scholars referred to in the previous note.

characteristics of the signs material elsewhere in the gospel. Finally, the figure of the Beloved Disciple, a figure found only in later layers of the gospel material, plays a central role in the miracle. Consequently it is most likely that it was not part of the signs material.[175]

---

[175]The issue here is not whether a traditional miracle has been joined with a post-resurrection appearance in order to form the present narrative. I would agree that that may well be the case. Rather, the issue is whether this miracle can be traced to that particular groups of miracles that were included in and developed by the author of the signs material. I find no evidence for that. Rather, I would conclude that the author of a later edition took a miracle *from another source* and joined it with material dealing with a resurrection appearance.

4

The Structure and Theology
of the Signs Material

As can be seen from the previous chapter, a considerable amount of the signs material remains in the gospel. This material is sufficiently extensive to enable us to recover both the structure as well as the overall theology of this first edition of John. It is our purpose here to describe in some detail this structure and theology.

1. The Structure of the First Edition of the Gospel

In what follows, we will attempt to sketch in a preliminary way the overall orientation of the signs material. It should be recalled that such an effort will necessarily not be able to project what the full structure of the signs material was in its original form since it is clear that much of that material has been edited out of the present form of the gospel. Just as we called attention to the amount of material still present in the gospel, here we are forced to recall that we clearly do not have it all! We have called attention throughout chapter 3 to the various sections of the gospel where there is evidently a considerable amount of the original edition of the gospel now missing. Consequently, we must be extremely cautious in stating conclusions which depend for their validity on the *absence* of material. For example, there is no mention of the Holy Spirit in the material we have isolated. But it is methodologically improper to conclude that therefore the signs material did not have a theology of the Spirit. It may simply be that that material has been replaced by what the community saw to be a more adequate formulation of its Spirit doctrine at a later time since there is clearly a considerable focus on the role of the Spirit in the subsequent editions of the gospel.

There is a still further limitation to the inquiry as it can be conducted at the present time. While we have identified a considerable amount of material from the first edition, it is unlikely that we have identified *all* of the signs material, even as it exists in the present state of the gospel. Not all of the signs material would necessarily be so clearly marked by the characteristics we have identified. At least theoretically, a more complete analysis would require a comparison with all of the other material of the gospel, a task that is reserved for another time. It is my opinion that the foregoing analysis of the signs material has uncovered well over ninety percent of the material actually present in the gospel. Consequently, I do not think the analysis of the remainder of the gospel will yield any major surprises with regard to the content or theology of the signs material, but it is well to be aware of such possibilities.

It is good to be aware of the limitations of one's enterprise, and the cautions expressed above are an attempt to do that. But we should not conclude therefore that there is little that can be known of the structure and theology of the signs material. The reverse is true! I think it is possible to indicate quite clearly many of the main lines of its structure. The project here will be to do this in the form of a sketch, but as we shall see there is considerable gain to be had from such a sketch.

A. THE NATURE AND ARRANGEMENT OF THE SIGNS

Certainly the most important element of the signs material was the attention it called to the magnitude of Jesus' signs.[1] Two elements of the signs themselves call for attention. First, the manner in which the

---

[1] It is generally recognized that the signs source concentrated on the miracles of Jesus. However, there is some disagreement about whether the signs source focused on the *power* in the miracles. Brown (*Gospel* 525-26) sees the miracles in John as being primarily focused on symbolism and not as on acts of power helping to establish the kingdom. Schnackenburg on the other hand distinguishes between the source "in which particularly great and astonishing miracles were narrated" and later symbolic interpretation of them (II 95). Nicol (*Semeia* 42-44) would agree.

signs are presented calls attention to their greatness. Secondly, they are arranged so as to indicate that the miracles of Jesus got greater and greater throughout his ministry, thus becoming clearer and clearer demonstrations of his power.

In the call of Nathanael, we have only a "private sign," yet it demonstrates Jesus' supernatural foreknowledge. In the first Cana miracle, Jesus changes the water in each of six stone jars into wine. Here the "mathematics" of the miracle indicate its magnitude. Each jar is said to hold two or three measures, thus giving a total of about 120 gallons of wine.[2] Although the miraculous is introduced in a "modest and discreet way,"[3] the result of the miracle is stupendous. And not only is there a great quantity of wine, but this wine is better in quality than all the wine served previously (2:10).

Just as the number six focused attention on the magnitude of the sign at Cana, in the story of the Samaritan woman the indication that Jesus knew of all five husbands is intended to reveal that there is nothing about the life of this woman that he does not know. As the woman herself says to the townspeople: "Come, see a man who told me all that I ever did."

Although there is no single element in the healing of the official's son which focuses the attention on the miraculous, various features of the story combine to demonstrate the tremendous power of Jesus. The boy was "at the point of death;" he was in a town fifteen miles distant. We are told he was healed by a word, at the very hour when Jesus spoke.

The healing in chapter 5 again uses numbers to indicate the greatness of the miracle: the man had been ill for thirty-eight years.[4] Yet only a word from Jesus is enough to heal the man.

The element of magnitude associated with the multiplication of the loaves is perhaps dulled by our familiarity with this miracle which appears in all the gospels. But the enormity of the miracle is indicated by the several numerical references within the account. The men in the

---

[2]A "measure" was approximately eight gallons.

[3]Brown, *Gospel* 101.

[4]So also Schnackenburg, *Gospel*, II, 95. Brown (*Gospel* 207) describes the numbers as "one of the ways of underlining the hopelessness of the case." It is unlikely that there was a symbolism intended (e.g., Israel wandering in the desert for thirty-eight years) since the numbers are not further developed.

crowd numbered five thousand, not to mention the women and children. The amount of food necessary is indicated by the statement that not even two hundred days' wages would be enough to buy a sufficient amount of food so that each could have a mouthful. But from five barley loaves and two dried fishes, Jesus provides enough to feed the crowd to satisfaction, and, in addition, to fill twelve baskets with leftovers. Whether or not the numerical emphasis is the addition of the author or simply traditional, the overall effect of the miracle clearly is to put the power of Jesus into greater relief than in any of the previous miracles.

But it is with the last two miracles that the sense of the increasing magnitude of the signs becomes clearest. In chapter 9 we hear that the healing of one *born* blind was something never before heard of (9:32). The peculiar wording of the statement would seem to put particular emphasis on the fact that the man had been born blind. The implication is that one might well be able to heal a person who had been blinded later in life, but not one born blind. But Jesus does what has never been heard of. The magnitude of this miracle is further attested by the two other references to it in the material that follows. In 10:21, the crowds ask whether Jesus could be possessed since a possessed person could not heal the blind. In 11:37 the people of Judea speculate that if Jesus could have healed a blind person surely he could have prevented Lazarus from dying. In this last statement we are able to sense the crowds' "ranking" of the miracles: giving sight to the blind man is more difficult than healing the sick. But once Lazarus is dead there is no thought of his being raised (not even by Martha and Mary).

The final miracle is the climax of the ministry: the raising of Lazarus. Martha, as do the Judeans, expresses the conviction that Jesus could have healed Lazarus (11:21); she does not expect Lazarus to be raised from the dead. The reality and finality of the death of Lazarus is indicated in the statement of Martha not to roll back the stone from the grave because it was already the fourth day and there would be an odor (11:39). Yet Jesus calls forth Lazarus from death simply by the force of his word!

The magnitude of the Lazarus miracle is also attested by other features. It is this miracle which leads the Sanhedrin to take action. The Pharisees and the chief priests convene the Sanhedrin and make an official decision to kill Jesus because "If we allow him to continue thus, everyone will believe in him and the Romans will come and destroy the Temple and the nation" (11:48). In addition, the impression the miracle has made on the people is indicated by the fact that others who have heard about the miracle come out from Jerusalem (11:9) not only to see Jesus, but also (in the most curious detail of the gospel) to see Lazarus!

These features within the signs themselves are the strongest indication of the theological orientation of the material, but as we have seen repeatedly, they are only one part of the presentation of the signs. In addition to the signs themselves, there are the repeated references to the signs. We called attention to the various adjectives used to call attention to the magnitude of the signs: "such signs," "so many signs," "such great signs." Finally, it is important to see that this emphasis on the signs is one intended by the author of the signs material himself (and not just a feature of traditional material taken over by him). This is evident from the attention he calls to the signs when he speaks, at the conclusion of the public ministry, of Jesus having performed "so great signs" (12:37) and again in the conclusion to this gospel when he says that Jesus did many other signs but "these are written that you may believe" (20:31).

Thus throughout the signs material, there are consistent features indicating the great power evident in Jesus' signs and demonstrating the increasing magnitude of those signs, features which made them clearer and clearer proofs of his power. To these miracles, the only proper response in the eyes of the narrator is belief.

B. THE BELIEF OF EVER INCREASING NUMBERS OF PEOPLE

Closely related to the magnitude of the signs throughout Jesus' ministry is the reaction to them on the part of the witnesses. This is evidenced by the numerous statements of belief which demonstrate so regularly the reaction of the people (2:23; 3:26; 4:1, 39, 43-45, 53; 6:14; 7:31; 10:40-42; 11:45; 12:9, 18-19, 42). It is also demonstrated by the repeated emphasis on the diverse social and geographical origin of believers. This is present most explicitly in the stereotyped formulas of belief, but also elsewhere in the signs material: the people of Jerusalem (2:23; 7:31; 11:45; 12:9); various Judeans (3:26; 4:1; 10:40-42); Samaritans (4:39); people in Galilee (4:43, 53; 6:14); the Greeks (12:20-22); even the authorities (12:42). We have called attention to this repeatedly in the previous two chapters and there is no need to detail it here. However, the final climax of the public reaction to Jesus is captured well in the words of the Pharisees in 12:19 "You see that you can do nothing; look, the [whole] world has gone after him."

C. THE INCREASING HOSTILITY OF THE RELIGIOUS AUTHORITIES

Yet in spite of the signs and the people's reaction to them, we find that the reaction of the religious authorities to the signs provides another clear pattern within the signs material. Just as the signs and the belief of the people increase throughout the ministry, so does the hostility of the authorities. This hostility also culminates in the raising of Lazarus and eventuates in the arrest of Jesus in 18:1-3. We have detailed this in chapter 2 and so here we need only call attention to the way the increase in hostility parallels the development of the signs and the popular belief in Jesus.

All three of these elements coordinate to form the basic structure of the signs material: the signs of Jesus are greater and greater, inspiring greater and greater belief on the part of the common people. Yet alongside this increasing belief of the people there is the increasing hostility of the religious authorities, who eventually take action to put Jesus to death.

2. The Christology of the First Edition

If the presentation of the signs follows a definite pattern, the insight into the meaning of those signs is also portrayed consistently within the signs material. Recalling again that in the present form of the gospel we certainly do not have the signs material in its complete form, nevertheless, three elements can be identified which characterize the christology of the signs gospel: a low christology, a Moses typology, and a final recognition of Jesus as Messiah and Son of God.

A. A LOW CHRISTOLOGY

In what follows we will see that the signs material is marked by a low christology. In none of its articulation of the identity of Jesus does the signs material go beyond what could be called the traditional Jewish expectations regarding the promised one. This framework of traditional expectation is evident both in the titles given to Jesus as well as in the accusations that are made against him by the religious authorities.

1) Low Christology in the Titles Given to Jesus

We saw in our discussion of the theological differences between the first and second editions of John that the first edition concentrates on a low christology while the second edition introduces a much higher one. The discussion throughout the signs material is whether God is with Jesus (3:2), whether or not Jesus is from God (9:16, 29, 30), or whether God has spoken to him (9:29).[5] Jesus is spoken of as a prophet (4:19; 9:16) and "the" Prophet like Moses (6:14; 7:40, 52). He is spoken of as Messiah (1:41; 4:29; 7:26-27, 31, 41-42), as the one of whom Moses and the prophets spoke (1:45), the son of God (1:49) and the king of Israel (1:49).

Even Messiah, which in other contexts could be taken as an adequate title for Jesus, was first a traditional title. And as can be seen from its use alongside other titles, such as Elijah and the Prophet, the meaning of "Messiah" in the first edition is quite traditional. This is true also of the title "Son of God." Although the title could be used to refer to the ontological relationship of Jesus to the Father, this title could also be understood in a traditional sense insofar as it referred to the "special adoptive relationship" which was present between the Israelite King and Yahweh (cf 2 Sam 7:14; 1 Ch 22:10; Ps 22:7; 89:28) or even in some cases to the pious Israelite as an individual (Ps 73:15; Wis 2:13). In the first edition of the gospel of John, the tenor of the discussion never rises above that of the traditional meanings of these titles.

Although some of these titles (Messiah, Son of God) continued to be considered appropriate for describing Jesus even within the later edition of the gospel (as can be seen from their use both in the later

---

[5]Thus I would disagree with Nicol (*Semeia* 92) who states: "In S, however, Jesus performs all the semeia by his own authority, and God is never mentioned—Jesus himself stands in the place of God."

edition(s) of the gospel of John and elsewhere within early Christianity), within the first edition their meaning does not begin to approach in profundity that associated with them or with other descriptions of Jesus in the second edition of the gospel.

2)The Low Christology in the Accusations Against Jesus by the Religious Authorities

That the first edition of the gospel had a low christology is confirmed not only by a review of the titles that are given to Jesus, but also by the accusations that are leveled against Jesus by the religious authorities. The authorities assert that anyone who knows the Law will know that he cannot be worthy of belief (7:48-49). The Scriptures confirm that he cannot be the Prophet like Moses (7:52). In the discussion of the man born blind, the Pharisees reject the possiblity that Jesus is from God. His crime is that he is a sinner who violates the Sabbath. God has not spoken to Jesus (9:29). When Jesus is finally condemned by the Sanhedrin, it is not for religious reasons but lest the Romans come and destroy the Temple and the nation (11:48).

3) A Brief Comparison with Some Christological Statements of the Later Editions of the Gospel

When we turn to the later material of the gospel, we see that the accusations against Jesus are of a radically different type. The issue is his claim to identity with God, his claim to divinity. In every major discourse involving the "Jews," the issue is Jesus' claim to divinity! The "Jews" in 5:18 say that Jesus "called God his own Father, making himself equal with God." In the discussion with the "Jews" in 6:30-50, the issue is how Jesus can claim to have "come down from heaven." In chapter 8, when Jesus speaks about his word as witness to himself, the discussion begins with a discussion of knowing Jesus' Father (8:14-20). But almost immediately we find the words of Jesus that they will die in their sins unless they believe that "I Am" (8:24). There can be no higher title of Jesus than the application of this Septuagint form of the name of Yahweh to Jesus. Later in the same chapter (8:58), Jesus speaks of his existence before the time of Abraham and then repeats his appropriation of the "I Am" title for himself (cf also 1:1; 17:5). In chapter 10, the Jews again charge Jesus with blasphemy (10:33). They accuse him of blasphemy "because you, being a man, make yourself God."[6] Thus there can be no doubt that there is a radical distinction between the christological affirmations of the two editions of the gospel.

B. A MOSES TYPOLOGY: A BACKGROUND FOR THE JOHANNINE SIGNS

1) The Signs Given To Moses

The clearest background for the Johannine signs is that of the description in Exodus and Numbers of the signs given Moses.[7] The signs given Moses are to be a proof to the Israelites that Yahweh is with him. The rod which becomes a serpent and Moses' hand which becomes leprous are to be "signs" that the Israelite people may "believe that the Lord, the God of their fathers, the God of Abraham, the God of Isaac, and the God of Jacob, has appeared to you" (4:1-5, cf. also vv7-9). In addition Moses is to work signs before the Pharaoh to show that Yahweh has appeared to him (7:3).

Num 14:11 also speaks explicitly of this theology of signs. The Israelites, now in the desert, have begun to grumble against the Lord and have ceased to believe: "And the Lord said to Moses, 'How long will this people despise me? And how long will they not believe in me, in spite of all the signs which I have wrought among them?'" In Num 14:22 we hear that those Israelites "'who have seen my glory and my signs which I wrought in Egypt and in the wilderness and yet have put

---

[6]This continues to be true within the trial of Jesus before Pilate where the Jews urge Jesus' death "because he has made himself Son of God."

[7]This was not always recognized. At one time it was thought that the Hellenistic "divine man" more closely paralleled the Johannine miracle tradition. For a presentation of the chief characteristics of the "divine man" theology as well as of the characteristics in John which suggested a parallel, see Nicol, *Semeia* 48-51, and the literature referred to there. Nicol himself presents a detailed review of the material he would assign to the first edition ("S") and finds so many Jewish elements as to exclude the possibility of a divine man presentation.

The Moses typology in the gospel has been the topic of frequent discussion. See especially T. Glasson, *Moses in the Fourth Gospel* (Studies in Biblical Theology 40; London: SCM, 1963); H. Teeple, *The Mosaic Eschatological Prophet* (JBL Monograph Series 10; Philadelphia: Society of Biblical Literature, 1957) and W. Meeks, *The Prophet King. Moses Traditions and the Johannine Christology* (NovTSupp 14; Leiden: E.J. Brill, 1967).

me to the proof these ten times and have not hearkened to my voice'" will not be allowed to enter the promised land.

These examples could be multiplied,[8] however, the theology of the Mosaic signs is clear. First, the signs are given by the Lord to Moses precisely to prove his divine mission both to his own people and also to the hostile Pharaoh. Second, they reveal the glory of the Lord. Third, they are meant to inspire belief. Fourth, the signs also result in unbelief because Yahweh hardens the hearts of some (e.g., the Pharaoh).

2) Parallels with the Johannine Signs

When we compare this presentation with that of the signs in John we find a remarkable parallel. First, there is the repeated discussion of the meaning of the signs of Jesus in terms of his being "from God" (3:2; 9:16, 24, 29, 31). Second, in John, the signs are said to reveal the glory of God (2:11, also implicit in 12:41-43). Third, there is the belief that the signs inspire. We have seen this repeatedly above. Here we notice that at the time of the Exodus the people believe but the Pharaoh does not. When they are in the desert, even the people fail to believe. In the signs' gospel, it is the people who by and large believe, but the authorities fail to believe. This failure to believe becomes the motif with which the public ministry of Jesus closes, soon after the decision of the authorities to put Jesus to death (12:37). This failure to believe is described in the words of Isaiah as due to the blindness and hardness of heart of the authorities. Thus the religious authorities in John become the parallel of the Pharaoh.

3) Other Evidence of Moses Typology

In addition to the portrayal of Jesus' signs against the backdrop of Moses and the Exodus, several times the Moses typology becomes explicit in the portrayal of Jesus.

a) References to the Prophet like Moses.

The Prophet like Moses as an eschatological figure is based on the statement of Deut 18:15-18: "The Lord your God will raise up for you

---

[8]Also 4:1-31 passim; 7:3, 9; 10:1-2; 11:2, 9, etc.

a prophet like me from among you, from your brethren—him shall you heed." Although this statement occurs in what was originally intended to be general legislation concerning the role of the prophet in Israel, it later came to be taken as a prediction of a specific prophet to come in the eschatological age. The figure of this prophet plays a prominent role in the gospel of John, a prominence not found in the synoptics. The title itself appears five times: 1:21, 25; 6:14; 7:40.[9] This concentration on the identification of Jesus with the prophet is all the more striking in the light of the fact that such identification occurs only in John (and only in the signs material!).[10]

b) Explicit References to Moses.

In the discussion with the blind man, the Pharisees make an explicit comparison (obviously intended to be ironical) between being a disciple of "that person" and being a disciple of Moses. The Pharisees claim that they follow Moses but that the man formerly blind is a disciple of Jesus. The Pharisees know that God has spoken to Moses, but they do not know where this man is from. That is, they ignore the thorough-going witness of the signs and fail to see that in a pre-eminent sense God was with Jesus also. Of course, given the complete orientation of the signs material, the reader has been amply prepared to see Jesus as the one like Moses (only superior) and so recognizes their error.[11]

---

[9]It will be recalled that there is strong textual evidence for the definite article before "prophet" in this verse. In addition two other times Jesus is referred to as "a" prophet (4:19 by the Samaritan woman and 9:17 by the man born blind). Although these are not specifically associated with "the" Prophet, it is not unlikely that these were intended to be evidence of partial recognition of the status of Jesus. In other words if they recognized Jesus as a prophet attested by signs (as each of them clearly does) then it would be a short step to the association of this prophet with the Prophet-like-Moses.

[10]There are several references, esp in Mt and Lk to Jesus as a prophet (Mt 11:9; 13:57; 16:14; 21:11; Mk 8:28; Lk 7:16, 39; 9:8, 19; 24:19), but nowhere does the title "the" Prophet occur.

[11]Curiously it is the second and later editions of John which make the Moses typology most explicit. In fact all but two of the explicit mentions of Moses occur outside of the signs material (1:17; 3:14; 5:45-46; 6:32; 7:19-24). The only signs material in which Moses is mentioned explicitly is 9:27-28. Yet this frequency of the name of Moses does not give an adequate picture. In these instances it is not so much Moses himself who is the point of comparison but the Law given through Moses.

Perhaps the text closest to comparing the two is 1:17 (the Law came through Moses, but grace and truth came through Jesus). This verse does not come from the

C. JESUS AS MESSIAH AND SON OF GOD.

In spite of the clear emphasis on the parallels between Moses and Jesus within the signs material, it is not correct to see a Moses typology as the ultimate identification intended by the author. Throughout the signs material there are repeated references to other titles, and it is ultimately these which are judged more adequate.[12]

Within the scene of the call of the first disciples, we find curiously enough no mention of the prophet like Moses. Rather, Jesus is identified first as Messiah (1:42) and then in a more general sense as "the one of whom Moses in the law and also the prophets wrote" (1:45). Finally, Nathanael, in what is evidently intended to be the climax of the passage, identifies Jesus as "king of Israel" and "son of God." Of course it is correct to say that within the signs material, these latter titles do not have the same implications that are attached to them within the context of the later editions. Nevertheless, they affirm that Jesus is the

---

signs material. In 3:14, Jesus is not compared to Moses but to the serpent which Moses lifted up. In 5:45-47, Moses is the one who writes about Jesus; there is no actual comparison between Moses and Jesus. In 7:19-24, the focus is on the true meaning of the Law: if the Jews understood the Law they would not condemn Jesus for healing on the Sabbath. The Discourse on Bread (6:30-50) seems at first to compare Moses and Jesus. But even here the comparison is really between Moses and the Father as persons who give bread. In this discourse, Jesus is the bread rather than the giver. Consequently even here the Moses typology is not as explicit and direct as in the signs material.

[12]Fortna (*Signs* 230-31) suggests a Mosaic background for the signs material. However he prefers to see this as one part of a more general Old Testament typology involving allusions also to figures like Elijah, Elisha, and Joseph. While I would agree that such allusions may be present, I would see a continuing problem to be the articulation of the relation between the Moses typology and the final titles given to Jesus.

Nicol (*Semeia* 79-94) attempts to describe a line of development in which signs which were originally associated with a Mosaic prophetic figure come also to be associated with a kingly figure who is called the anointed one. While this is in a general sense true, it is difficult to establish on grounds outside of the NT use of the titles. It would seem certain from Jn 7:40-44 that the prophetic figure continued to be distinct from the "anointed one." The complexity of the issue is underscored by the fact that in some traditions, as W. Meeks has shown, Moses is thought of in kingly terms Likewise, in both Jewish literature of the time and in the New Testament, David the king was also considered to be a prophet! See, for example, the discussion in M. de Jonge, "The Earliest Christian Use of *Christos.* Some Suggestions," *NTS* 32 (1986) 321-343 esp 334-335. The precise relationship between these two eschatological figures (as well as between the corresponding titles) in the understanding of earliest Christianity is yet to be definitively articulated.

expected one of Israel. All of these titles are able to be integrated with one another: the Messiah, who was to be king of Israel and therefore (adoptive) son of God, is the one of whom Moses and the prophets wrote. It is in terms of these titles that the narrator speaks again in his conclusion: "... these [signs] are written that you may believe that Jesus is the Christ, the Son of God..." (20:31). The title of Messiah also appears on the lips of the Samaritan woman (4:25, 29).[13] It is the fact that Jesus tells the woman her past life that makes her think of him as the Messiah since the Messiah "will show us all things."

The next time the title of Messiah is discussed is chapter 7. There it, along with the title of the prophet, becomes a major topic of discussion. In 7:26-27 the first (in this chapter) feature of popular expectation of the Messiah becomes evident: "...when the Christ appears, no one will know where he comes from." This is used as an argument against Jesus being the Messiah since they know where he comes from. In the next passage of signs material, however, yet another feature of the Messiah comes to the fore: "When the Christ appears will he perform more signs than this man has done?" (7:31).[14] Finally, in 7:41-42 a comparison is made whether Jesus is the prophet or the Christ. The fact that Jesus is from Galilee argues against his being the Messiah since the Scripture says that the Christ is descended from David and comes from Bethlehem.[15] We learn very little in terms of the christological

[13]As was explained in chapter three, I am inclined to think that the title of prophet in 4:19 is an addition by the editor in order to introduce his addition in vv20-24 and that the original title was that of Messiah. The title of prophet is applied to Jesus in 9:17. There it is part of the signs material.

[14]This and other Jewish expectations about the Messiah according to the Fourth Gospel have been studied by M. de Jonge in his article by that title [*NTS* 19 (1972-73) 246-70, now reprinted in *Stranger* 77-116]. Pointing to the fact that the Messiah is not associated specifically with signs in Jewish expectations, de Jonge (and others) conclude that the statement in 7:31 reflects a Christian rather than a Jewish belief.

While the association of signs with the Messiah is not found in a specific form in Jewish writings, it does not seem necessary to find such a specific passage since the concept of a norm for determining the legitimacy of the Messiah/prophet is itself typical of Jewish thought.

[15]This statement has given rise to much discussion. Is it intended to be ironical, in the sense that the reader is expected to know of the Davidic descent of Jesus and his birth in Bethlehem and so exhibiting the ignorance of the common people? Or does the text actually betray an ignorance of the tradition of the Bethlehem birth of Jesus even on the part of the author? Since the answers to these questions in the current text

views of the author from these exchanges however, simply because they are so fragmentary and inconclusive. The one piece of new information is that the signs can be seen as indicative of the Christ as well as of the Prophet.[16]

The discussion in chapter 7 is the last mention of the title within the signs material apart from the affirmation of Jesus as Christ and Son of God in the conclusion to the gospel. There we get a "controlling" view of the previous discussion in the affirmations about Jesus made by the author. Jesus is the Christ, the Son of God, and in the last analysis it is this, more than the previous discussion of the title within the signs material, that clarifies the way in which the discussion of the prophet like Moses is to be associated with Jesus. Since the title of "the" prophet does not occur, it becomes clear that for the author of the signs material the elaboration of the Mosaic background of Jesus is just that, a typological background. But the author's basic affirmation is the one which is standard throughout early Christianity: Jesus is the Christ, the son of God.[17]

D. JESUS AND JOHN THE BAPTIST

Because of the consistent (and unique within the gospel tradition) emphasis on a comparison between Jesus and John, many think that the gospel had for at least part of its purpose, the refutation of followers

of the gospel are provided by the later editors, it is not possible to determine the intention of the first author.

[16]We are speaking here of the view within the gospel itself. There is perhaps an historical problem in that there are no texts outside of the New Testament which associate the working of signs with the appearance of the Davidic Messiah (M. de Jonge *Stranger* 91-94). I am not convinced, however, of de Jonge's conclusion that the discussion in 7:31-32 reflects an inter-Christian dispute.

[17]The absence of apocalyptic elements in the signs material is noteworthy. This is one indication of the difference in portrayal between the Johannine miracles and those of Mark. However, this does not mean that the miracles should be viewed against the background of the Hellenistic model of the divine man (*theios anēr*). This conception of the *theios anēr* itself has been called into question by C. Holladay, *THEIOS ANĒR* in Hellenistic-Judaism (Missoula: Scholars Press, 1977). In addition it should be remembered that there is a strong tradition of signs and wonders in the parts of the Old Testament which are not apocalyptic. Therefore to say "non-apocalyptic" does not imply "Hellenistic."

of John who continued to argue that John and not Jesus was the Messiah. This is a difficult issue, made more difficult by the fact that, within the gospel, material dealing with John occurs in all three editions of the gospel. We see clear evidence that the role of John was of interest to the author of the second edition also. For example, it is in the second edition (3:26-29) that we find the theological elaboration of John's role vis-a-vis Jesus. And it is there that we find (5:33-36a) that John is to be counted as a witness to Jesus, although not an essential one. In addition, it is within the material added to the Prologue (which undoubtedly came from the last stratum of the gospel) that we also find evidence of John witnessing to the light. Each of these references to John the Baptist clearly has to be judged independently and within the context of the theology of the material in question.

But there is no evidence of a polemic against John the Baptist in the signs material. John's role as a herald is clear and he is contrasted with Jesus as one who "did no sign" (10:41).

Regarding the references to John in the signs material we may with some certainty affirm that in these passages we have vestiges of a very early (and possibly more accurate?) tradition both about the calling of the first disciples and also about the relationship between the ministry of Jesus and John as well as the possibility that Jesus himself baptized. That this tradition was not seen to conform to other elements of the early tradition is evident from the "correction" found in 4:2, inserted at a later time, which states that Jesus himself did not baptize but only his disciples.

E. SUMMARY OF THE THEOLOGY OF SIGNS

Evident within the signs gospel is a theology which is very Jewish and very traditional. It was written for Jews against a backdrop of the traditional view of Moses: Jesus was the Christ and the Son of God, but he was also the Prophet like Moses, who would save his people in the last days, just as Moses had saved them at the Exodus.

It has close affinity with the Baptist movement and records that the first disciples of Jesus had previously been followers of John the Baptist. It gives us details of the life of Jesus that we know from no other source: that he himself baptized and was seen as a rival to John the Baptist for a time; that he made several trips to Jerusalem and that his ministry extended longer than is described in the synoptics.

It is also a document that shows considerable familiarity with the customs [the water for the footwashing 2:6] and feast of the Jews [it is the only gospel to mention the feast of Tabernacles (7:2) and the feast of Dedication (10:22)]. In addition, it specifically identifies the places where the events took place (Aenon near Salim, Jacob's well, Bethesda, etc.).

Theologically, it is a document with a preoccupation with christology, at least as far as we can tell from the material that survives within the present edition of the gospel. Strikingly absent are references to the Spirit which so dominate the presentation of the later editions. The christology, as it can be judged from what remains, focuses almost exclusively on the importance of the miraculous. Yet it must be said that the document is positive and could well have served as a missionary (or kerygmatic) document; the presentation of the signs is "so that you might believe" (20:30).[18]

3. Place of Composition, the Date, and the Character of the "Signs Community"

A. PLACE OF COMPOSITION

The signs material focuses on the ministry in Judea and was very likely the product of a Christian community there. This emphasis on Judea is evident in several ways. First, Jesus is presented as making regular trips to Judea/Jerusalem and as spending considerable time there each trip. While it is difficult to know exactly the number of trips to Jerusalem in the signs material,[19] there are clear indications of trips in chapter 2 (cf 2:23), followed by a withdrawal to Galilee (cf 4:1ff). Jesus then appears again in Jerusalem at the feast of Tabernacles (chapter 7). He withdraws across the Jordan (10:40-42) and then returns

---

[18]Nicol (*Semeia* 144) correctly points out that in this sense it is considerably different from the later material of the gospel where there is little hope of conversion and where there is little positive estimation of "the Jews."

[19]The major problem is the trip stated in 5:1. As was mentioned in the discussion in chapter 3 above, it is possible that this material originally occurred after the multiplication of the loaves in the signs edition and that the order has been reversed in the second edition. But a resolution of this problem requires a detailed study of the second edition.

to Bethany again (12:1-11) and then eventually to Jerusalem (12:12ff).

Apart from the trips themselves, the ministry of Jesus is associated more with Judea than with Galilee (or any other area). Only the changing of water to wine at the wedding in Cana, the identification of the Samaritan woman's past life, the healing of the official's son and the multiplication of the loaves are described as taking place outside Judea. The remainder of the material focuses on activity in Judea: the call of the first disciples (1:39-49),[20] the discussion with Nicodemus (3:1-3), Jesus' baptizing ministry (3:22-24),[21] the healing of the paralytic at the pool (5:1-9), the discussions at Tabernacles (chapter 7 *passim*), the healing of the blind man (9:1-41), the withdrawal across the Jordan (10:40-42), the return to Bethany where he heals Lazarus (11:1-45), the withdrawal to Ephraim (11:54), the return to Jerusalem before the feast (12:1-20).[22] Finally, there is the evident location of the post-resurrection appearances (except for the appearance in chapter 21) in Judea.[23]

In addition there is the mention of the Judeans by name in 3:25 and throughout chapters 11 and 12, and possibly in 1:19. This is unique to the gospel of John.

B. DATING OF THE SIGNS MATERIAL

In spite of the fact that the gospel of John is known for the several anachronistic features which give the impression of a report far

---

[20]This represents a considerably different view from that of the synoptics. Not only are the first of Jesus' disciples portrayed as previously disciples of John the Baptist, they are presented as in Judea and with the Baptist at the time of their call rather than in Galilee fishing.

[21]The withdrawal of Jesus to Galilee is only because of increasing hostility of the Pharisees (4:1-54).

[22]Of course the last supper and the passion occur in Jerusalem, but these are located there in all of the gospels.

[23]The majority of the resurrection material in the present version of the gospel occurs in Judea and this is certainly significant. However, much of the resurrection material in the present version of the gospel is not from the signs material, consequently it is uncertain whether the original version of the appearances had the same orientation. However, given the emphasis on Judea elsewhere in the original version, it is certainly likely.

removed from the ministry of Jesus itself,[24] the signs material contains much information which is historically specific and geographically accurate (particularly within Judea!) and which is not found elsewhere in the gospels. This confirms the association of the signs material with Judea and in addition indicates its early age.

First, we have called attention to the consistent presentation of certain religious terms first in Hebrew and then in Greek translation. This needs no further comment.

Second, geographical references are generally much more specific in this material than in the remainder of the gospel. We know through the signs material some places not otherwise mentioned in the gospels: Bethany beyond the Jordan (1:28),[25] Aenon near Salim (3:23),[26] Jacob's well (4:5-6),[27] the Sheep Pool at Bethesda (5:2), Siloam (9:7),[28] Ephraim (11:54),[29] the Stone Pavement (19:13). All of these are or show signs of being in Judea.

Some of the locations mentioned in John, which were previously considered to be simply symbolic creations, have been confirmed by archaeologists relatively recently.[30] The mention of the Stone Pavement

---

[24]These anachronistic features include the location of the official expulsion from the synagogue within the ministry of Jesus, the anachronistic and inaccurate use of "Jews" to refer to religious authorities, the abstract form of Jesus' words and discourses (so different from those of the synoptics), the nature of the theological issues (esp high christology, the references to "your" Law), the lack of narrative sense (for example, in the hostility of the Jews). All of these are more appropriate to the end of the century than to the ministry of Jesus. We have called attention before to the comments of scholars (e.g., Dodd, *Tradition*) that the gospel on the other hand contains information which seems peculiarly accurate and early. Our identification of the material of the signs edition also provides an objective way of accounting for these changes since it will be noted that all of these later, anachronistic features occur outside the signs material in the later editions of the gospel.

[25]This is not the town near Jerusalem mentioned in 11:18. There are no longer any remains of this Bethany.

[26]The place is yet unidentified.

[27]The reference to Gerizim, however, does not seem to come from the earliest material.

[28]This pool is situated at the southern end of the eastern hill of Jerusalem. Into it flowed the water from the spring of Gihon. It is mentioned in Isaiah 8:6.

[29]The location of this town is uncertain.

[30]The discovery is described in detail in J. Jeremias, *Rediscovery*. The pool was trapezoidal and 165-220 feet wide and 315 feet long. It was divided by a partition in the

(19:13) as the place where the judgment seat of Pilate was located has also been identified by many with the stone pavement of the lower level of the fortress Antonia.[31] All of this points to an early date for the signs material and its association with the southern part of Palestine. The dating of the complete gospel is generally put between 90-110AD. One of the main reasons for assigning a date of 90AD is the reference to synagogue exclusion which seems to have become formal about that time. However, if this is the case, then clearly the signs material antedates 90AD. No more precise dating is possible although a date of perhaps 70-80AD for the signs material is not unreasonable.

C. CHARACTER OF THE "SIGNS COMMUNITY"

The Johannine community was Jewish-Christian in composition. The clearest evidence for this comes not from the signs material but from the second stage of the community's history where we find the bitter struggle over exclusion from the synagogue. However, it is most likely that the community which gave birth to the signs material was the same as that responsible for the second edition. The Jewish background is evident of course in the Old Testament background of the portrayal of the ministry of Jesus, the Moses typology, the use of the Old Testament. In addition, there is the constant focus on the ministry of Jesus in southern Palestine. These features would tend to confirm the theory that the community was Jewish-Christian.

About the identity of the author, nothing can be discovered from the signs material itself.

center, running from side to side. Because of the central partition it is also possible to speak of there being two pools (the place name as given in the Dead Sea Scrolls [3Q15] is plural) although the gospel text indicates that it was also spoken of as a single pool. There were colonnades on the four sides and on the partition. These are the porticoes mentioned in the gospel. Stairways in the corners permitted descent into the pool.

[31] The identification of this site, however, is not as certain as is that of Bethesda. The location of the praetorium itself is somewhat disputed. Some would associate the praetorium with the Herodian Palace on the West Hill of Jerusalem. There is mention in Josephus and in Philo that this was the usual residence of the Roman procurators. Others would identify the praetorium with the fortress Antonia, a Hasmonean castle. This was just north of the temple and was the place where Roman troops were stationed during the festivals. This is the location where the stone pavement, an area of about 2,300 square yards, was discovered. For a discussion see Brown, *Gospel* 881-82.

The mention of the portico of Solomon (10:23) should perhaps be grouped with the accurate references to locations in Jerusalem not mentioned elsewhere in the gospels; however, its association with the signs material is not certain.

5

A Glimpse at
the Second Edition of John

Up to this point, we have focused our attention on the first edition of the gospel of John, how it was composed, its theology, its background, the date of its writing, and its place of origin. But as we have pointed out, the signs gospel is only the first of the three editions of the gospel.

It has been said repeatedly in this book that it was not the intention of the original author to employ the signs as symbols or as pointers to some reality of a spiritual nature beyond themselves. Yet R. Brown states: "In John the primary function of the miracles seems to be one of symbolism."[1] Explaining this more concretely, Brown says, "If Jesus heals the official's son and grants him life (iv 46-54), the explanation that follows this miracle and that of Bethesda makes it clear that the life which Jesus communicates is *spiritual* life (v 21, 24). If Jesus restores the blind man's sight, the interchange that follows (ix 35-41) shows that Jesus has given him spiritual sight and reduced the Pharisees to spiritual blindness."[2]

But I have contended throughout that this is true only in the sense that the original version of the gospel was taken over and re-edited from a different theological perspective. It is not because the term "sign" has anything of the symbolic in it, but only because an author

[1]Brown, *Gospel*, 526.
[2]Brown, *Gospel*, 529.

with a different theological perspective saw *everything* on the material level as symbolic of something more real and more important in the spiritual realm. That this is true is evident both from the fact that not all of the signs are developed symbolically and from the fact that elements of the gospel which are not miraculous are developed as symbols of the spiritual.

In spite of the explanation given by Brown and quoted above, the healing of the man at Bethesda is less an example of Jesus' ability to give life than is the Lazarus miracle. And in fact it is the Lazarus miracle which contains the more explicit elaboration of the symbolism of physical life and eternal life. Some of the signs are developed symbolically (the ability to give bread, the ability to give sight, the ability to give life) but others are not (the healing of the official's son, the healing of the man at Bethesda).[3]

Sometimes the symbolism is not directly connected with the power of Jesus demonstrated in the sign but only tangentially related to it (the giving of living water, the spiritual worship, the spiritual food in the story of the Samaritan woman). In only one case did we find the possibility of an inherent symbolism: the changing of water into (eschatological?) wine at Cana. And curiously there the symbolism is not developed!

Consequently on the basis of a critical understanding of the editorial history of the gospel, we have come to see that the use of symbolism (with some minor exceptions) is something which came into the gospel after the time of the first edition. The study of these subsequent editions is, of course, the subject of another book and cannot be treated in detail here. However, we can look at a few examples of how the second edition incorporated the signs. Such examples are instructive of the process by which the second edition was composed and may ultimately shed more light on the first edition.

What follows is meant to be suggestive of the orientation of the second edition. All of the passages referred to below occur outside the

---

[3]Some (e.g., Brown) have suggested that the healing of the official's son and the healing of the man at Bethesda are meant to be related to the two themes of 5:20-30, the ability to give life and to judge. This very well may be true. Nevertheless, this is not a symbolic development (as is the comparison of material and spiritual bread in chapter 6). If anything, the two miracles are *examples* of those two powers, not symbols of them.

criteria whereby given material is attributed to the second rather than the third edition. Detailed presentation of the characteristics of the third edition vis-a-vis those of the second and first editions must await the commentary referred to in the introduction.

1. The Circumstances of the Second Edition

The second edition took place at a critical time in the history of the community, at the time when the community was experiencing a wrenching separation from its native Judaism. About the year 90AD, the Jews determined through a series of "Benedictions" that those who were Christians should be expelled from the synagogue. There are clear indications in the gospel of John that this also entailed persecution, perhaps even martyrdom for one's beliefs.[4] In the material of the second edition, there is such hostility evident on the part of "the Jews" and such defensiveness evident on the part of the community that it is clear that the community was intent on explaining its own belief in a legitimating way and at the same time explaining why such persuasive grounds could be so completely rejected by their fellow Jews.

2. The Theology of the Second Edition

During this period of persecution and of the obviously permanent rejection of Jesus as Messiah on the part of their fellow Jews, the Johannine community took its reflection on the mystery of Jesus and of belief in him to a theological level considerably deeper than that of the first edition of the gospel. Whereas in the first edition of the gospel, the signs had been the chief indicator of who Jesus was, the community now stressed another element of the tradition: the role of the Spirit in

---

[4]9:18-23, 12:42, and 16:4 are the classic texts which illustrate this set of conditions. The first of these (9:18-23) is clearly identified as coming from the second edition by the repeated use of "Jews" in the hostile sense. The second is complicated by the mixture of terms characteristic of the first and second editions which indicates that the passage has been edited still further (probably at the time of the third edition). The most influential study of this Johannine context of persecution and synagogue exclusion is that of J.L. Martyn, *History and Theology in the Fourth Gospel* (Nashville: Abington, 1979).

belief. In the second edition, the question of belief and unbelief is addressed on a level considerably more profound than *apparently* was the case at the time of the first edition.

From the second edition of the gospel we see that the community concluded that it was not simply seeing signs that brought about belief; belief had a broader scope and deeper foundation. In addition to the signs there were other "witnesses" (the term used in the second edition) to Jesus: there was John the Baptist (although he was not an essential witness), the words of Jesus himself, the "works" (the term used in the second edition), and the scriptures (cf. 5:31-40). But beneath and behind all of these was the Spirit. Unless one possessed the Spirit, one could not respond to any of the witnesses with belief.

A. THE SPIRIT AND BELIEF

Although the Spirit had certainly been part of the tradition from the beginning, as it had for all of Christianity, the role of the Spirit in the Johannine tradition at the time of the second edition becomes all important. This becomes evident in the way the signs material is elaborated. The most important passage for understanding the view of the Spirit at the time of the second edition of the gospel is the Nicodemus episode.

We observed above that 3:1-2 belonged to the signs material within the gospel. One of the major reasons for identifying a break in "strata" after 3:2 is the fact that the response of Jesus to the question of Nicodemus really does not take up his question about the signs.[5] Nicodemus asks about the value of signs, and Jesus speaks of the need for rebirth. Two elements of this discourse are particularly important. First, there is a structure within the ensuing dialogue that becomes paradigmatic for other such dialogues within the gospel. However, here it occurs in a fuller form. Jesus tells Nicodemus that he needs to be reborn. Nicodemus, misunderstanding Jesus, takes the statement on the purely physical level.

The second important element in the discourse is the content itself. This discourse is essential for understanding the "epistemology" of the

---

[5]As we have seen, this is a common pattern within the gospel, occuring here, in 3:27; 7:28; 33; and 12:23.

second edition. Jesus repeats his statement that Nicodemus must be reborn of the water and the Spirit and unless this occurs he will not be able to "see" (v3) or "enter" (v5) the Kingdom of God. Why? Because (v6) "that which is born of the flesh is flesh, and that which is born of the Spirit is Spirit." Jesus then goes on to explain that the Spirit is like the wind: "The wind blows where it will, and you hear the sound of it, but you do not know whence it comes or whither it goes; so it is with every one who is born of the Spirit."

Jesus here is calling for a new form of existence. Just as physical birth involves reception of a "natural" spirit from God, so spiritual (re)birth by means of reception of the Spirit is necessary to live on a spiritual plane. It is only then that one is able to "see" or "enter" the Kingdom of God. Not only does this dialogue with Nicodemus involve a misunderstanding, but also it contains an explanation of what causes the misunderstanding (lack of rebirth from the Spirit) and what its cure is (obviously, birth from the Spirit). This is the principle by which one will perceive the "real" meaning of Jesus' words (and so avoid misunderstanding) necessary to make the transition from the fleshly/material perception of reality (and indeed existence on that level of reality).[6] It is the principle which is operative in all such misunderstandings throughout the gospel![7]

The additions to the signs material in the story of the Samaritan woman were described above, noting that vv10-15, 20-24, 31-38 and 40-42 were editorial additions. The consistent pattern of editing is patent. In the first addition (vv10-15), Jesus asks the woman for a drink of water then reverses the procedure by offering her "living" water. The woman takes living water on the purely physical, material

---

[6]In discussion of the Nicodemus episode, there is a tendency to focus on the title Jesus uses to correct Nicodemus [cf M. de Jonge, "Nicodemus and Jesus: Some Observations on Misunderstanding and Understanding in the Fourth Gospel" (ch 2 of *Stranger* 29-48)]. However, there are really two facets to the discussion, each of which is equally important: vv3-10 discuss the "how" (birth from the Spirit); vv11-21 discuss the Son of man and the proper response to him. See, for example J. Neyrey, "John III—A Debate over Johannine Epistemology and Christology," *Nov T* 23, 2 (1981) esp 118-121. De Jonge's article is very insightful regarding various aspects of the low christology discussed in detail in the previous chapter, particularly when read against the backdrop of the literary analysis I have provided.

[7]Compare the way such additions involving material of the second edition consistently take the issues of the first edition to the level of the spiritual and cause misunderstanding: 4:10-15, 19-24, 31-38; 6:30-50; 7:28-30, 33-36, etc.

level to refer to a spring. In fact, the living water that he is offering her is the Spirit (cf 7:37-39; 19:34), the principle of "eternal" life (v14). However, lacking the very Spirit (i.e., living water, cf. 7:37-39) that Jesus speaks of, the woman sees it only on the material level and continues to misunderstand when Jesus says that this water will mean she will never be thirsty again. The woman responds on the purely material level that it would be nice not to have to come to the well every day for water.

The second insertion is handled the same way. First, the woman asks a question (v20) about the correct physical place of worship (Gerizim or Jerusalem). Jesus responds by saying that the time is coming and is here now, when the true worshipers will worship neither on Gerizim nor in Jerusalem, but "in Spirit and in truth." Jesus adds that it is this sort of worship that the Father seeks because God is spirit and he seeks those who will worship in Spirit and in truth. Once again the woman poses a question on the physical level and the response of Jesus is on the spiritual. Although this episode does not detail the misunderstanding as closely as in the previous two passages, the parallel is clear: it is worship in the Spirit which is important, not "physical" worship.

Finally, in the last major addition to the story, the disciples themselves become for a time the victims of misunderstanding. They bring food from town for Jesus (vv31, cf v8). He responds that he has a food they know not of. They in turn take him on the purely material level and suppose that someone else has brought him food. Once again the topic of Jesus' speech is misunderstood by taking it on the material level when in fact it should be understood on the spiritual.[8]

Such examples could be multiplied. A review of chapter 7, noting the various passages of signs material and the way they are elaborated by material from the second edition, provides another clear parallel. Throughout the chapter a series of discussions takes place in which the opponents of Jesus constantly pose questions (in the first edition) on a purely material level and Jesus (in the first edition) on a purely material

---

[8]The purpose of the addition in vv40-42 is clear. It focuses on the importance of the word of Jesus as opposed to his "signs." Such a correction of simple signs faith is evident throughout: cf 1:50-51; 2:24-25; 4:44; 4:50 (where the belief in the "word" of Jesus seems to be what redeems the miracle from the excessive focus on "signs and wonders").

level and Jesus (in a passage of the second edition) provides answers on a spiritual plane, resulting in continued misunderstanding. The analysis of chapter 7 clearly shows that the process of symbolization is not restricted to the signs material itself but rather was a technique used in a variety of material by the author of the second edition as a means of demonstrating the role of the Spirit for belief (and unbelief).

B. THE WORKS AND THE WITNESSES TO JESUS

If the Spirit is the principle of belief, the witnesses to Jesus are the means of belief in the second edition. This new view of the "evidence for Jesus" is given paradigmatically in Jn 5:31-40. First, there is John the Baptist (5:33-36a). He witnessed to the truth. But his witness is not essential because there is a still greater witness. Second, there are the works which the Father has given Jesus to bring to completion (v36b). They testify that the Father has sent Jesus. Third, there is the witness of the Father himself whose word they have heard through Jesus but which the Jews do not have abiding in them because they do not believe Jesus (vv37-38). Finally, there are the Scriptures which witness to Jesus (vv39-40).

The understanding of this larger context of belief is important for understanding the second edition as a whole, for it is these witnesses and the response to them which serves to structure much of the second edition. While the disciples are shown to respond to these witnesses, the Jews do not, in spite of all the opportunities that are given them. Nevertheless, within the second edition, the signs of Jesus are not neglected, they are put within a larger context of belief. Now designated as "works" they are not the exclusive focus of attention but constitute one of four witnesses to Jesus.

A brief look at one aspect of the belief of the disciples in the second edition illustrates well both how the witnesses structure the presentation and how the material of the first edition is incorporated within this larger context.

It is one of the curiosities of the gospel of John that the disciples' belief is presented as coming so easily and so early within the gospel. At the beginning of the gospel the disciples are the focus of attention, appearing in every pericope between their first mention in 1:35 and 2:22. Yet after 2:22 their role is minimal until the Last Supper where they again come to play a major role.[9] The role of the disciples in 1:35-2:22 is therefore intended to be of some importance to the author.

In the first instance (1:35-50), the disciples come to Jesus on the basis of the witness of John the Baptist. Although in turn one disciple gets another, the beginning of the process clearly is the witness of John. This material which comes from the first edition is shown to have given rise to the first belief of the disciples.

Immediately following this first meeting with Jesus, the disciples and Jesus appear at a wedding feast at Cana, where Jesus works the first of his (public) signs. In 2:11 we are told that this was the first of his (public) signs[10] and that the disciples saw his glory and believed in him. Two elements here are of importance. First, it is because they saw his glory that the belief was considered appropriate. Second, this is the only passage in the gospel where the disciples are shown to have believed on the basis of a sign.

Following this there is a brief stay at Capernaum and then a trip to Jerusalem. All of this is material of the first edition.[11] While the material of the first edition will be resumed in 2:23, two passages from the second edition now intervene. They are marked as belonging to the second edition by the term "Jews" (2:18, 20) and by the use of "sign" in the sense characteristic of the second edition (2:18) and by the characteristic dialogue between Jesus and the authorities in 2:18-20.

This material describes Jesus' entry into the Temple and the expulsion of the sellers and money-changers. In v17 we are told that the disciples remembered that it was written: "Zeal for thy house will

---

[9]The disciples play a minor role in 4:8, 31 and then reappear in 6:60-71, where we hear of the defection of some, the faith of Peter and the first prediction of the betrayal of Judas. They appear at the beginning of the story of Lazarus but again in a minimal role.

[10]In the analysis of this material I have referred to this as the first of the public signs, since the miraculous knowledge of Nathanael's whereabouts also functioned as a sign within the first edition. However, in the second edition this is overlooked and the function of the Cana miracle is stressed since it is witnessed by all the disciples.

[11]The mention of the stay at Capernaum (2:12) has not been discussed since it does not contain any of the criteria discussed in this book. Yet it is likely that it comes from the first edition. Dodd, who lists this verse among his "transitional passages" attributes it to a prior tradition, pointing out that it "does not in any way contribute to the development either of the narrative or of the thought of the gospel," nor is it the product of any particular interest of the evangelist (*Tradition* 235).

consume me." The scene then switches to a confrontation between "the Jews" and Jesus in which "the Jews" demand a sign of authority for doing this. Jesus responds with the statement about destroying "this" Temple, which is then interpreted by the author in terms of referring to Jesus' resurrection. Finally, in v22 we are told that these two events (the cleansing of the Temple and Jesus' prediction of the destruction of the Temple) become the basis of the disciples' belief after Jesus was raised from the dead: "When therefore he was raised from the dead, his disciples remembered that he had said this; and they believed the scripture and the word which Jesus had spoken." In this verse we are told explicitly that the disciples found both the Scripture and the word of Jesus to be other bases for belief when he was raised from the dead!

Although the disciples now drop out of focus until the Last Supper, we have in four passages seen examples of how they have responded to each of the four witnesses to Jesus: to John the Baptist (1:35-49), to the sign at Cana (2:1-11), to the scriptures (2:13-17, 22) and to the word of Jesus (2:18-22). They are portrayed as models of belief for the Johannine community; they did not fail to see the witness to Jesus in any of the forms in which it was made manifest.

Of course the presentation of belief is somewhat anachronistic since the belief in the word and the Scripture does not occur until after the resurrection of Jesus. However, this is in keeping with the theology of the second edition which sees the possession of the Spirit as the basis of all forms of believing response to Jesus (cf 3:3-10) and which conceives of the giving of the Spirit as taking place only after the glorification of Jesus (7:37-39; 20:22). But this anachronism itself is an indication of the desire of the author to portray the disciples as models of believing response right at the beginning of his gospel even if it meant including forms of belief which did not actually occur until after the public ministry.

In addition, from the way in which this section of the gospel is laid out, the manner in which the author of the second edition was able to take the material of the first edition and make it serve his wider theological vision becomes quite clear.

C. THE "WORKS" OF JESUS AND A HIGH CHRISTOLOGY

Another significant element of the theology of the second edition is its christology. Again, I do not intend to provide a full description but only to sketch some of the ways in which christology undergoes a transformation in the second edition.

Whereas in the first edition Jesus had been conceived of almost exclusively in terms of traditional Jewish categories, in the second edition, a much clearer awareness of his divinity emerges. The discourse in 10:22-39 is a clear example of this higher christology. Not only do the linguistic characteristics of this passage clearly identify it as belonging to the second edition, but also the christology is in clear contrast with the earliest material of the gospel.

This passage, which is essentially an elaboration of the witness value of the works of Jesus for "the Jews", is identified as belonging to the second edition both by its use of the characteristic term for religious authorities: "Jews" (vv24, 31, 33); and by the use of the characteristic term for miracle ("works") which also appears several times (vv25, 32, 33, 37, 38). Finally, the christology is radically different from that of the signs material. The discourse begins with a request by "the Jews" for Jesus to tell them plainly whether he is the Christ. Although this title is traditional, it becomes apparent that it is enveloped within a significantly different christology. Jesus responds that he has told them and they do not believe. His "works" witness to him but they do not believe because they are not of his sheep. The Father is the one who has given him the sheep, and he and the Father are one.

The Jews then take up stones to stone Jesus and he asks them which one of his works was the cause for their stoning him. They in turn respond that it is not because of a good work "but for blasphemy because you, being a man, make yourself God." Jesus responds in terms of his being consecrated and sent into the world by the Father. In v36 he says it even more clearly: "Do you say ... 'You are blaspheming,' because I said, 'I am the Son of God'? If I am not doing the works of my Father, then do not believe me; but if I do them, even though you do not believe me, believe the works, that you may know and understand that the Father is in me and I am in the Father.'"

Here the miracles of Jesus are spoken of as demonstrating something much more profound than in the first edition. They show that when he speaks of God as his Father, and of being "in the Father and the Father in him," he is truthful. He is now "Son of God" and "equal with God" in the full sense of these words.

Clearly, the "works" of Jesus are meant to lead to a more profound conclusion than were the signs. Through the works, one sees that the miraculous activity of Jesus is an extension of the activity of the Father. As God acts on the Sabbath, so does Jesus, because of the same prerogative of freedom from the Sabbath law (5:19). The "works" of Jesus are intended to be part of the larger "work" (i.e., the entire ministry) given to him by the Father. But this larger work is simply to bring to completion the work of the Father. Thus rather than being pictured primarily against the background of Exodus, the works of Jesus are portrayed against the background of God's creative activity.

Conclusion

Our intention has been to describe the signs of John. Our brief discussion of the second edition has only been to give some clues to the way the first edition has been incorporated into the second. Our description of the second edition is, of course, far from complete. It is hoped, however, that a clearer picture of the signs material, its structure, theology and background will pave the way for a more intelligent and more critical reading of the gospel in all its complexity. Such a reading is the most certain way to understand both the theology of the gospel in its present form, but also the developing theological awareness of this first-century community. Finally, such a reading will also help in understanding the unique history of this community and the relation between this history and the community's theology.

THE SIGNS IN JOHN: A FINAL LOOK BACK

As was indicated in chapter 1, there have been numerous attempts to solve the Johannine Problem (the numerous indications of a complex literary history for the gospel of John) throughout the era of modern biblical studies. Although there is general agreement among scholars that the gospel has undergone three stages of development and although there is considerable agreement about the basic type of material which constitutes each of these stages of development, the study of the development has not borne great fruit for the study of the gospel. In my opinion this failure is due to the fact that the analysis of the gospel has not been able to provide sufficiently clear and objective criteria and because the analysis has not been extended to the entire gospel in a consistent way and in sufficient detail as to remove the numerous ambiguities. When the transitional passages are attributed to the evangelist while the miracle narratives themselves are attributed to the sources, one has not achieved a consistent explanation of either language or theology within the gospel.

In terms of results, I think it is fair to say that the foregoing analysis differs from previous attempts by attributing the majority of the transitional passages to the source rather than to the Evangelist—or, in my terms, by attributing the transitional material to the signs material rather than to the second edition. My analysis also finds considerable signs material within chapter 7, a section of the gospel which is all but ignored in most studies of the signs in John. Finally, I have included somewhat less material of the Passion, and especially of the post-resurrection appearances within the signs material.

By now the reader should be thoroughly aware of how different the criteria are that I have employed from those commonly employed in the signs analysis of the gospel. Yet at the same time, those familiar with the literary analysis of the Hebrew Scriptures will recognize clearly how similar my criteria are in many respects to the criteria used in the classical studies of the Pentateuch. These criteria are, I would judge, considerably more objective than those used previously in the literary analysis of the fourth gospel. If we are now able to account in a consistent way for the obvious differences between such designations of the religious authorities as "Pharisees, chief priests, and rulers" on the one hand, and "Jews" on the other; and if we are able to account for the obvious differences in the use of "sign" and "work" for the miracles of Jesus, then we have come a long way toward understanding the text and language of John. And, as was indicated earlier, this more consistent explanation has become possible only because of the individual studies of the language usage of the gospel which have gone before.

Another seeming benefit of the present analysis is that the same set of criteria have been applied to the entire gospel. We have not chosen certain sections of the gospel for analysis because those sections seemed to contain traditional material. The same criteria have been applied to the entire text.

It was mentioned above that by including material from the transitional passages and from chapter 7, the present analysis provides a different perspective on the extent of the signs material. But such results also provide a much clearer and more distinct picture of the theology involved in each of the editions. It is now clear, in all specific cases, how the "easy belief" and the "low" christology of the gospel are the product of the first edition and how the basis of faith in the word and the scriptures (as well as in the miracles)—a much more restrained view of belief—and the higher christology are the product of the gospel's second edition. Although there has been a general recognition of this by scholars for a considerable time, it is only when one is able to account for these differences concretely and by correlating them with other characteristics of the material that one can have a reasonable degree of certainty that one has really identified most, if not all, of the material of the first edition.

Finally, as we have seen above, the gospel of John contains material which by all rights appears to preserve some of the more primitive traditions within the New Testament. Yet, at the same time, the gospel of John is known for containing some of the most anachronistic material within the New Testament. Perhaps the greatest anachronism of all is the divergent use of terms for religious authorities. To refer to the authorities as "Jews" in a blanket way certainly mirrors a condition of the community far removed from the more historically accurate designations of them as "Pharisees," "chief priests" and "rulers." Some parts of the gospel clearly seem to reflect rabbinic debates of the later first century, even employing terminology that is anachronistic. Yet alongside of these is the considerable accuracy of the references to the pool of Bethesda, the stone pavement, the only occurrences of the Hebrew form of Christ (*Messias*). This list could be extended to considerable length, but I think the way in which the present theory accounts for these various elements in a consistent way throughout the gospel is some indication that the signs material is different, both in extent and in nature, from what it was previously thought to be.

Appendices

Appendix A

TEXTS OF THE SIGNS MATERIAL

[NOTE: Secondary texts, those not identified by the primary criteria, are introduced by an "*"]

1.	1:19-28	The Interrogation of the Baptist
2.	1:35-49 (without v43)	The First Disciples Come to Jesus
3.	2:1-11	Jesus Changes Water into Wine
4.	2:23-3:2 (without 2:24-25)	A Report Of Jesus' Signs and the Reaction of Nicodemus
5.	3:22-26	The Continued Success of Jesus and the Concern on the Part of John's Disciples
6.	4:1-4	A Transition: Jesus Begins a Journey Through Samaria
7.	4:5-42 (without vv10-15, 20-24, 31-38, 40-42)	Jesus Demonstrates His Knowledge of the Samaritan Woman's Past
8.	4:43-45 (without v44)	A Transition: Jesus Comes into Galilee
9.	4:46-54 (without v48)	Jesus Heals an Official's Son at Cana
10.	5:1-9	Jesus Heals a Man Ill for Thirty-Eight Years
11.	6:1-3	A Transition: Jesus Crosses the Sea of Galilee
12.	6:4-14 (without v6)	Jesus Multiplies the Loaves and Fishes
13.	*6:16-21	Jesus Crosses the Sea of Galilee Miraculously
13a.	6:26	(not part of SM).
14.	7:25-27	A Fragment of a Discussion at Tabernacles
15.	7:31-32	The Belief of the Crowds and the Reaction of the Pharisees

16.	*7:40-44	The Debate Continues
17.	7:45-52	The Debate Among the Religious Authorities
17a.	8:12-13	(not part of SM)
18.	9:1-41 (without vv2-5, 18-23, 35-41)	Jesus Heals a Man Born Blind
19.	10:19-21	Division Among the People
20.	10:40-42	Still Other Believe in Jesus
21.	11:1-45 (without vv2, 4-5, 7-10, 15b-16, 21-27, 40-42)	Jesus Raises Lazarus from the Dead
22.	11:46-53 (without vv51-52)	The Sanhedrin's Decision to Put Jesus to Death
23.	11:54-57	The Aftermath of Sanhedrin's Decision
24.	*12:1-8	Jesus in Bethany
25.	12:9-11	Crowds of Judeans Come to Bethany
26.	12:18-19	The Action of the Crowd and the Reaction of the Pharisees
27.	*12:20-22	The Greeks Want to See Jesus
28.	12:37-42	The Conclusion of the Public Ministry
29.	18:1-3 (without vv4-6, 9)	Jesus is Arrested
30.	*18:19-24	The Hearing Before Annas
31.	18:28-29, 33-35	The Transfer of Jesus from Caiaphas to Pilate and Pilate's First Questioning of Jesus
32.	18:39-19:6a	The Release of Barabbas, the Scourging, Mockery, and the Cry for Crucifixion
33.	19:13-16	The Final Questioning and Judgment by Pilate
34.	19:17-25a	The Crucifixion of Jesus
35.	*19:39-42	Nicodemus Removes the Body of Jesus for Burial
36.	20:1, 11, 14-16	The Appearance of the Risen Jesus to Mary in the Garden
37.	20:30-31	The Conclusion of the Signs Material

Appendix B

Summary Listing of Characteristics

LINGUISTIC

	1	2	3	4	5	6	7	8	9	10	11	12	13
1. "Pharisees" "Chief Priests," "Rulers" as The Terms For Religious Authorities	x		x		x								
2. "Signs" As The Term For Miracles		x	x				x		x		x		
3. "Jews" With the Meaning "Judeans"	x			x									
4. Translations of Place Names and Religious Terms	x						x			x	x		

IDEOLOGICAL

	1	2	3	4	5	6	7	8	9	10	11	12	13
5. Stereotyped Formulas of Belief					x	x		x					
6. Tandem Belief					x			x	x				
7. Emphasis on Quality and Quantity of Signs					x	(x)	x		x	x	(x)	x	x
8. Emphasis on the Variety of Groups Which Believe in Jesus	x	x	x	x	x	x	x				x	x	
9. Reaction of the Pharisees to the Signs		x		x									
10. The Increasing Hostility of the Pharisees		x		x									
11. The People's Reaction to the Religious Authorities													
12. Division of Opinion Regarding Jesus													
13. The Predominance of Narrative	x	x	x	x	x	x	x	x	x	x	x	x	x

THEOLOGICAL

	1	2	3	4	5	6	7	8	9	10	11	12	13
14. A Belief Based on Signs					x	x	x			x	x	x	x
15. Belief Presented as an Easy Affair					x		x	x	x	x	x	x	x
16. A Traditional Christology	x	x		x		x					x	x	x
17. The Supernatural Knowledge of Jesus	x					x							

OTHER

	1	2	3	4	5	6	7	8	9	10	11	12	13
18. The Occurrence of Terms Used Only Once	x			x									
19. References to Previous Signs Material	x												
20. Specific and Accurate Geographical References	x							x		x			
21. Contrast With Surrounding Theology													
22. Questions/Statements With a Response That Is Not Consistent					x	x		x					

	14	15	16	17	18	19	20	21	22	23	24	25	26	27	28	29	30	31	32	33	34	35	36	37
1.	x	x		x	x		x	x	x		x	x	x	x		x	x	x	x					
2.		x			x	x	x	x			x		x								x			
3.					x		x		x		x													
4.					x												x		x		x			
5.		x					x	x			x		x											
6.											x													
7.		x			(x)		x	(x)	x		x	x	x								x			
8.					x		x	x			x	x	x	x										
9.		x			x			x			x	x												
10.		x			x		x		x	x		x	x	(x)	(x)	(x)	(x)	(x)						
11.						x	x		x		x													
12.	x		x		x	x		x	x									x						
13.	x	x	x	x	x	x	x	x	x	x	x	x	x	x	x	x	x	x	x	x	x	x	x	x
14.		x			x	x	x				x	x	x											
15.					x		x	x	x		x	x	x									x	x	
16.	x	x	x	x	x																			
17.																								
18.	x										x												x	
19.					x	x								x		x	x	x						
20.					x	x											x	x	x	x				
21.											x		x	x	x	x								
22.	x	x										x			x									

Appendix C

SOME RECENT PROPOSALS REGARDING
THE SIGNS MATERIAL IN JOHN

Bultmann's Signs and Passion Material

Bultmann's semeia source includes the following (minor modifications within a given verse are not mentioned): 38-44: 1:35-49; 2:1-12; 4:4-7, 9, 16-19, 25-26, 28-29, 30, 40, 46-47, 50-54; 6:1-3, 5, 7-13, 16-22, 25; 7:2-4, 6, 8-10; 5:2-3, 5-15, 18; 7:19-23; 9:1-3, 6-14, 16-21, 24-28, 34, 35-38; 10:40-42; 11:2-3, 5-7, 11-15, 17-19, 33-34, 38-39, 41, 43-44; 12:37-38; 20:30-31.

Bultmann did not think the Passion account came from the same source as the signs. Nevertheless, his basic Passion account would include the following: 18:1-2, 4-5, 10-12, 15, 17-23, 25-29; 19:13, 29, 15, 38-40, 6, 1, 16, 2-3, 17-19, 23-24, 30, 25, 31-34, 36-42; 20:1, 6-7, 11-13, 19-20, 23-28. (The list is taken from D.M. Smith *Composition* 48-51. The irregular numbering reflects Bultmann's rearrangement of the text.)

Fortna's Gospel of Signs

A listing of Fortna's signs material is more difficult because of the complexity of his analysis and because he believes that in a number of instances the material has been rearranged. The following list does not indicate that, in many cases, Fortna attributes only part of a given verse to the source: 1:6-7, 19-34 (without vv22, 24-25, 28-31); 3:23-24; 1:35-50 (without v37); 2:1-12; 4:46-54; 21:2-14 (without vv9, 13); 6:1-25 (without vv4, 6, 23-24); 11:1-4, 11; 4:4-42 (without vv8, 10-15, 20-24, 27, 31-39, 41); (11:17-45 without vv21-27, 29-31, 35-37, 40, 42); 9:1-8 (without vv4-5); 5:2-9, 14; 2:14-19 (without v17); 11:47, 53; 12:1-8 (without v6), 12-15; very brief fragments of the last supper in chaps. 12 and 13; 18:1-5, 10-13, 24, 15-16a, 19-23, 16b-18, 25-28, 33, 37-38; 19:15; 18:39-40; 19:6, 12-14, 1-3, 16-20, 23-24, 28-30, 25, 31-34, 36-38; 3:1; 19:39, 41-42; 20:1-20 (without vv4, 6, 13, 15), 30-31. (*Signs* 235-245).

Nicol's Semeia Source

Of the theories reviewed here Nicol's is the shortest. The S identified by Nicol is confined to the material of the six miracles plus the call of the first disciples, the story of the Samaritan woman, and the walking on the water ("the bulk of" 1:35-51; 2:1-11; 4:5-9, 16-19, 28-30, 40; 4:46-54; 5:2-9b; 6:1-22 except for v4, parts of vv12 and 14; 9:1-3a, 6-7; 11:1-3, 6, 11-15, 17-19, 33-39, 43-44 (*Semeia* 30-40).

The Miracles in Boismard's Analysis

Because of the nature of Boismard's theory, his analysis does not correspond exactly to the type of theory represented by Bultmann, Fortna, and Nicol. Boismard believes there is a Document C (also titled Jean I) which comprised the first edition of John. This document was utilized to a certain extent by Luke and Mark. It constituted a complete gospel running from the ministry of the Baptist to scenes of the Risen One. It did not have any of the great discourses and had only five "signs." It was composed in Palestine and was influenced by Samaritan thought. It was an account structured by the geographical regions of Jesus' ministry: (1) Samaria, (2) Galilee, (3) Jerusalem, (4) Bethany. The only feast mentioned was the feast of Tabernacles.

The five miracles included in this edition are: the wedding at Cana; the healing of the son of the royal official; the miraculous catch of fish; the healing of a blind man; the raising of Lazarus.

This document was re-edited and amplified by a member of the Johannine school, resulting in the document described by Boismard as Jean II-A. Jean II-A added the call of Andrew and Peter, two miracles from the synoptic tradition, and some of the discourses of Jesus. This was done in Palestine. It kept the order of the original document.

The miracles added at this time are: the multiplication of the loaves; the healing of the cripple; and the healing of the blind man.

After the community moved from Palestine to Ephesus; the community found itself confronted with certain hostile Jewish-Christian groups as was Paul. The evangelist then produced a new version (Jean II-B). This edition included more material from the synoptic tradition. This edition added the framework of Jewish feasts, giving priority to the feast of Passover rather than to the feast of Tabernacles as had been the case in the first edition. This edition was influenced by Paul,

Luke and Qumran—and has some similarity with the Johannine epistles.

Finally, a third author (Jean III) added some passages originally composed by Jean II-B but parallel to Jean II-A. He also reversed the order of chapters 5 and 6 and added glosses of an apocalyptic orientation. Finally, he modified the anti-Jewish tendencies of Jean II-B.

Because of the difference of approach and the complexity of the redaction as proposed by Boismard, the verses attributed to each of these levels are not given here. They are available in Boismard and Lamouille, *Evangile* 11-35.

Schnackenburg's Signs Source

In the introduction to his commentary on the gospel of John, Schnackenburg provides a brief analysis of the signs. In his discussion of the individual signs, however, his analysis is somewhat more complex although he frequently feels unable to reach a definitive conclusion regarding individual verses. His list includes: 2:1-11 (except for 11b-c); 4:46-54; 6:1-21; 5:2-9; 9:1, 6f; 11:1a, 3, 17, 33-34, 38, 39a, 41a, 43-44; 20:30 (*Gospel* 64-67).

Selected Bibliography

TEXTS

Aland, K., et al, *The Greek New Testament* (London: United Bible Societies, 1975).

Septuaginta (Ed. A. Rahlfs; 2 vols; 5th ed.; Stuttgart: Württenbergishche Bibelanstalt, 1952).

The Revised Standard Version of the Bible (New York: National Council of the Churches of Christ in the U.S.A., 1973).

REFERENCE WORKS

Bauer, W., Arndt, W.F. , Gingrich, F.W., *A Greek-English Lexicon of the New Testament and Other Early Christian Literature* (Chicago: University of Chicago, 1957).

Blass, F., Debrunner, R., Funk, R.W., *A Greek Grammar of the New Testament and Other Early Christian Literature* (Chicago: University of Chicago, 1967).

Hatch, E., Redpath, H.A., A *Concordance to the Septuagint and Other Greek Versions of the Old Testament (Including the Aprocryphal Books)* (Oxford: Clarendon, 1897.

The Interpreter's Dictionary of the Bible. An Illustrated Encyclopedia (New York: Abingdon Press, 1962).

Kittel, G., Friedrich, G. (eds.), *The Theological Dictionary of the New Testament* (7 vols.; Grand Rapids: Wm. B. Eerdmans, 1964-71).

Liddell, H.G., Scott, R., *A Greek-English Lexicon* (Oxford: Oxford University, 1940).

Metzger, B., et al, *A Textual Commentary on the Greek New Testament* (London: United Bible Societies, 1971).

Moulton W.F., Geden, A.S., *A Concordance to the Greek Testament* (4th ed.; Edinburgh: Clark, 1963).

COMMENTARIES

Barrett, C.K., *The Gospel According to St. John* (2nd ed.; Philadelphia: Westminster, 1978).

Beasley-Murray, G.R., *John* (WBC 36; Waco: Word, 1987).

Bernard, J.H., *A Critical and Exegetical Commentary on the Gospel of St. John.* (ICC; 2 vols; Edinburgh: Clark, 1929).

Brown, R.E., *The Gospel According to John,* (AB 29,29a; Garden City: Doubleday, 1966-70.

Bultmann, R., *The Gospel of John. A Commentary*, (Philadelphia: Westminster, 1970).

Schnackenburg, R., *The Gospel according to St. John* (Vol. 1; New York: Herder and Herder, 1966; Vol. 2, 3; New York: Crossroad, 1980-82).

GENERAL WORKS

Ashton, J., "The Identity and Function of the *Ioudaioi* in the Fourth Gospel" *NovT* 27 (1985) 40-75.

Bacon, B.W., *The Fourth Gospel in Research and Debate* (New Haven: Yale University, 2nd ed.; 1918).

—————, *The Gospel of the Hellenists* (New York: Holt, 1933).

Becker, J., "Wunder und Christologie. Zum literarkritischen und christologischen Problem der Wunder im Johannesevangelium," *NTS* 16 (1969-70) 130-148.

Bergmeier, R., "Glaube als Werk? Die 'Werke Gottes' in Damaskusschrift II, 14-15 und Johannes 6, 28-29," *RevQ* 6 (1967) 253-60.

Bertram, G., "ergon," *TDNT* 635-52.

Blinzler, J., "Eine Bemerkung zum Geschichtsrahmen des Johannesevangelium," *Bib* 36 (1955) 20-35.

Boismard, M.-E., Lamouille, A., *L'Évangile de Jean* (Synopse de quatre Evangiles, vol.3; Paris: Cerf, 1977).

—————, *La vie des Évangiles. Initiation a la critique des textes* (Paris: Cerf, 1980).

_____, "Aenon, près de Salem (Jean 3,23)," *RB* 24 (1973) 218-229.

_____, *Du Baptême à Cana (Jean 1, 19-2, 11)* (Paris: Cerf, 1956).

_____, "Le caractère adventice de Jn 12,45-50," *Sacra Pagina.* (ed. J. Coppens; Miscellanea Biblica. Congressus Internationalis Catholicus de Re Biblica; vol. 2; Gembloux: Duculot, 1959) 189-92.

_____, "Les traditions johanniques concernant le Baptiste," *RB* 70 (1963) 5-42.

_____, "Un procédé rédactionnel dans le quatrième évangile: la Wiederaufnahme," in *L'Èvangile de Jean: Sources, rédaction, théologie* (Bibliotheca Ephemeridum Theologicarum Lovaniensium 44; Leuven: University Press, 1977) 235-241.

Bowman, J., "Samaritan Studies," *BJRL* 40 (1957/8) 298-327.

Bratcher, R.J., "'The Jews' in the Gospel of John," *BT* (1975) 401-09.

Bull, R.J., "An Archaeological Context for Understanding John 4:20," *BA* 38 (1975) 54-59.

Carson, D.A., "Current Source Criticism of the Fourth Gospel: Some Methodological Questions" *JBL* 97 (1978) 411-29.

Church, W., "The Dislocations in the Eighteenth Chapter of John," *JBL* 49 (1930) 375-83.

Cuming, G.J., "The Jews in the Fourth Gospel," *ExpTim* 60 (1948-49) 290-92.

Dauer, A., *Die Passionsgeschichte im Johannesevangelium. Eine traditionsgeschichtliche und theologische Untersuchung zu Joh 18, 1-19, 30* (Studien zum Alten und Neuen Testament; Müenchen: Koesel, 1972).

de Jonge, M., *Jesus: Stranger from Heaven and Son of God* (SBLSBS 11: Missoula: Scholars Press, 1977).

_____, "The Beloved Disciple and the Date of the Gospel of John," *Text and Interpretation. Festschrift M. Black* (ed. E. Best and R. McL. Wilson; Cambridge: Cambridge University, 1979) 99-114.

_____, "The Earliest Christian Use of *Christos.* Some Suggestions," *NTS* 32 (1986) 321-343.

de la Potterie, I., "Ad Dialogum Jesu cum Nicodemo (Jo. 2, 23-3, 21)," *VD* 46 (1969) 141-50.

Dodd, C.H., *Historical Tradition in the Fourth Gospel* (Cambridge: Cambridge University, 1965).

_____, "The Prophecy of Caiaphas: John xi. 47-53," Chapter 5 of *More New Testament Studies* (Grand Rapids: Wm. B. Eerdmans, 1968) 58-68.

Eissfeldt, O., *The Old Testament: An Introduction* (New York: Harper and Row, 1965).

Fortna, R.T., "Christology in the Fourth Gospel: Redaction Critical Perspectives," *NTS* 21 (1974-75) 489-504.

_____, "From Christology to Soteriology. A Redaction Critical Study of Salvation in the Fourth Gospel," *Int* 27 (1973) 31-47.

_____, *The Gospel of Signs. A Reconstruction of the Narrative Source Underlying the Fourth Gospel* (SNTSMS 11; Cambridge: Cambridge University, 1970).

_____, *The Fourth Gospel and Its Predecessor* (Philadelphia: Fortress, 1988).

_____, "Source and Redaction in the Fourth Gospel's Portrayal of Jesus' Signs," *JBL* 89 (1970) 151-66.

_____, "The Theological Use of Locale in the Fourth Gospel," *ATR Supp. Series 3* (1974) 58-94.

Fuller, R., "The 'Jews' in the Fourth Gospel," *Dialog* 16 (1977) 31-7.

Glasson, T.F., *Moses in the Fourth Gospel* (SBT 40; London: SCM, 1963).

Graesser, E., "Die antijüdische Polemik im Johannesevangelium," *NTS* 10 (1964-65) 74-90.

Gutbrod, W. *"Ioudaios, Israel, Hebraios* in the New Testament," *TDNT* 3 375-91.

Hahn, F., "Der Prozess Jesu nach dem Johannesevangelium," *EKK* 2 (1970) 23-96.

Hartmann, G., "Die Vorlage der Osterberichte in John 20," *ZNW 55* (1964) 197-220.

Hirsch, E., *Das vierte Evangelium in seiner ursprünglichen Gestalt* (Tübingen: J.C.B. Mohr, 1936).

_____, *Studien zum vierten Evangelium* (BHT 11; Tuebingen, J.C.B. Mohr, 1936).

_____, "Stilkritik und Literaranalyse im vierten Evangelium," *ZNW* 43 (1950-51) 128-43.

Holladay, C., *THEIOS ANER in Hellenistic-Judaism* (SBLDS 40; Missoula: Scholars Press, 1977).

Jocz, J., "Die Juden im Johannesevangelium," *Judaica* 9 (1953) 129-42. 42.

Kundsin, K., *Topologische Überlieferungsstoffe in Johannes-Evangelium* (Forschungen zur Religion und Literatur des Alten und Neuen Testaments 22; Göttingen: Vandenhoeck and Ruprecht, 1925).

Kysar, R., *The Fourth Evangelist and His Gospel. An Examination of Contemporary Scholarship* (Minneapolis: Augsburg, 1975).

_____, "The Source Analysis of the Fourth Gospel: A Growing Consensus?" *NT* 15 (1973) 134-152.

Leistner, R., *Antijüdaismus im Johannesevangelium?* (Theologie und Wirklichkeit 3; Bern/Frankfurt a. M.: H. Lang, 1974).

Lindars, B., *Behind the Fourth Gospel* (Studies in Creative Criticism 3; London: SPCK, 1971).

Lowe, M., "Who were the *Ioudaioi?*" *NovT* 18 (1975) 101-30.

_____, "*Ioudaioi* of the Apocrypha," *NovT* 19 (1976) 51-90.

Lütgert, W., "Die Juden im Johannesevangelium," *Neutestamentliche Studien für Georg Heinrici zu seinem 70. Geburtstag* (Leipzig: Hinrichs, 1914) 147-154.

Martyn, J.L., *History and Theology in the Fourth Gospel* (2nd ed; Nashville: Abingdon, 1979).

_____, "Source Criticism and *Religionsgeschichte* in the Fourth Gospel," *Jesus and Man's Hope* (vol. 1; Pittsburgh: Pittsburgh Theological Seminary, 1971) 247-273.

Meeks, W.A., "Am I a Jew?' Johannine Christianity and Judaism," *Christianity, Judaism, and Other Greco-Roman Cults: Studies for Morton Smith at Sixty* (SJLA 12; vol. 1; Leiden: E.J. Brill, 1975) 163-186.

————, "Galilee and Judaea in the Fourth Gospel," *JBL* 85 (1966) 159-169.

————, "Moses as God and King," *Religions in Antiquity: Essays in Memory of Erwin Ramsdell Goodenough* (Studies in the History of Religions 13; Leiden: E.J. Brill, 1968) 354-371.

————, *The Prophet-King. Moses Traditions and the Johannine Christology* (NovTSupp 14; Leiden: E.J. Brill, 1967).

Mendner, S., "Johanneische Literarkritik," *TZ* 8 (1952) 418-32.

————, "Nikodemus," *JBL* 77 (1958) 293-323.

————, "Die Tempelreinigung," *ZNW* 47 (1956) 93-112.

Meyer, R., "Ochlos," *TDNT,* vol.5, 582-90.

Milik, J.T., *Discoveries in the Judean Desert,* III (1962).

Neirynck, F., "The 'Other Disicple' in Jn. 18, 15-16," *ETL* 51 (1975) 113-141.

————, "L'Epanalepsis et la critique littéraire. À propos de l'Évangile de Jean," *ETL* 56 (1980), 303-338.

Neyrey, J., "John III—A Debate over Johannine Epistemology and Christology," *NovT* 23 (1981) 115-127.

Nicol, W., *The Semeia in the Fourth Gospel* (NovTSupp 32; Leiden: E.J. Brill, 1972).

Richter, G., "Die Deutung des Kreuzestodes Jesu in der Leidensgeschichte des Johannesevangeliums (Jo. 13-19)," *BLE* 9 (1968) 21-36.

————, "Zur Formgeschichte und literarischen Einheit von Joh 6,31-58," *ZNW* 60 (1969) 21-55.

————, "Die Fusswaschung Joh 13, 1-20," *MuTZ* 16 (1965) 13-26.

————, "Zum gemeindebildenden Element in den johanneischen Schriften," *Kirche im Werden. Studien zum Thema Amt und*

Gemeinde im Neuen Testament (ed. J. Hainz; München: Schoeningh, 1976).

_____, "Praesentische und futurische Eschatologie im 4. Evangelium," *Gegenwart und kommendes Reich:* Schülergabe Anton Vögtle zum 65. Geburtstag (ed. P. Fiedler, D. Zeller; Stuttgart: Katholisches Bibelwerk, 1975) 117-152.

_____, *Studien zum Johannesevangelium* (Leiden: E.J. Brill, 1976).

_____, "Zur sogenannten Semeia-Quelle des Johannesevangeliums," in *Studien zum Johannesevangelium,* 281-87.

_____, "Zur Frage von Tradition und Redaktion in Joh 1, 19-34," *Studien zum Johannesevangelium,* 288-314.

Roberge, M., "Jean VI, 22-24. Un problème de critique littèraire," *Laval Theologique et Philosophique* 35 (1979) 139-151.

_____, "Jean VI, 22-24. Un problème de critique textuelle," *Laval Theologique et Philosophique* 34 (1978) 275-289.

Robinson, J.M., Koester, H., *Trajectories Through Early Christianity* (Philadelphia: Fortress, 1971).

Ruckstuhl, E., "Die literarische Einheit des Johannesevangeliums, der gegenwärtige Stand der einschlägigen Forschungen) (Studia Friburgensia, n.f. 3; Freiburg: S. Paul, 1951).

Sabbe, M., "The Arrest of Jesus in Jn 18, 1-11 and Its Relation to the Synoptic Gospels," in *L'Évangile de Jean: Sources, rédaction, théologie* (Bibliotheca Ephemeridum Theologicarum Lovaniensium 44 (Leuven: University Press, 1977) 203-234.

Schnackenburg, R., "Die Erwartung des 'Propheten' nach dem Neuen Testament und den Qumran-Texten," *Studia Evangelica; Series 5, 18;* (Berlin: Akademie-Verlag, 1959) 622-39.

_____, "Entwicklung und Stand der johanneischen Forschung seit 1955," *L'Évangile de Jean. Sources, rédaction, théologie* (ed. M. de Jonge; BETL 44; Gembloux: Duculot, 1977) 19-44.

_____, "Die johanneische Gemeinde und ihre Geisterfahrung," *Die Kirche des Anfangs. Festschrift Heinz Schürmann zum 65. Geburtstag* (ed. R. Schnackenburg, J. Ernst, J. Wanke; Leipzig: St. Benno, 1977) 277-306.

204   *Selected Bibliography*

——————, "Zur Traditionsgeschichte von Joh 4,46-54," *BZ* 8 (1964) 58-88.

Schneider, J., "Zur Komposition von Joh 7," *ZNW* 45 (1954) 108-19.

——————, "Zur Komposition von Joh 10," *Coniectanea Neotestamentica 11* (Lund: Gleerup, 1947) 220-25.

——————, "Zur Komposition von Joh. 18,12-27," *ZNW* 49 (1958) 111-119.

Schwank, B., "Ortskenntnisse im vierten Evangelium? Bericht über ein Seminar in Jerusalem," *ErbAuf* 57 (1981) 427-442.

Schwartz, E., "Aporien im vierten Evangelium," *Nachrichten von der königlichen Gesellschaft der Wissenschaften zu Göttingen* (1907) 342-372; (1908) 115-148; 149-188; 497-560.

Schweizer, E., *Ego Eimi . . . Die religionsgeschichtliche Herkunft und theologische Bedeutung der johanneischen Bildreden, zugleich ein Beitrag zur Quellenfrage des vierten Evangeliums* (FRLANT 38; Göttingen: Vandenhoeck und Ruprecht, 1939).

Shepherd, Jr., M., "The Jews in the Fourth Gospel: Another Level of Meaning," *ATR Supplementary Series 3* (1974) 95-112.

Smith, D.M., *The Composition and Order of the Fourth Gospel. Bultmann's Literary Theory* (New Haven: Yale University Press, 1965).

——————, "Johannine Christianity: Some Reflections on Its Character and Delineation," *NTS* 21 (1974-75), 222-48.

——————, "The Milieu of the Johannine Miracle Source: A Proposal," *Jews, Greeks and Christians. Religious Cultures in Late Antiquity: Essays in Honor of W.D. Davies,* (ed. R. Hamerton-Kelly, R. Scroggs; SJLA 21; Leiden: E.J. Brill, 1976) 164-180.

——————, "The Setting and Shape of a Johannine Narrative Source," *JBL* 95 (1976) 231-241.

Spitta, F., *Das Johannesevangelium als Quelle der Geschichte Jesu* (Göttingen: Vandenhoeck und Ruprecht, 1910).

Strachan, R., "Is the Fourth Gospel a Literary Unity?" *ExpT* 27 (1914-16), 22-26, 232-37, 280-82, 330-33.

Teeple, H.M., *The Literary Origin of the Gospel of John* (Evanston: Religion and Ethics Institute, 1974).

_____, "Methodology in Source Analysis of the Fourth Gospel," *JBL* 81 (1962) 279-86.

_____, *The Mosaic Eschatological Prophet* (SBLMS 10; Philadelphia: SBL, 1957).

Temple, S., "A Key to the Composition of the Fourth Gospel," *JBL* 80 (1961) 220-232.

_____, "The Two Signs in the Fourth Gospel," *JBL* 81 (1963) 169-74.

_____, "The Two Traditions of the Last Supper, Betrayal, and Arrest," *NTS* 7 (1960-61) 77-85.

Tenney, M.C., "Literary Keys to the Fourth Gospel. The Old Testament and the Fourth Gospel," *BSac* 129 (1963) 300-08.

_____, "Literary Keys to the Fourth Gospel. The Author's Testimony to Himself," *BSac* 129 (1963) 214-23.

Thyen, H., "Entwicklungen innerhalb der johanneischen Theologie und Kirche im Spiegel von Joh 21 und der Lieblingsjüengertexte des Evangeliums," in *L'Évangile de Jean: Sources, rédaction, théologie* (Bibliotheca Ephemeridum Theologicarum Lovaniensium 44; Leuven: University Press, 1977) 259-299.

Topel, L.J., "A Note on the Methodology of Structural Analysis in Jn. 2, 23-3, 21," *CBQ* 33 (1971) 211-20.

van Dyke Parunak, H., "Oral Typesetting: Some Uses of Biblical Structure," *Bib* 62 (1981) 153-168.

van Unnik, W.C., "De Verbinding *tauta eipōn* in het Evangelie van Johannes," *Ad Interim* (Kampen: J.J. Kok, n.d.) 61-73.

von Wahlde, U.C., "A Redactional Technique in the Fourth Gospel," *CBQ* 38 (1976) 520-33.

_____, "The Terms for Religious Authorities in the Fourth Gospel: A Key to Literary Strata?" *JBL* 98 (1979) 231-53.

_____, "Faith and Works in Jn vi 28-29: Exegesis or Eisegesis?" *NovT* 22 (1980) 304-315.

————, "The Witnesses to Jesus in John 5:31-40 and Belief in the Fourth Gospel," *CBQ* 43 (1981) 385-404.

————, "The Johannine 'Jews': A Critical Survey," *NTS* 28 (1982) 33-60.

————, *"Wiederaufnahme* as a Marker of Redaction in Jn 6, 51-58," *Biblica* 64 (1983) 542-49.

Wellhausen, J., *Das Evangelium Johannis* (Berlin: Georg Reimer, 1908).

Wendt, H.H., *The Gospel According to St. John* (ET; Edinburgh: T.T. Clark, 1902).

————, *"Die Schichten im vierten Evangelium* (Göttingen: Vandenhoeck und Ruprecht, 1911).

White, M.C., *The Identity and Function of Jews and Related Terms in the Fourth Gospel* (Ann Arbor: University Microfilms, 1972).

Wilkens, W., *Die Entstehungsgeschichte des vierten Evangeliums* (Zollikon-Zurich: Evangelischer Verlag, 1958).

————, "Die Erweckung des Lazarus," *TZ* 15 (1959) 22-39.

————, "Evangelist und Tradition im Johannesevangelium," *TZ* 16 (1960) 81-90.

————, *Zeichen und Werke: ein Beitrag zur Theologie des 4. Evangeliums in Erzählungs und Redestoff* (Zürich: Zwingli, 1969).

Subject Index

Boldface indicates major treatment.

Anachronism 62, 82n.41, 172, 173n.
24, 184, 188
Aporias 12, **17-20**, 18, **26-28**, 30, 34,
38n.31, 63, 77, 138, 150
Apocalyptic 169n.17
Baptist, John the 19n.4, 49, 49n.55, 50,
51, 67, 67n.5, 68; 68n.10, 69, 79, 80,
169-170, 179, 182, 183
Belief 184
   an easy affair 48, **58-59**, 70, 80, 82,
84, 88, 90, 93, 96, 97n.74, 99, 115,
119, 123, 127, 128, 131, 188
   based on signs 51, **58**, 60, 73, 90, 91,
93, 165
   criticism of 89, 90, 92, 93, 100, 93n.-
64, 97n.74, 181n.8
   stereotyped formulas **46-48**, 48, 50,
59, 74, 76, 85, 104n.85, 105, 115,
123, 133
   tandem aspect/chain reaction **48-49**,
70, 71, 84, 88, 93
Beloved disciple 70n.14, 138n.140,
A148, 148n.164, 149, 151, 151n.
167, 155
Bethesda 45, 96n.69, 99n.76, 171, 173,
174n.31, 177n.3
Blasphemy 50, 53, 163, 185
Cephas 44, 70, 71
Chief priests 19, **31-36**, 31, 31n.10, 33n.-
16, 34, 37, 40n.34, 42, 45n.44, 51,
52, 54, 55, 56, 67n.2, 105, 125, 126,
127, 135, 141, 144, 145, 146n.160,
147, 148, 159, 187, 188

Christology **59**, **161-163**
   High 44n.43, 59, 96n.68, 100, 106n.-
92, 144, 145, **184-186**, 188

equal with God 55, 60, 72, 96n.
68, 163, 185
   making self God 20, 164, 164n.6,
185
   Low 20, 106, 110, 152, **161-164**,
180n.6, 188
   Come down from heaven 163
   God has spoken to him 162
   God his own Father 72, 163
   God is with him 77, 162
   from God 20, 51, 52, 59, 77, 112,
113, 114, 162, 165
   the one Moses wrote of 71, 162
   "a" prophet 59, 86, 87, 108n.95, 114,
162, 166n.9, 166n.10, 168n.13, 168n.-
14
   a sinner? 59
   teacher 71
Christ (see Messiah)
Criteria, defined
   ideological 28, 28n.7, **46-56**
   linguistic 28, **30-46**
   style **29n.8**
   theological 29, 30, **57-65**
Dead Sea Scrolls 174n.30
Discourse material 23, 57, 57n.66, 36n.-
22
Dislocation, accidental 21, 21n.7, 22
Divine man 169n.17
Division among the authorities 110
Duplicate material 19, 23
Ecclesiastical redactor 22
Editions, general description
   First 13, 16
   Second 13, **176-186**, 183
   Third 14, 138n.140
Ego Eimi/I Am 59, 72, 101n.80, 135n.-
136, 136, 163

Author Index

This is a bibliographical index, citing only
the first appearance of a work.

Scripture Index

Old Testament

Boldface indicates major treatment.

New Testament